The Undead in the 21st Century

Genre Fiction and Film Companions

Series Editor: Simon Bacon

THE UN DEAD
IN THE 21ST CENTURY

A Companion

Edited by Simon Bacon

PETER LANG
Oxford • Bern • Berlin • Bruxelles • New York • Wien

Bibliographic information published by Die Deutsche Nationalbibliothek. Die Deutsche
Nationalbibliothek lists this publication in the Deutsche Nationalbibliografie; detailed bibliographic
data is available on the Internet at http://dnb.d-nb.de.

A catalogue record for this book is available from the British Library.

Library of Congress Cataloging-in-Publication Data

Names: Bacon, Simon, 1965– editor.
Title: The undead in the 21st century : a companion / Simon Bacon, [editor].
Other titles: Undead in the twenty-first century
Description: Oxford ; New York : Peter Lang, 2022. | Series: Genre fiction
   and film companions, 2631-8725 ; volume no. 10 | Includes
   bibliographical references and index.
Identifiers: LCCN 2022019703 (print) | LCCN 2022019704 (ebook) | ISBN
   9781789977363 (paperback) | ISBN 9781789977295 (ebook) | ISBN
   9781789977301 (epub)
Subjects: LCSH: Zombies in motion pictures. | Zombies in literature. |
   Zombies in popular culture.
Classification: LCC PN1995.9.Z63 U63 2022 (print) | LCC PN1995.9.Z63
   (ebook) | DDC 398/.45—dc23/eng/20220610
LC record available at https://lccn.loc.gov/2022019703
LC ebook record available at https://lccn.loc.gov/2022019704

Cover design by Peter Lang Ltd.

ISSN 2631-8725
ISBN 978-1-78997-736-3 (print)
ISBN 978-1-78997-729-5 (ePDF)
ISBN 978-1-78997-730-1 (ePUB)

© Peter Lang Group AG 2022
Published by Peter Lang Ltd, International Academic Publishers,
Oxford, United Kingdom
oxford@peterlang.com, www.peterlang.com

Simon Bacon has asserted his right under the Copyright, Designs
and Patents Act, 1988, to be identified as Editor of this Work.

All rights reserved.
All parts of this publication are protected by copyright.
Any utilisation outside the strict limits of the copyright law, without
the permission of the publisher, is forbidden and liable to prosecution.
This applies in particular to reproductions, translations, microfilming,
and storage and processing in electronic retrieval systems.

This publication has been peer reviewed.

Contents

Acknowledgements ix

David Punter
Prologue: The Revolution of the Undead xi

Simon Bacon
Introduction 1

PART I Undead Cultures in the Global Present 17

Mikel J. Koven
Hereditary (Ari Aster, 2018) – Folk Horror and the Undead 19

Cristina Santos
La Llorona (Various, 2006–2019) – Mexican Undead 27

Iain Robert Smith
Go Goa Gone (Raj and D. K., 2013) – Bollywood Undead 37

John R. Ziegler
Wakening (Danis Goulet, 2013) – Métis-Cree Undead 45

Naomi Simone Borwein
Killer Native (Bjorn Stewart, 2019) – Australian Aboriginal Undead 53

Katarzyna Ancuta
Seoul Station (Sang-ho Yeon, 2016) – South Korean Undead   65

PART II   The Undead and Never-ending Present   73

Dara Downey
The Haunting of Hill House (Mike Flanagan, 2018) – Domestic Undead   75

Tyler Unsell
The Girl with All the Gifts (Colm McCarthy, 2016) – Undead Classroom   83

Antares Leask
ZOMBIES 2 (Paul Hoen, 2020) – Anti-racist Undead   93

Natalie Wilson
Deadgirl (Marcel Sarmiento and Gadi Harel, 2008) – Undead Rape Culture   101

Brandon R. Grafius
The Nun (Corin Hardy, 2018) – Religious Undead   109

Laura R. Kremmel
Saint Maud (Rose Glass, 2019) – Medical Undead   119

Jeffrey Andrew Weinstock
Bubba Ho-tep (Don Coscarelli, 2002) – Ageing and the Undead   127

Gina Wisker
Relic (Natalie Erika James, 2020) – Undead Heritage   137

Contents

PART III Undying Identity   145

Leah Richards
AHS: Hotel (Ryan Murphy and Brad Falchuk, 2015–2016) and
The Strain (Guillermo del Toro and Chuck Hogan, 2014–2017) –
Undead Children   147

Sara Williams
Suspiria (Luca Guadagnino, 2018) – Undead Motherhood   155

Valerie Estelle Frankel
Game of Thrones (David Benioff, 2011–2019) – Undead Masculinity   165

Madeleine Mackenzie
Dorohedoro (Q Hayashida, 2000–2018) – Transgender Undead   175

Martine Mussies
'The Zombie Mermaid' (Katelynn E. Koontz, 2018) – Undead
Mermaids   185

Gwyneth Peaty
Bloodthirsty (Amelia Moses, 2021) – Undead Celebrity   193

Antonio Alcala Gonzalez
Behemoth (Nergal and others, 1991–present) – Extreme Metal and
the Undead   201

PART IV Undead Futures   207

Persephone Braham
Wicked Weeds (Pedro Cabiya, 2011 [trans. 2016]) – Meta Undead   209

Jay Treagus and Nicola Young
Get Out (Jordan Peele, 2017) – The Undead and Afrofuturism   217

Mikaela Bobiy
Les Revenants (Fabrice Gobert, 2012–2015) – Environmental Undead   225

Catherine Pugh
Antisepticeye (Seán McLoughlin, 2016) – Online Undead   235

Ildikó Limpár
Westworld (Lisa Joy and Jonathan Nolan, 2016–present) – Posthuman Undead   249

Lorna Piatti-Farnell
Marvel Zombies (Robert Kirkman, Sean Phillips and Arthur Suydam, 2005–2006) – Undead Superheroes   257

Simon Bacon
The Cloverfield Paradox (Julius Onah, 2018) – Universal Undead   265

Roger Luckhurst
Epilogue: The Death of Death – *Zero K*, Don DeLillo (2016)   273

Bibliography   281

Notes on Contributors   307

Index   315

Acknowledgements

To begin I'd like to say a huge well done to all the contributors to the book for actually getting their chapters completed under the difficult conditions that the world has thrown at us over the past few years. I would also like to thank Laurel Plapp at Peter Lang for all her help and patience during the production and completion of this book, and indeed with all the books in the *Genre Fiction and Film Companions series*. Many thanks also to all those on FB and Twitter, particularly the members of SCMS Horror Studies Group, the International Gothic Association, Open Graves, Open Minds, and the Manchester Centre for Gothic Studies, who have offered their help and ideas at various stages during this book and have also stood in when contributors have had to pull out. Many thanks also to Jason@SMurnau, who helped with the original cover design of the book, Anthony Hogg for his encouragement and suggestions in getting the project together and for the support of the Vampire Studies Organization (https://vampirestudies.org/) and *The Journal of Vampire Studies*, and all those I have forgotten who offered help and advice along the way. Most importantly I want to thank my amazing wife Kasia for her unending help, patience and support, without whom none of this would get done or be worth doing. Also, our two ever-growing monsters, Seba and Majki, who always manage to provide some light relief and distraction no matter how stressful things get. And last but by no means least the constant support (and sernik Magdi) of Mam i Tata Bronk.

David Punter

Prologue: The Revolution of the Undead

Forty years ago, in the first edition of *The Literature of Terror*, I said this about the twentieth-century horror film:

> The beast may come from the stars or from 20,000 fathoms, from Mars or from beneath the earth, from the moon, Venus, the ocean floor or the black lagoon [...] but wherever it comes from it generally might as well not have bothered: the moral virtues of the clean-cut American hero, sometimes backed up by clean-cut American tanks and guided missiles, prove far too strong – or unattractive – for it to withstand. (Punter 1980: 352)

In the twenty-first century, things have changed. It is no longer so easy to put the monster – the aberrant, the deformed, the grotesque, the zombie – back in its box. Many texts – literary, filmic, televisual – remain unresolved; the invasion continues, often up to the point where it is difficult, as comically envisioned at the conclusion of *Shaun of the Dead* (2004), to tell the difference between the zombie and the 'normal' human being.

And at the heart of this lies the problem, precisely, of 'human being'. In his *Economic and Philosophic Manuscripts* (1844), Marx described four kinds of alienation, or estrangement, which are the product – and the motor force – of capitalism. The one that interests me is estrangement from 'species-being', of which he has this to say:

> Estranged labour turns [...] Man's species being, both nature and his spiritual species property, into a being *alien* to him, into a *means* to his *individual existence*. It estranges from man his own body, as well as external nature and his spiritual essence, his *human* being. (ed. Struik 1964: 114)

It might seem surprising to hear Marx, even the young Marx of 1844, speaking of the spirit; yet how else are we to define the zombie, that cardinal example of the undead, except as a human body without a spirit or soul – or vital spark, or any of the other myriad ways in which we have tried down the millennia to define what it is that makes us human? We might want to consider a few instances of how we have under capitalism attempted to dehumanise work and productivity. 'Manpower'; 'hands'; 'workforce'; and now, above all, 'human resources', as though these resources – living, breathing people who have to live by the work they do, generally in the absence of what we laughably call a state-sponsored 'safety net', as though even the attempt to attain life security through labour is tantamount to the risky activities of a trapeze artist – are simply another disposable on the balance sheet. We are all the precariat now.

Yet we have a reassurance: we may no longer be valued for our labour (whether that be by hand or mind), but we are valued for our consumption. Indeed, we are so valued that we figure largely in terms of the algorithm, the set of predictions of desire that determine the focus of advertising. Human being is now an effect of an algorithm defined as a set of instructions: for that set of instructions, individual behaviour no longer matters; what matters is the mass, the aggregate, the maximisation of sales capacity.

It is not clear at this moment, in the third decade of the twenty-first century, in what age we are living: it might be the Anthropocene, it might (optimistically) be a stage of late capitalism, it might be an age of neoliberal global consensus. But whatever it is, it seems to be an age in which the undead are proliferating. What are these undead? In this book, you will find many examples, and I would not want to rehearse them here, nor would I want to attempt a general definition of the many forms in which they occur and recur. But one thing, I think, is of vast significance, which is that they are, literally, all over the place. We can find them in the West, we can find them in Japan; we can find them in Korea, we can find them in Africa. In Max Brooks's emblematic *World War Z* (2006), their ubiquity and the ways in which different national governments and traditions attempt to deal with them form the entire substrate of the novel.

And we see this not only in our dealings with the undead, but also in our dealings with the perhaps wider sphere of the Gothic. The term 'global Gothic' is now much used, and a valuable term it is; but it is also, of course, a hybrid term, signifying the numerous conjunctions between a history of terror with its origins firmly rooted in Europe and North America and a huge variety of folk traditions with their roots equally firmly in different cultures, different histories. The 'globality' does not refer to a common set of interests, but to a worldwide cultural spread which, although inflected by the local, in the end threatens to absorb the local and either turn it into a version of the dominant, or locate it in a space denoted as the exotic.

Where the undead are, there are bodies; and where there are bodies, there is usually war. It is perhaps not necessary to detail the connections between capitalism and war: suffice to mention the many fictions of manipulated shortages of goods and services which lead to otherwise avoidable conflict, and the close links between governments and the armaments industry. War, of course, pre-dates capitalism; but now it has become an essential part of the economic machine.

And this leads me to a consideration of a text about the undead, Ahmed Saadawi's *Frankenstein in Baghdad*. This is not obviously a zombie text; it does not deal in hordes, or slavering greed, or (exactly) in mindless bodies. It was written in Arabic in 2013, but not translated into English for five years, until 2018, even though in 2014 it had made Saadawi the first Iraqi winner of the prestigious International Prize for Arabic Fiction. Once translated, it was immediately shortlisted for the Man Booker International Prize. Set, of course, in Baghdad, in the years 2003 to 2005, the novel begins from the contentious claims of an alcoholic junk dealer, Hadi, that he has constructed an undead creature from the bits and pieces of broken bodies he finds every day on the war-torn streets of the city. This contention is never fully validated: Hadi is a known liar and storyteller, and rarely certain of his own memories. Amid a large cast of other characters, our main point of focalisation is a young journalist named Mahmoud, who runs across the trail of this creature at various points and in various different ways, all the while having to struggle with the uncertainties of trying to follow a journalist's calling in a city where news is rarely verifiable and almost never true.

The creature, whatever it is, is certainly undead. And although it is a single entity, it also represents myriads, because it is composed of the body parts of all those who have suffered from Iraq's endless wars. But unlike many recent examples of the undead, this creature, although monstrous, is also perceived as heroic:

People in coffee shops spoke of seeing him during the day and vied to describe how horrible he looked. He sits with us in restaurants, goes into clothing shops, or gets on buses with us, they said. He's everywhere and has an amazing speed, jumping from roof to roof and wall to wall in the middle of the night, they added. No one knew who his next victim would be, and despite all the assurances from the government, people grew more convinced with every passing day that he would never die. They were well aware of the stories of bullets passing through him. They knew he didn't bleed and didn't let anyone catch a glimpse of his face. The definitive image of him was whatever lurked in people's heads, fed by fear and despair. It was an image that had as many forms as there were people to conjure it. (Saadawi 2018: 260)

Of course, this paragraph is an account of the Frankenstein mythos, a version of the monster created by a human but failing to be answerable to its supposed master. It focuses on the perceived immortality of the undead; on our ability to remake the creature's form in almost any way we want, as we have seen in countless film versions; on the essential link with fear; on the horror of ugliness; but also, most importantly, on the everyday-ness, the mundanity, of the so-called monster.

The point here is that what Saadawi is recounting is that in a city like war-torn Baghdad, the sighting of deformity or mutilation is hardly strange at all; it is indeed the stuff of common life. Everybody is accustomed to the monstrous as it blurs the line between life and death; indeed, the monstrous, whether physical or ethical, is what is to be expected. And it is what we live with every day; we are no longer able to register whether what is sitting beside us on a bus is human or zombie, alive or dead, a 'natural' creature or a composition of body parts. How do we register the human when the thin line between life and death has proved permeable?

Of course, we do not all live in war zones. Many of us are privileged to pass our lives in protected spaces where we believe we need not fear our fellow human. And yet, is that really true? In Stephen King's novel *Cell* (2006), one of the characters remarks, 'We are all refugees now' (252), and surely this marks one of the most looming of contemporary fears, which is bifurcated at root: our fear of being driven from or supplanted in what we consider to be our native land, which then replicates itself in our fear of the refugee considered as usurper. Politicians of many stripes fuel our fears of the invading hordes, and one way to handle this paranoia is to treat them as less than human, to fail to see their faces, to credit them with malevolently supernatural powers;

in short, to attribute to them all the terrifying powers which the undead have traditionally exercised.

Weaving through *Frankenstein in Baghdad*, alongside the tale of the creature and interlocking with it, there is also a tale of capitalist profiteering, focused on two characters in particular, Hadi himself and Faraj the real estate agent. Hadi's junk business is based on the dead; to him, the dead are indispensable. In one particular incident amid the bomb-fuelled mayhem of Baghdad,

> Ambulances came to pick up the dead and injured, then fire engines to douse the cars and tow trucks to drag them off to an unknown destination. Water hoses washed way the blood and ashes. Hadi watched the scene with eagle eyes, looking for something in particular amid this binge of death and devastation. Once he was sure he had seen it, he threw his cigarette to the ground and rushed to grab it before a powerful jet of water could blast it down into the sewer. He wrapped it into his canvas sack, folded the sack under his arm, and left the scene. (Saadawi 2018: 20)

What Hadi is actually looking for here is body parts, but this is only an extension of his normal activity of searching for the goods that the dead and disappeared may have left behind; it is on this that his business is founded. After one such disappearance, we hear, 'by midday Hadi had sold half the stuff to people living in the area and felt he would make a good profit' (Saadawi 2018: 235). This is an almost exact reimagining of what Brecht had to say so many years ago in *Mother Courage* (1939): that war is primarily a means of gaining profit (Brecht 1986). And Saadawi underlines this through his depiction of Faraj: he

> had many relatives and acquaintances, and when the regime fell, they were the means by which he imposed authority, winning everyone's respect and legalising his appropriation of the abandoned houses, even though everyone knew he didn't have the papers to prove he owned them or had ever rented them from the government. (Saadawi 2018: 12–3)

War for Faraj is a process of acquiring property, preferably the property of the dead, who appear to have no further claim on it. And the creature, composed of body parts, residues of interminable wars, emerges as the culmination of a reappropriation of the bones of the dead: as the physical form of the reanimated undead, he too signifies a form of capitalist enterprise.

The ending of the novel is emblematic of twenty-first-century developments in the depiction of the undead. For political reasons, Hadi is found guilty of the many murders committed by the creature, even though few of his neighbours believe he could possibly have been responsible. But 'reduced to a state of childlike elation, no one could see, or even tried to see, those timid eyes looking out from behind the balconies and windows of the abandoned Orouba Hotel' (Saadawi 2018: 271). Those timid eyes, we are led to believe – rendered timid by his increasing realisation of the things he has done – belong to the creature, who has survived yet again and will, we may presume, continue to exist as long as the dead bodies mount up and Baghdad fails to find, or be permitted to find, peace. As I said at the beginning of this prologue, one of the distinguishing features of the twenty-first-century undead is that they can no longer be banished; after all, those clean-cut American heroes whose operations were so successful even fifty years ago are now no longer the solution to successive waves of terror, they are instead at least part, perhaps indeed the instigators, of the problem.

So perhaps what we can say about the undead now is that they are a function of estrangement: as we grow apart from our species being, then the boundaries between life and death become ever more permeable. Or, in another way of looking at it, the undead are the residues: they are what is left over as we are increasingly reduced to algorithms, the statistical objects of mass consumerism – whether that be in the consumption of goods or of political lies. No wonder, then, they are in a continual state of rising up, nor that we should be – as perhaps at first seems odd – attracted to them; for the undead, I think, are no longer our obvious enemies; instead they are coming more than ever to represent the leftover bits of ourselves, crying out to be noticed, shouting from the sidelines that the capitalist war machine cannot ever fully eradicate what we might ironically call 'the human remains'. And the end point of that structure of irony is that the undead are now in a process of transformation; they are changing from being objects of fear and becoming the repository of what is human within us, the forgotten, abandoned selves peeping out with 'timid eyes' as human being, whatever that might be, continues to be under threat of vanishing before the might of the capitalist war machine.

Simon Bacon

Introduction

There is something inherently undead about the twenty-first century, not just because our age seems to have chosen the shambling zombie slowly plodding toward inevitable entropy as its cultural emblem, but also because we seem inescapably caught between life and death: unable to decide if we want to save ourselves or the planet we live on or just let it all burn as we party like tomorrow will never come. This ambivalence or uncertainty finds form in how many words have been created to try to categorise the current era, such as the Anthropocene,[1] Capitalocene (Moore 2017),[2] Necrocene (O'Brien 2016),[3] Virocene (Fernando 2020),[4] Entropocene (Robbins 2017),[5] Eremocene (Wilson 2014),[6] Disanthropocene (Cohen 2016)[7] and Limbotopia (Gomel 2022).[8] All these view humanity as something of a 'dead man walking' (or shambling) to a point of self-destruction, irrelevance or exhaustion. In this sense, the undead, or undeadness, is a mode of being in the twenty-first

1 Generally assigned to the time period from which human activity on the Earth had potential global impact.
2 More directly related to how capitalist ideologies – as a patriarchal endeavour – have driven the increasingly negative effects of 'mankind' on the planet.
3 Related to the increasing amount of extinction events (death of entire species) that are occurring across the globe.
4 A reflection on how viruses are increasingly determining the future of humanity and therefore the planet.
5 Based on the third law of thermodynamics where all closed systems naturally develop towards entropy and that such a process is currently happening to the Earth.
6 Related to the idea of the Necrocene and that humanity will become increasingly 'lonely' on the Earth as diversity decreases.
7 Talks to a time when we more clearly see the minor 'scale' of human existence in relation to the immense scale of planetary time.
8 Related more specifically to the undead nature of society which, zombie-like, continues to move with little purpose beyond instant gratification.

century which finds expression in our all-consuming yet 'mindless' lifestyles, where we are led by the overwhelming desires of 'now' yet are numb to, and irrevocably detached from, the environment around us. Indeed, an inherent part of being undead is that, in a very real sense, tomorrow never really arrives: it is just an endless continuation of today, or a purposeful attempt to return to the past to avoid tomorrow. Within this then are more focused manifestations of undeadness that express our anxieties around how detached, or undead, we have become to our own environments and even our own skins – a form of cultural and individual repression created by our sublimated realisation that all is not well whilst we choose to carry on regardless. In this way, the more we repress our anxiety of the increasingly dangerous and unstable situation of the world, the more extreme our undead monsters become as they give shape to the anxieties we repress. An obvious example of this would be the comparison between Bram Stoker's *Dracula* (1897), where a group of friends are threatened by the vampire, and Richard Matheson's post-Second World War novel *I Am Legend* (1954), where the entire world is turned into shambling vampires. In the twenty-first century this becomes even more extreme, as seen in *Daybreakers* (2009), where militarised vampires hunt down surviving humans to turn them into cattle for a blood-producing factory.

The undead, giving physical form to our repressed anxieties, no longer threaten just ourselves or our close friends and family, but the entire world, and moreover they plan to do it with insatiable malicious intent. In this way, the impending apocalypse, or extinction event, can only be deferred, never prevented. Consequently, whether zombies, vampires, hungry ghosts, ecological contagion or vengeful AIs, the undead express the central cultural fears of the twenty-first century, which can be further seen to relate to both our alienation from ourselves and the purposeful ignoring of the obvious signs from across the globe that things are going cataclysmically wrong. The undead, then, as an expression of these repressed fears, can provide ways in which to investigate the causes of our deepest anxieties, both individually and collectively, providing strategies that can lead to their resolution or, at the very least, be recognised and accepted.

Undead 2.0

For most of the twentieth century, the word 'undead' would have made people think of vampires, supernaturally energised revenants rising from the grave to suck the life out of their nearest and dearest. At the end of the nineteenth century, Bram Stoker had originally planned to call his novel 'The Dead Un-Dead', based on the idea that Dracula was dead yet still alive in some way. More recently, however, and arguably since George A. Romero's *Night of the Living Dead* (1968), the word has become even more closely related to the figure of the zombie, from the spiritually-possessed-voodoo kind to the rampaging-zombie-horde-heralding-the-start-of-the-apocalypse kind. As noted by Kyle William Bishop, a 'multiplicity of zombies' (2015: 5), or the five ages of the undead, has defined its taxonomic rise from Haitian sorcery to capitalist slave, to all-consuming consumerist, then to the rage caused and released by neoliberalism, and finally to a rhizomic apocalypse of anxiety and discontent that spreads across the popular imaginary. Of note within this, and with the body of the zombie itself, are its indelible signifiers, or traces, as Jack Halberstam would call them (1993: 349), of imperialism (Loza 2017: 7) and slavery, specifically in its relation to blackness and otherness (Wilentz 2012). Subsequently, one should always be aware, as with all origin points of specific monsters, that they carry the discriminations, prejudices and bigotries of their times. However, as observed by Marina Levina and Diem-My T. Bui, the 'multiplicity' is more centred on the idea of the undead (2013: 1–2) than on just zombies, and such a limited view can no longer contain the burgeoning amount of undying entities that rise from our unconscious to feed upon our life-essence. Consequently, the twenty-first-century undead can be many different kinds of manifestations – from a biological jouissance to a primordial god, from a supernatural manifestation to artificial intelligence – though all are united by their inherent vampiric characteristics of a dependence upon humanity for sustenance and of lifespans beyond human existence and comprehension. This last is of particular importance, as it relates directly to humanity's not always openly acknowledged realisation of its insignificance in the face of environmental or planetary time. (Jeffrey Cohen talks of this in relation to his term 'Disanthropocene' and how short the human lifespan is in relation to that of the planetary ecosystem, which itself relates to Timothy Morton's idea of 'hyper objects').[9] In this way the immortality of the undead is in direct correlation to the anxiety we experience, and often repress, at our total insignificance in the face of the world around us and its complete disregard for us. Equally, the undead's insatiable need to consume us is a reflection of our own unstoppable desire to drain the world of its resources. As such, they more obviously become our dark reflections, alter egos or doppelgängers that are necessarily intent on our destruction. They also differ from most traditional monsters, killers and fiends in that they do not stop; they can be outrun, they can be evaded, they can be obstructed, but they cannot be stopped. Whether it is the lone monster from *It Follows* (2014), which just walks towards its prey with little sense of urgency, slowly working its way through humanity one transgressive person at a time, or the psychotropic creatures causing millions to commit suicide in *Bird Box* (2018), these entities can be seen to drain human life or emotional energies in some way. What is also of note in many of these kinds of twenty-first-century undead is that, although they express a wider cultural anxiety, they possess a very specific face or form for the individual they are currently pursuing or feeding upon. In *It Follows*, the creature is not only invisible to others apart from its intended victim but often changes its appearance to confuse them or look like someone they know. Similarly, in *Bird Box*, the possibly alien entities appear to show a different face to everyone that sees them, as evidenced in the multiple and completely unique drawings made of them.

Inherently within this is the idea of excess that, in part, is produced by and resonates with a similar kind of extremity as seen in the temporal character of the undead themselves, so that as the immortality of the undead is representative of an excess of time that is beyond our comprehension, the manifestation of the undead stretches our emotional and physical responses beyond their normal limits. There is a sense, then, that the mere apprehension of the appearance of the undead causes heightened emotional states, a sense of the 'fight or flight' instinct constantly being triggered.

9   Morton talks of objects so immense that the concept of time relates differently to them, as seen in huge objects such as planets or stars, but equally in things like plastic that once created never decompose.

Unsurprisingly, these feelings of continual dread and existential threat become connected to extremist or excessive states in popular culture. This sees these states being given expression and/or validation through fundamentalist discourses related to the fallout of the War on Terror, the rise of religious extremism and terrorism, the increase in populist politics, the seemingly inevitable decline of the ecosystem, and the extinction of humanity itself, so that the undead of the popular imagination become the embodiment of continual and never-ending existential dread (see Phillips 2021). Such a heightened state of living would seem contrary to the idea of an undead, zombie-like society, yet as seen in films like *World War Z* (2013), *Army of the Dead* (2021) and even *The Silence* (2019) – the 'veeps' in *The Silence*, whilst not zombies, act like an undead horde – such collectives are extremely easy to arouse, distract and redirect. However, once the undead are brought forth or unleashed, they never give up, and even when they seem to have been eradicated completely, there is only ever a brief respite before it begins again.

The idea of never-ending repetition or resurrection of the undead in their attempt to destroy us – or rather the world that has created and unleashed them – can then be more clearly seen to act like a form of trauma that is impelled to continue. Such traumas, whilst being identified as endemic to our culture in the early twenty-first century (see Bracken 2002; Kaplan 2005; Ataria 2017), are created around the notion of an originary event, and an ongoing inability to recognise or be able to reintegrate that event and its consequences into our lives and how we relate to the world around us. The twenty-first-century undead and the kinds of trauma that create them in the first place, the dark aporia that lies between us and meaningful connection to the environment around us, is a wound that can never be healed, and the traces of the passing of the undead are all potential triggers to opening the maw of undeath once again. And so the vampire will not only rise from the grave but, reflecting the excess and depth of the traumatic aporia, it will not come singly but as a plague that will spread unstoppably amongst the faithful (*Midnight Mass*, 2021); the zombie horde will never be completely destroyed, but is waiting to be reanimated in even greater numbers (*The Girl with All the Gifts*, 2016); the curse of Sadako can no longer be ended by burning video tapes, as she is now a computer virus released onto the internet (*Ring*, 2002–present); and the undead spirit of violence will never be satiated as it spreads from house to house across the world (*Grudge*, 2004–present).

Alongside this is the increasing number of natural environments that are shown as unwelcoming or expressly malignant towards human intervention, and more particularly a white, privileged colonial kind of intrusion. Here, the undead 'gods' of times before the Anthropocene enact a form of reverse colonisation by intruding into the present and creating exclusion zones where humanity is no longer welcome, except as a food source, revealing both how disconnected we are from the world around us and how small our conception of time and our importance within it have become. Films such as *The Ritual* (2017), *Midsommar* (2019), *In the Tall Grass* (2019) and *No One Gets Out Alive* (2021) show how pervasive these areas of exclusion have become, from territories on the periphery of 'civilisation' to those not just in the midst of the 'modern' privileged world but even in bustling city centres, displaying how we have become unwelcome strangers in both rural and urban environments in a world we call our own. More clearly, this communicates how in the twenty-first century we have become inherently unhomely in our own environment.

One other aspect of the undead is worth mentioning here, namely how they are shown to be equally at 'home' in the future as in the present, and often in a way that humanity is not. From *The Walking Dead* (2010–22) to the *Terminator* franchise (1984–2019), and from *Annihilation* (2018) to *The Girl with All the Gifts*, the undead and undying have become more integral to the evolving world, whilst we have become increasingly extraneous and peripheral, creating an environment that is openly antagonistic to human life as we currently know it. Here, then, the anxiety is that we are detached not only from the here and now, but also from any possible future that might emerge from it. This again highlights the disparity between human and planetary time, and that 'life', as a universal force that constantly mutates and changes to whatever shapes and forms are best suited to its continuance regardless of any specific expression of it, has little regard or 'time' for humanity if it is no longer suited to the environment it is in. In this sense, the undead in the twenty-first century are not against life – indeed, they express its continuation beyond what we conceive of as 'death' – but rather express just how removed humanity is from recognising its own place within life. To paraphrase Count Dracula, 'time is on their side', and while there is still 'time', they will continue.

Undead Configurations

The undead in the twenty-first century are a many-splendoured thing, not just in their various shapes and manifestations but also in the categories and meanings they signify or represent. No longer just signalling a past that will not let us go, they take on the mantle of existential anxieties around the very meaning of individual identity and humanity itself, and not just in the present, but in the many possible futures that might occur, with or without humans. Indeed, one of the main complications of looking at the undead is that they are purposely outside human conceptions of life and normality – though we often try to humanise them to make them containable in some way – which makes them necessarily super-normal,[10] super-natural and beyond ideas of human longevity. Something of this is suggested in Elaine Showalter's idea of the undead being a 'third' thing, neither dead nor alive but something else (1992: 197). She tends towards linking this to a form of inherent queerness, and there is much that is queer about the undead in being decidedly non-binary yet also resisting definitive categorisation. Nils Bubandt builds on this, describing 'undeadness' as a state of indeterminacy (see Bubandt 2022). He further sees this inability to fully grasp or categorise the world as a way of linking contemporary society to cultures where folklore and superstition still hold sway, and where the undead provide the most fitting way to describe phenomena that occur in the world around them. As intimated earlier, this sees the undead less as a single thing or event, but is as much a way of understanding the world as it is of being in it. Recognising the undeadness of the world, and how it describes our relation to it, then becomes a fundamental way of investigating what has gone wrong with that relationship, as will be discussed further below. Indeterminacy also finds resonance in Timothy Morton's 'hyperobjects', mentioned previously, not necessarily in terms of objective size but more in how they 'defy overview and resist understanding' (Morton 2013: 1). Positioning them beyond human

---

10   Designer Jasper Morrison uses the words Super Normal to describe objects that are anonymously designed but inevitably exceed the everyday, and the world of the specific and unique (Morrison 2015).

comprehension (one might almost add, 'not of this world') further points to their inherently unhomely nature, or rather how they appear unhomely to the world as we know it; as noted above, our 'knowledge' of the world is such that humanity is always central to its ultimate meaning.[11]

The notion of the unhomely is important when considering the undead and has been mentioned above. Largely coming from Sigmund Freud's 'unheimlich' and his theories around the uncanny, it speaks to how the familiar, the heimlich, can suddenly become unfamiliar, or unheimlich (Freud 2003). To illustrate this, Freud uses the short story of 'The Sandman' (1816) by E. T. A. Hoffman, which centres on a lifelike doll that a young man is convinced is a beautiful girl and subsequently falls in love with. Although this exemplifies what has more recently been termed the 'uncanny valley' – where robots appear 'creepy' when they look too human – Freud saw the larger story as relating to castration anxiety, which more obviously focuses on male (human)-based fears within the story rather than on how the uncanny can more clearly talk to how we as individuals and as a culture relate to our environments. (The young man is so wrapped up in his own emotive reaction that he is oblivious to the wider world around him.) More useful for how 'unhomely' is used in this Companion is how Martin Heidegger relates the idea of the uncanny, the unhomely, as being fundamental to our experience of reality – not unlike the mode of being undead described previously – and that it provides a way for us to investigate reality and achieve some level of authenticity (Buchoul 2013). Whilst Heidegger was certainly not thinking about the undead, how he saw the unheimlich as a tool to look at our place in the world beyond that presented on the surface is of great use here. As already noted, the undead are a manifestation of how out of place we are in the world; their unhomeliness is a reflection of our own, so that the more intensely we feel it, the more extreme the undead become, and this relates to Heidegger's sense of not-being-at-home. In this way, by investigating the nature of the undead (effectively our own feelings of being unhomely), we

---

11 A case in point is the dual nature of particles that can be seen to act as both waves and particles depending on the experiment used to observe them. Rather than being interpreted as our inability to fully comprehend the world around us, this duality is often used to show the importance of the presence of humanity to observe the universe to give it meaning.

might more clearly understand the real nature of our relation to the world around us and recalibrate our actions and conceptions of it and to it accordingly. The appearance of the excessive undead then acts as a kind of revelation, a revealing of our true place in the world. It is not coincidental that one of the words often associated with the undead is 'apocalypse', which in its biblical use means 'revelation'. In these terms, the undead are inherently apocalyptic: not necessarily harbingers of evil, but a signal of the impending end of the world as we know it. Consequently, the undead and the unhomeliness they embody and inspire are a signal that our world is so out of balance that it will end unless we do something about it by examining how and why we have become so unhomely.

Although much of what has been said points to the necessity of re-examining our undead, and more particularly our relation to them, the resistance that humanity displays towards this finds expression in other ways. In part, such resistance, largely expressed through denial and repression, directly causes the explosive nature of the undead as they erupt into the conscious world. However, on a more Freudian view, resistance also gives shape and impetus to a contrary desire for the world and human life to end (Freud 1990). Freud, of course, saw this drive towards death as an inherent part of life and a dualistic view of existence; in many respects, this is seen in the film *Nosferatu*, where the figure symbolising light and life, Ellen, is drawn towards darkness and death as seen in the vampire. This death drive sees us being pulled towards our own destruction, even though we know how bad that will be, and as somehow yearning to embrace the undead as a means of achieving the transcendental or sublime in some way; some eschatological views wish to precipitate the end of days so that they may transcend to heaven. However, Slavoj Žižek views it more as expressive of endless consumption and nearer to a 'zombie-drive' inherent to capitalism (Sigurdson 2013). This very much reflects the notion of the Capitalocene, which brings us back to the idea of undeadness as a mode of being in the twenty-first century.

A curious twist within this, and one which concerns the idea of 'embracing' the undead, is the relatively recent phenomenon of romantic relationships with zombies and other non-human entities. Although this would superficially speak to what has been said about the death drive, the point in these relationships is very rarely death but often the (re)humanising of the undead. This would seem to intimate two different directions here, with the first being a way to try and make the unhomely undead more heimlich and less uncanny. One of the few films to attempt this is *The Breed* (2001). It works to a point; and yet the body of the undead, whether zombie, vampire or whatever, even if (re)turned to human form in some way, is still one that might be hundreds of years old or has survived only on human brains and so can never configure a recognition of the difference between the human and planetary scales. What this does often reveal, though, is the porosity of bodies. One might expect this in the undead body (corpse), but its proximity also causes it in the human one. On one level this reveals a kind of hybridity between the undead and humanity, as seen in films like *Splinter* (2008), *The Girl with All the Gifts* and *Annihilation*, but also a Gothicisation of the body where it is 'continually in danger of becoming not-itself, becoming other' (Hurley 2004: 3). Kelly Hurley's identification of such bodies as being 'abhuman' sees the human body as one that has become porous, pliable and potentialised, constantly on the cusp of changing into something else. This further sees Gothicisation as closely akin to the idea of undead in terms of a mode of being where the homely becomes unstable and unfamiliar, and hence also intimating the ways in which our own bodies, that we often see as unchanging and impermeable, can become unstable and consequently unhomely to ourselves. This further suggests that it is impossible for the human body to remain absolute and separate from its environment, and that it will inevitably change with its surroundings. In this configuration, the environment no longer waits for humanity to decipher the meaning of the undead rampaging across the globe, but rather rewrites the nature of the human body, seeing it as a living palimpsest that can be forcibly wiped clean and reintegrated into an ever-evolving world. Terms like Virusocene capture some of this, although the 'Symbiocene' (Everard 2016) addresses it more directly, seeing a future of inevitable and irrevocable entanglement between us and the environment. This, too, signals the end of the world as we know it, but also marks the beginning of a world where we more clearly recognise the environment and our place within it.

The Face of the Undead

In very general terms, then, the undead as described above can be loosely grouped into four areas: Undead Cultures in the Global Present, The Undead and Never-ending Present, Undying Identity, and Undead Futures. These are variously intersected by cultural and individual fears around identity, sexuality, ethnicity, belonging and the environment, which will inevitably create further currents, trends and resonances revealing the intricacies and complications of the undead and how they are implicated within the very fabric of being in the twenty-first century.

This collection begins with 'Prologue: The Revolution of the Undead' by David Punter, which sketches out what we might expect of the recent undead in comparison to their former, slightly less apocalyptic selves. This then moves to 'Part I: Undead Cultures in the Global Present', which more broadly looks at the idea of undead national and ethnic identities in the face of homogenising globalism. Here, examples from contemporary Folk, First Nation, Aboriginal, South American, Indian and Korean traditions configure the traumas of all-consuming colonial intent and the resistance of undying traditions and mythologies. The first chapter, '*Hereditary* (Ari Aster, 2018): Folk Horror and the Undead' by Mikel J. Koven, discusses more generally the elements that constitute 'folk Horror' and how they play into contemporary texts like *Hereditary*. Koven further argues that the undead nature of the folklore behind such narratives is one that is constantly accumulating and 'consuming' new elements, so that it is as undying as the monsters it often describes. This is followed by 'La Llorona (Various, 2006–2019): Mexican Undead' by Cristina Santos, which continues the theme of the colonising and globalising of traditions but in ways that change and transform the original meanings of mythic characters. Here, the undead figure of La Llorona, which began as a manifestation of the monstrous feminine and a point of opposition to dominant patriarchal ideologies, has been reduced to stealing milk from the fridge in the middle of the night in the service of contemporary capitalist society. Next is Iain Robert Smith's '*Go Goa Gone* (Raj and D. K., 2013): Bollywood Undead', which continues this theme of the globalisation of traditional characters and modes of expression with negative and positive results. Focusing on the film

Go Goa Gone, Smith shows the incursion of the zombie into Indian cinema as a point both of evolution and of cultural homogenisation. '*Wakening* (Danis Goulet, 2013): Métis-Cree Undead' by John R. Ziegler proceeds in a similar vein, focusing on a very particular example of North American Métis-Cree folklore around the figure of the 'weetigo', but also highlights points of burgeoning resistance and agency. Broadly configured as a cannibalistic spirit, the weetigo has been associated with the colonising settlers and seen as a means for re-establishing and recolonising their own lands and identities, revealing the undead nature of their own lore and myths. Naomi Simone Borwein, in '*Killer Native* (Bjorn Stewart, 2019): Australian Aboriginal Undead', also examines the ongoing processes of globalisation, but describes ways in which it is appropriated and repurposed in indigenous culture. Here, the all-consuming zombie is integrated into Aboriginal Dreamtime narratives revealing the entanglement of joint histories and ongoing traumas of a violent past. Part I ends with '*Seoul Station* (Sang-ho Yeon, 2016): South Korean Undead' by Katarzyna Ancuta, which describes how a culture can absorb and reappropriate the global dead to its own ends. Ancuta shows how the zombie narrative in South Korea is used to critique local and national governments and their dehumanising treatment of the poor and the homeless.

'Part II: The Undead and Never-ending Present' considers aspects and spaces of everyday life that have become points of extreme anxiety in relation to neoliberalism and globalisation, such as mental health, ageing, misogyny, racism, education and the Church, that complicate the relationships and entanglements between tradition and modernity, patriarchal ideology and sexual and ethnic equality. It begins with '*The Haunting of Hill House* (Mike Flanagan, 2018): Domestic Undead', where Dara Downey considers the most heimlich environment that we know, the family home. Yet here, under the guise of tradition and the (super)natural order, the home is shown to be a form of patriarchal, normative undead ideology that consumes all that comes under its influence. Related ideas are found in Tyler Unsell's '*The Girl with All the Gifts* (Colm McCarthy, 2016): Undead Classroom', which considers the nature of education and the necessity of its ongoing evolution. Unsell notes the undead nature of certain perspectives on teaching and the need to change alongside the students and environment. Antares Leask, in '*ZOMBIES 2* (Paul Hoen, 2020): Anti-Racist Undead', also focuses on a teaching environment, although here education involves a change of ideological viewpoint. Exampled here is how, even in a school of monsters, otherness and acceptance, there are ongoing negations. This is followed by '*Deadgirl* (Marcel Sarmiento and Gadi Harel, 2017): Undead Rape Culture' by Natalie Wilson, which focuses on older high school students, specifically male ones. Here it is 'institutionalised' misogyny and the objectification of women that create an undead environment that is perpetuated by men and yet, literally, comes back to kill them. '*The Nun* (Corin Hardy, 2018): Religious Undead' by Brandon R. Grafius moves to another Western cultural institution, the Church. Grafius notes the centrality of the Catholic Church in many horror texts as a point of help and hope in the bid to alleviate or expiate the pull towards undeadness and possible transcendence. '*Saint Maud* (Rose Glass, 2019): Medical Undead' by Laura R. Kremmel considers people requiring end-of-life care and the effect it has on those who care for them. Both the terminally ill patient and the carer are positioned in a liminal, undead state between life and death that might or might not lead to an existence beyond. Jeffrey Andrew Weinstock, in '*Bubba Ho-tep* (Don Coscarelli, 2002): Ageing and the Undead', considers care homes and those who end their days there caught between life and death. Within this is an examination of the undead trials of old age and the quest to remember and be remembered. The final chapter in this part, '*Relic* (Natalie Erika James, 2020): Undead Heritage' by Gina Wisker, further studies the effects of old age and dementia, and the role of daughters and granddaughters as carers. Here, though, the liminal, undead positioning of the increasingly 'monstrous' grandmother is not just a singular event but one which will inevitably be revisited on those of her own bloodline.

Next is 'Part III: Undying Identity', which examines growing cultural anxieties around gender and/or identity positions. Beginning with those that are in many respects overdetermined – undead and unchanging – this part then moves on to those that are in a state of undying flux, caught between a past of determined cultural meanings and a present where they are Gothicised and hybrid. '*AHS: Hotel* (Ryan Murphy and Brad Falchuk, 2015–2016) and *The Strain* (Guillermo del Toro and Chuck Hogan, 2014–2017): Undead Children' by Leah Richards focuses on instances of vampiric children. Of note here is how the inherent monstrosity of the children is utilised to bring out an undead response in the mother figures' nether-narratives. Sara Williams, in 'Suspiria (Luca Guadagnino, 2018): Undead Motherhood', takes this further to a representation of a truly monstrous and undead mother. Mother Suspiriorum is the undead spirit of the gaping maw at the repressed heart of patriarchy and the undead, undying feminine that threatens to consume it. In 'Game of Thrones (David Benioff, 2011–2019): Undead Masculinity', Valerie Estelle Frankel shifts the focus to forms of male identity positions that are as undead as the characters that embody them. Of particular importance here is the stereotypical, or undead, responses they provoke in the characters around them. In 'Dorohedoro (Q Hayashida, 2000–2018): Transgender Undead', Madeleine Mackenzie further examines masculine identity positions in relation to various degrees of trauma. Here, the protagonist, in multiple, often undead embodiments, finds identity in their true self beyond the impositions of the worlds around them. Something of this carries over into '"The Zombie Mermaid" (Katelynn E. Koontz, 2018): Undead Mermaids' by Martine Mussies, which more obviously focuses on hybrid bodies and identities. The zombie mermaid purposely defies categories, self-identifying as a 'misfit', an ineffably indeterminate status that inherently makes it one of the undead. This is followed by an examination of the pressures not to be a 'misfit' and to conform to what the world requires you to be in 'Bloodthirsty (Amelia Moses, 2021): Undead Celebrity' by Gwyneth Peaty, which focuses on the world of celebrity. Like the music industry shown in this example, celebrity creates 'products' to consume and be consumed, and this chapter sees the twenty-first-century popular obsession with 'being known' as one which monsterises us all. Next is Antonio Alcala Gonzalez with 'Behemoth (Nergal and others, 1991–present): Extreme Metal and the Undead', a consideration of the intersection between one of the oldest undead manifestations in the Western world, that of Satan and Extreme Metal music. Here, both the Devil and the music that appropriates him are shown to be purposely beyond all normative and binary categorisation to create an identity position that is uniquely other.

The collection ends with 'Part IV: Undead Futures', which considers ways in which ideas of the undead are used to configure the future. These futures can be seen as agentic or evolutionary in some way, as seen in Afrofuturism and Afrofuturismo, and yet can also reveal deeper and darker anxieties around our changing relationship to the environment, the technologies that structure our lives and even the future itself. Persephone Braham, in '*Wicked Weeds* (Pedro Cabiya, 2011 [trans. 2016]): Meta Undead', considers the origin of zombie narratives from the Caribbean islands, such as Haiti. Whilst these narratives have been largely configured to negativise the region, Braham points to new stories that reinvent and subvert the figure and the meaning of the Caribbean zombie. '*Get Out* (Jordan Peele, 2017): The Undead and Afrofuturism' by Jay Treagus and Nicola Young examines the undead technologies of whiteness. Here, through an Afrofuturist lens, the control of these technologies can be wrested from undead hands and put into the hands of those whom they were formerly used to control. This is followed by '*Les Revenants* (Fabrice Gobert, 2012–2015): Environmental Undead' by Mikaela Bobiy, which also considers technologies, though in this case those used to control and upset the balance of the environment. The environment responds in kind, upsetting the balance of human life, death and memory, so that the local community becomes entrapped in an undead world it cannot escape. The theme of technology continues in 'Antisepticeye (Seán McLoughlin, 2016): Online Undead' by Catherine Pugh, which focuses on how the nature of the internet is inherently conducive to the undead. The gap between real and online identities is full of spectral presences and ghosts, a place of anxiety where the unreal, or unliving, can hold sway over reality. Ildikó Limpár's '*Westworld* (Lisa Joy and Jonathan Nolan, 2016–Present): Posthuman Undead' continues the idea of technology and manufactured, or undead, identities, but in the offline world of a futuristic theme park. Here, non-human machines find not life exactly, but rather a kind of humanity in being neither alive nor dead but becoming 'aware'. This is followed by Lorna Piatti-Farnell's '*Marvel Zombies* (Robert Kirkman, Sean Phillips and Arthur Suydam, 2005–2006): Undead Superheroes', which also features manufactured identities, in this case those that are designed to be ideologically aspirational. However, when ideology becomes undead, its heroes no longer save humanity but promise a future without them. In the final chapter, '*The Cloverfield Paradox* (Julius Onah, 2018): Universal Undead' by Simon Bacon, it seems that the future itself wants to devour humanity with a parallel world intent on destroying our own. The volume concludes with 'Epilogue: The Death of Death – *Zero K*, Don DeLillo (2016)' by Roger Luckhurst, who, using the lens of the authors late novel, examines a possible tomorrow where humanity is frozen in time. This cryogenic future, which is already taking shape in our own time, is one where death as we know it will vanish from the world to be replaced by an undeath that will never end.

Part I

Undead Cultures in the Global Present

Mikel J. Koven

Hereditary (Ari Aster, 2018)

Folk horror lives in the intersection of three separate discourses: satanism/witchcraft/paganism, the rural, and folklore. These discourses exist independently of one another, but when combined, the space of overlap defines the terrain of folk horror. The analysis of the folk horror film needs to treat each discourse separately before one can see how each informs the other in interpretation of the film and its (possible) wider significance.

Folk horror is contemporary horror cinema's most distinct subgenre in the twenty-first century. Originally the term was used to distinguish the (explicitly) British films *The Witchfinder General* (Michael Reeves, 1968), *Blood on Satan's Claw* (Piers Haggard, 1971) and *The Wicker Man* (Robin Hardy, 1973) from the dominance of Hammer's 'campy' horror films of the late 1960s and early 1970s (Simpson 2013). The films depicted, exclusively, British folklore survivals and belief traditions of previous centuries persisting into 'today', despite two of the above-mentioned films being set in historical pasts and only *The Wicker Man* set contemporaneously.

As far back as 2011, Ben Wheatley's *Kill List* revived the folk horror film, which has since increased in popularity and expanded beyond British cinema, with examples from the USA (*The Witch*, Robert Eggers, 2015), South Korea (*The Wailing*, Na Hong-Jin, 2016), Germany (*Hagazussa*, Lukas Feigelfeld, 2017) and India (*Tumbbad*, Rahi Anil Barve, 2018), to name a representative few. However, and despite the contemporary vogue for folk horror film production, the subgenre often has little to do with a concept of the 'undead' specifically. While most of the films considered to be folk horror focus on witchcraft in some form or other, witches, despite being supernaturally empowered, are still very mortal creatures; that is, they can die without resurrection. The same applies to the supernatural agencies which do said empowering (Satan, the Devil, other demons and pre-Christian gods), none of which are 'undead', as they never lived as mortal in the first place. To be 'undead', one must first have been 'dead' and then somehow resurrected (regardless of agency). To be 'dead' suggests a former 'life' and therefore being 'mortal'. Gods, devils and demons who never lived as mortal cannot be considered 'undead', as they never mortally 'died'. Unlike vampires, zombies or ghosts, the witches and supernatural forces/entities which populate folk horror films do not meet the most liberal of definitions of the 'undead'.

Despite these definitional characteristics, Ari Aster's breakthrough feature film, *Hereditary* (2018), seems to yolk elements of folk horror with the supernatural thriller, and in so doing uses folk horror as a discourse, a commentary on 'the undead' in the twenty-first century, through a return to the traditional ghost story. In the film, Annie Graham (Toni Collette) is trying to move past the recent death of her mother, Ellen (Kathleen Chalfant), with whom she had a strongly ambivalent relationship, while she attempts to complete an art exhibition making miniature dioramas of her own life. She has a strained relationship with her 16-year-old son, Peter (Alex Wolff), but does not want to repeat Ellen's mistakes. Her relationship with her 13-year-old daughter, Charlie (Milly Shapiro), is also difficult, with Charlie displaying autistic-like behaviours, or an emerging personality disorder. Within weeks of Ellen's death, Charlie is killed in a freak accident, for which Peter was responsible. Peter is wracked with guilt, and Annie blames Peter for Charlie's death. The deaths of both her mother and daughter, and the increasing tension between her and Peter, lead Annie (sceptically at first) to explore spiritualism and contacting the dead through a spirit medium, via a chance friendship with Joan (Ann Dowd), who recently lost her grandson. As Annie gets deeper into the spiritualist world, becoming increasingly obsessed with contacting Charlie, the supernatural events in her home increase, leading to more tragedy. In this regard, Aster's narrative focuses on the spiritual emptiness of the twenty-first century, a universe as sterile as Annie's dioramas – perfect and unchanging – but suggests that, despite such emptiness, we still strive for evidence of meaning in all our existential pain. What does Ellen's parental negligence and abuse *mean*? What does Charlie's death *mean*? The Church has failed us, and science has failed us, on that one fundamental question of 'Why does this hurt so much?' and, as a twenty-first-century meditation on this kind of existential pain, the film suggests there is no place we can go to for answers.

Hereditary (2018)

In the film's final minutes, Aster shifts gears abruptly. With Peter the only apparent survivor of the supernatural events which have rocked the Graham household, he is drawn to the family treehouse, and there discovers that everything the family has gone through, including Ellen's negligent mothering, has all been to find the perfect host to embody the demon Paimon in Peter. Annie's family have for generations been leading priests of this cult dedicated to breeding the perfect host for their god, and even the chance encounter, and subsequent friendship, with Joan has all been part of the plan to embody Paimon. What begins as a traditional ghost story, albeit with twenty-first-century existential angst, turns into an explicit folk horror film in the tradition of *The Wicker Man* or *Blood on Satan's Claw*. It is this aspect of the film's folk horror connections that I wish to confine most of my commentary to.

As noted at the outset of this chapter, folk horror consists of three intersecting discourses. Each discourse functions as commentary on the topic, as exemplified by the film. In this regard, the film should be seen as symptomatic of a larger set of discourses, outlined below.

To begin with witchcraft, Satanism and paganism are not synonyms: they are vastly different belief/disbelief traditions. This is not a case for their interchangeability. Alan Cameron offers a rigorous deconstruction of the Latin etymology of the word 'pagan' in the late Roman period. Space does not permit me to go into much detail of this history, but to summarise, while a popular understanding of the word refers to 'country dweller' (2011: 26), a more nuanced definition, such as Cameron's, notes the word's particular use to refer to those born 'outside' the Church – that is, outside of Christianity; in the early Christian writings, 'pagan' was a non-pejorative means to refer to non-Christians (2011: 23–4). As the word becomes the standard way to refer to a non-Christian *by a Christian*, 'pagan' was never self-defining but used to refer to the Other (2011: 27). Witchcraft, furthermore, needs to be read as a *less neutral* reference to those selfsame outsiders to Christ. This should suggest not a vilification of those who self-identify *as* witches in contemporary society but how the Church vilifies those who are not part of its own membership. Satanism is more direct in that it emerges (particularly under Anton LeVey in 1966 with his 'Church of Satan') as an oppositional group *to* Christianity. The connection of Paganism, witchcraft and Satanism, particularly in folk horror films, is as an oppositional faith-based group, in specific opposition to

Christianity, despite any explicit Christian group to oppose within the diegesis. Christianity, in this regard, is the structured absence to which all folk horror films (at least within the Christian West) refer, despite actual referents to such groups. To use *The Wicker Man* as an obvious example, a base level of understanding is that the deeply Christian Sergeant Howie (Edward Woodward) is the outsider to Summerisle; that is, ironically pagan to the pagan community in the film. A more nuanced reading, such as I am suggesting here, indicates that not to be the case. Despite Howie's outsider-status to Summerisle, he represents an implicit norm (for the audience) to which the islanders, despite their dominance (and ultimate success) in the film, are oppositional. Christian hegemony structures the existence of the Pagan because that definition is imposed on them by Christendom. Pagans never define themselves but appropriate the label from those who see them *as* outsiders.

The obvious connection in *Hereditary* is with the cult of Paimon at the heart of the film's diegesis. This is not the connection I want to make, however. If we are to read Paganism as any antagonism Christianity holds towards those who are not its members, the Graham family are constructed as Pagan from the very beginning of the film. David Crow, writing for the website *Den of Geek* (2018), has no qualms conflating witches, Satanists and demons in his discussion of *Hereditary*, thereby, intentionally or not, reflecting that the belief community of Paimon worshippers are simply the Other to Christendom: they are simply 'pagan', and therefore suspicious, if not actually evil. The Grahams are outsiders in many ways, but Annie's difficulty in allowing herself to be absorbed into the bereavement group is particularly strained. The group exists to help families overcome bereavement, obviously, but that is not a space Annie can find any solace from. The intensity and intimacy of the narrative she tells in the group increasingly alienates Annie within the film frame, until she is alone. The only person Annie speaks to who is not family is Joan, and it is Joan who has to make the first move approaching Annie, flagging her down as she tries to drive away thinking she is safe in the isolation of her car. The Grahams are not (apparently) churchgoers of any kind, and even the funerals – of Ellen and Charlie – are not religious services. Aster's camera lingers on the necklace around Ellen's neck as she lies in her casket, which is identical to the one around Annie's neck as she delivers her eulogy. Even in the shot around the grave at Charlie's funeral, there appears to be no officiating clergy. The only connection Peter has with the other high school students is through smoking weed, and even then he is very much on the margins of those groups. We may relate to the Grahams' feelings of isolation and alienation, of wanting private mourning, but considering the film's discourse on paganism (understood as Christian antagonism to those who do not join its community), *Hereditary* suggests a series of provocations regarding belonging and community. The Christian (the cultural hegemonic) might read the film (at least until the denouement) as evidence of the importance of Church-based communities providing solace to the Grahams in the wake of these personal tragedies. However, as we learn by the end, the Grahams have always been part of a faith-based community, just one that the Church does not recognise and that the Grahams do not recognise themselves as belonging to. To read the Grahams as existing outside any dominant American religious context, to read them as *faith-less*, is to read the family as pagan to hegemonic ('normal') Christendom. So, the first discourse of folk horror in *Hereditary* is the discomfort and the uncanny, unheimlich nature of existing outside of Christendom; and if one *can* indeed, live (or die) outside of Christendom, what are the actual benefits of being inside this community?

The second discourse is the rural, specifically on the psychogeography of the rural landscape. The three key works on folk horror (Beam and Paciorek 2015; Scovell 2017; Ingham 2018) all put the rural landscape at the centre of folk horror, what Scovell has named his 'folk horror chain'. His 'causational narrative theory' (2017: 8) begins with the rural landscape itself, which in turn heightens a sense of isolation wherein 'skewed belief systems and morality' flourish, and which culminates in some kind of 'happening' or 'summoning' (Scovell 2017: 17–18; see also Paciorek 2015: 10–11). In *Hereditary*, the 'chain' might have been a structuring device for Aster's screenplay: the Grahams live in the country, which isolates them from others (children must be driven to school and for any normal socialisation activities). Even the unnamed town nearby is smaller than a typical American city, and it is this small town, isolated from the rest of the country, which has allowed the Paimon cult to flourish without drawing attention to itself. Finally, at the film's climax, the culmination ritual, which will see the ancient god/demon embodied in Peter, is the final stage of 'summoning' in this folk horror chain. For writers like Paciorek, Scovell and Ingham, folk horror is only focused on that chain. While these writers are correct on the importance of the rural in folk horror, by focusing only on the chain, other discourses are overlooked, namely the Pagan and the Folklore itself. The Paimon cult's isolation in the rural American landscape is what has allowed it to flourish (particularly in Mormon-dominated Utah, where the film was shot, which the rest of the country may see as cult-like); in a larger city, the inevitable culmination of the ritual might be less assured because of the distractions a city offers, including the existence of other faith-based communities.

The final discourse is folklore itself. Calling the subgenre 'folk horror' should put the folklore at the centre of any such discussion, but too often, at least in the existing scholarly literature, it is the folklore which gets the shortest shrift. Paciorek, for example, defines folk horror as having 'a rural, earthy association to ancient European pagan and witchcraft traditions or folklore' (2015: 9). In this definition, Paciorek touches upon the three key areas I note are part of the discursive combination in folk horror, but he is notably vague on what he means by 'folklore' (as are the other writers cited here). Space does not allow me a full deconstruction of their use of this word; however, to summarise, there is a common-sense understanding (much like with 'pagan') that we just understand that 'folklore' refers to 'Olde World' survivals of a pagan past in contemporary European culture. Prior to its replacement by the word 'folklore' in 1846 by William John Thoms, eighteenth-century antiquarians used the term 'popular antiquities' to refer to stories, songs, material culture and 'superstitions' which persist into the contemporary world, and which are purported to give insight into the world view of earlier generations. In truth, folklore is much broader than that, with the narratives, beliefs and material cultures of contemporary societies being as relevant for the folklorist to study as any old collection of witch superstitions. To say that folk horror films include 'folklore' is self-evident, in that *all* films, in one form or another, can be of folkloristic interest; this is not predicated on survivals from earliest times, although they do tend to connect with older traditions, of varying degrees, which require investigation. It is 'folklore' which is the true undead in twenty-first-century folk horror: not only the persistence of such folkloristic beliefs as are in evidence from *The Witch* or *Midsommar* (Ari Aster, 2019), but also the persistence of the putative belief that such 'antiquarian' materials are survivals of earlier generations.

The folklore in *Hereditary* is the discourse of demystifying the centrality of Paimon in the film. Aster himself has noted that he did not want to play the Devil card (Crow 2018), and so he looked to other demonic presences in the arcane literature, ultimately settling on 'King' Paimon, a demon of the higher ranks often depicted as riding on a dromedary and wearing a crown (much as Peter is crowned at the end of the film, but, alas, no dromedaries). As noted by Tony Sokol, 'King Paimon is one of Lucifer's most obedient devotees, rules 200 legions of angels, is connected to the tree of death and first appeared in an anonymously written grimoire from the mid-1600s called *Lesser Key of Solomon*' (Sokol 2018). The Kabbalistic *Book of Abramelin* (2006; first published in 1725 but said to date back to the fourteenth/fifteenth century) also refers to Paimon. *The Goetia* (the grimoire cited by Sokol; Anonymous 1995) was famously edited by Aleister Crowley, for the Hermetic Order of the Golden Dawn, to summon any number of arcane demons. However, the Paimon cult in *Hereditary* is not evoking the demon; they are creating a vessel for its physical embodiment. As Crow notes,

> some occultists argue Paimon is a name derived from Mesopotamian mythology and is actually a Middle Eastern goddess in origin. The idea of Western mythology turning a goddess into a demon and a female deity into a male spirit so it could be 'king' is an intriguing one. (Crow 2018)

As the film informs us, Charlie was the first intended body for Paimon to embody, but she was too weak, and so Peter is chosen (by the cult); presumably his masculinity makes him the stronger host. Crow quips, '[t]he patriarchy thrives even in the bowels of Hell' (Crow 2018). The issue of gender is a point also noted by Alexandra Hauke (2018): 'Similarly, as in many folk tales and horror narratives, the female characters fall victim to male hegemony. While Paimon's final form is inherently human, it is also unambiguously male'. This is ultimately the discourse of the film's use of folklore: it is not simply an annotated list of antiquated demonologies, but an examination of how that antiquated demonology is *used* in the film by Aster. Hauke is correct to see Aster's use of the lore as deeply problematic; despite the transformation of a Mesopotamian goddess into a male (or, at least, ambiguously sexed, according to the literature) demon by the patriarchal traditions in the arcane arts, Aster further problematises these assumptions by using 'strong' and 'weak' vessels for Paimon's embodiment. It is not sufficient to conclude the ambivalence of Aster's transformation of the lore, but that the role sex and gender play in the arcane arts is the discourse of the film's use of the folklore.

Folk horror is not done justice when the discussion solely rests on the psychogeography of 'the rural' (i.e., Scovell's 'folk horror chain'). Problematising the texts' use of 'the pagan' as well as its use of 'folklore' must also be considered. Within a discussion of *Hereditary*, such discourses raise issues of how the borders between community insiders and outsiders are maintained and patrolled, of how discourses of patriarchy, which permeate arcane occult literature from 'time immemorial', are adapted into contemporary cinematic texts, and what the combination of those three discourses has to say to us. Folklore never dies.

Cristina Santos

La Llorona (Various, 2006–2019)

La Llorona is the undead and undying myth of the ghost figure of the wailing woman dressed in white doomed to roam the earth as punishment for her past sins. From its earliest sources the legend of La Llorona finds its roots in powerful mythological Aztec warrior goddesses only to be consumed by colonisation and systemic racism, classicism, misogyny, and sexism. La Llorona's legend is a significant part of the Mexican and Mexican American cultural imaginary but has also been refigured into mainstream popular culture with certain cultural drawbacks. These contemporary versions are adaptations of the legend that reflect current socio-political contexts but, in some cases, La Llorona's cultural meaning is sacrificed for market consumption. This chapter considers a selection of representations of La Llorona as an ever-present undead figuration of colonial and feminist intersections of the sociocultural consumption of women within dominant androcentric discourses. Just as La Llorona consumes her victims so too is her historical and cultural inheritance recolonised to diminish her power by enclosing her within the symbolic. It is a continued negotiation of what Gloria Anzaldúa has called 'lo heredado, lo adquirido, lo impuesto' [the inherited, the acquired, the imposed] (1999: 104).

Many variants of the legend of La Llorona depict her as a maligned mother[1] guilty of drowning her children by focusing on the inequities of race, class, and gender experienced by women in patriarchally structured societies over various historical time periods. La Llorona's legend has also been used as a bogeyman story told to children to get them to behave, a cautionary tale to young women not to engage in premarital sex or seek partners outside their

1   See Santos 2016 and 2017.

social class or race, as well as the story of a vindictive ghost that entices wayward men to punish them for their indiscretions and/or abusive behaviour. The figure of La Llorona has proven to move beyond geographic, cultural, and historical boundaries; it has demonstrated a cross-cultural and trans-historical persistence, remaining a conclusive representation of the various ways that women continue to be victimised. The pre-colonial roots for La Llorona's legend are linked to the indigenous mythological figures of Coatlicue and Cihuacoatl, two warrior goddesses embodying female fertility, power, and strength and perceived as monstrous by the dominant patriarchal colonial discourse.[2] Indeed, the colonial discourse exemplifies the role of the European male's gaze that views the female indigenous body as an extension of the 'savage' land they have 'discovered' that also needs to be dominated and conquered.[3] Most importantly, Coatlicue and Cihuacoatl prophesize the fall of the Aztec Empire to the Spanish and establish foundational narratives of the relationship between women dressed in white and a mother's wailing for their lost children: 'Dear children, soon I am going to abandon you! We are going to leave' (Read and González 2000: 149).

La Llorona is also linked to the historical figure of La Malinche, an Aztec princess gifted to Hernán Cortés who served as his translator, lover, and eventual mother to his children. When La Malinche's story is fictionalised as part of the legend of La Llorona, the border between fiction and history is blurred. The legend describes that, to prevent Cortés from taking her son to Spain, La Malinche stabs her child in the heart before dropping his dead body into the lake surrounding Tenochtitlan. Her cries, 'Oh, hijo mío' [Oh, my child], are said to be heard today as her figure dressed in white with a white veil haunts the site of her son's death. These colonial roots establish key motifs that persist in subsequent iterations of the legend over time: a wronged woman so vulnerably situated within her sociocultural context that she sees infanticide and suicide as her only options and then haunts the site of the murder/suicide, wailing her lost child/children.

---

2   See Santos (2017: 64–9) for a discussion of the Aztec mytho-history of these indigenous warrior goddesses.
3   See Octavio Paz's discussion of the dualism *chingón/chingada* as part of the colonial coloniser/colonised dialectic (1961: 76).

Oral and written stories of La Llorona in a colonial context tend to focus on indigenous, mestiza and/or poor La Llorona figures who have been abandoned, abused and/or cheated on by their lover or husband. In earlier work, I have indicated that these oral and written iterations of the legend blend historical and fictional accounts, and that at times it is difficult to differentiate fiction and non-fictional elements (Santos 2017: 69–71). The dominant discourse underlying these versions depicts the colonial inheritance of indigenous or mestiza women being used by Spanish males, having their children only to be disowned and never given legal recognition of their relationship. These women find themselves abandoned, ignored, and silenced in life, and so in death they roam the streets at night dressed in white crying out for their dead children; allowed no rest in death because of their murderous actions, they haunt the living as a reminder of their own sad stories.

The film *J-ok'el/La Llorona: Curse of the Weeping Woman* (2007) references the Mayan name for La Llorona and the story of a Mayan woman who killed her children and committed suicide after being abandoned by her lover, a Spanish soldier. Unlike in the *Grimm* episode 'La Llorona' (2012) mentioned below, this La Llorona does not kidnap other children to replace her own that she has lost. Instead, she 'has been taking children that have suffered from something their parents have done to them [...] All the children come from broken homes' (*J-ok'el*, 2007); that is, the impetus to take the children is not purely selfish but rather a matter of saving them after they have been abandoned by their own mothers. Even though the *Grimm* episode modernises La Llorona's portrayal whilst remaining true to its cultural coding of her as a child kidnapper/killer, it does so by using the Hispanic character of Valentina, a retired police officer whose nephew was one of La Llorona's victims, to translate her story for the non-Hispanic Detective Grimm.

In contrast Roberto Castañeda's *Kilométro 31* (2007) interprets the legend as a cautionary message for young women not to cross social or racial lines in their relationships. The Spanish soldier in this filmic version takes on a poor indigenous woman as his lover because his legitimate wife is unable to provide him with children. The opening credits insinuate that the film is based on 'true events' that occurred during colonial times, thereby highlighting the denigrated status given to indigenous women during Spanish colonisation.

Figure 1. La Llorona, *Grimm*, Season 2, Episode 9, directed by Holy Dale (Universal Television, 2012).

Other modern-day versions of La Llorona depict a young wife abandoned by her husband because she is less attractive after having had his children, and her children become the obstacle to keeping her husband, finding a new husband, or winning back her lover.[4] An anonymous version has the mother drowning her children in the Rio Grande and describes her wailing for her lost children: 'Oh my children! I left you here, I left you here. Where am I going to find you?'[5] (Anonymous 2000: 95). These modern renditions add a dialectic of mother blame to the colonial criticisms of racism, classicism, and sexism. Sandra Cisnero's short story 'Woman Hollering Creek' (1991) reinscribes La Llorona's passive cry as the agentic 'La Gritona' [Woman Hollering], thereby recuperating female agency and solidarity whilst confronting issues of misogyny, domestic abuse, and Chicana identity.

4   See Santos for discussion of 'real' La Llorona figures that drown their children (2017: 83).
5   '¡Ay, mis hijos! Aquí los eché, aquí los eché, ¿dónde los encontraré?' (my English translation).

Figure 2. La Llorona. *The Curse of La Llorona*, directed by Michael Chaves (New Line Cinemas, 2019).

Andrés Muschietti's 2013 film *Mama* takes place outside Mexico and features the ghost of a white American woman who haunts a cabin in the woods. Mama is the ghost of a young woman who killed herself in the 1880s by jumping off a cliff whilst escaping from a mob of men who wanted to return her to the mental asylum, where she had been committed just for being an unmarried mother. The impetus here for Mama is to be reunited with her child who was precipitously taken away from her, a child she replaces with the two girls she saves from being killed by their father.[6] *Mama* refers back to versions of La Llorona's legend that depict the father as the perpetrator of infanticide, not because he refuses to legitimise their children's births or marry the mother due to her lower social class,[7] but rather as having suffered a mental breakdown after losing all his money in the stock market crash.

Music is another mediated space used to communicate La Llorona's suffering, and although it is rooted in the haunting sound of her cries, it has also migrated into mainstream popular culture. Popularised versions of the song 'La Llorona' have been performed by many, each adding their own verse to

---

6   There are variants of La Llorona's legend that depict the father as the murderer. The film *Shutter Island* (2010) can be read as an adaptation of La Llorona set in 1954 Boston that considers the psycho-emotional aftermath on the father after discovering that his wife had drowned their children in the backyard pond.
7   See story of former resident of Ciudad Chihuahua in Mexico collected by Robert A. Barakat (1969: 271).

Figure 3. La Llorona as a lost love. Directed by Lee Unkrich (Disney/Pixar, 2017).

the song yet maintaining the sense of suffering, lament, and pain in the performance. In *Mama*, Mama's wailing cry is emphasised in the film's music score with a haunting lullaby, a technique similarly applied in *The Curse of La Llorona* (2019) in the attempt to humanise La Llorona and emphasise her suffering and victimisation by a patriarchal society.[8] However, the Disney/Pixar production *Coco* modifies the song as a lament and a love song *for* La Llorona: 'I won't stop loving you // [...] // And even if it costs me my life, Llorona // I won't stop loving you'.

The series pilot 'Woman in White' for the television series *Supernatural* (2005–20) depicts La Llorona as the vengeful ghost of a woman who committed suicide after discovering her husband's infidelity. This Woman in White is vanquished by being forced to re-enter her home to be reunited with her dead children, at which point all three dissolve into a puddle of water. By returning La Llorona to the domestic space, this is a redomestication of the wandering ghost with its reintegration into a patriarchal discourse of power.

---

8   There is a rich tradition of songs that tell of La Llorona's stories and laments and even made it into the Disney/Pixar *Coco* (2017; see Figure 3).

Figure 4. 'Got Milk' advert aired in California in 2004, <https://www.youtube.com/watch?v=erhsuXTyDww>.

Furthermore, 'Woman in White' does not mention La Llorona by her original name but rather labels her by the colour of the clothes she wears; this in turn erases the power of her cry and of her cultural inheritance, thereby reverting La Llorona to the level of symbolic image. It represents what Domino Renee Perez identifies as La Llorona being whitewashed to enter the mainstream popular culture, the victim of cultural theft and appropriation as part of a 'politics of taking' (2012: 153). See, for example, the consumerisation of her image in the advertising images below.

In the horror trilogy *The Wailer: La Llorona* (2006), *The Wailer II: La Llorona II* (2007) and *The Wailer III: La Llorona III* (2012), although La Llorona's name is featured in the title of each film, her story functions more as a backdrop to the overall filmic narrative. The first film merely references the myth of an indigenous woman who drowns her children to please her lover, whilst the second film references cultural adaptations of indigenous and punitive iterations. The trilogy ends with a modern adaptation of the legend that has La Llorona seeking revenge on the descendants of her cheating husband

Figure 5. 'You see scary things out in the country'. Chevrolet car advert, <http://www.mccann.com.uy/Web/grafica/llorona.html>. Ad designed by McCann Worldgroup (Uruguay). The homepage for the company describes itself as follows: 'We help brands earn a meaningful role in people's lives' and 'It all starts with a truth. A powerful truth sets creativity free. Truth moves people and in turn the market' (2021). <https://www.mccannworldgroup.com/>. Accessed 29 March 2022.

by haunting the pool of the ancestral home. In these variations, La Llorona is a ghost whose cries have a 'mesmerizing Medusalike effect on male[s]' so that she can drown them at the bottom of the lake or river (Roberts 2018: 74).[9]

Contemporary variants and depictions of La Llorona continue to allude to the effects of Spanish colonisation and institutionalised patriarchy whilst also championing a dialectic of resistance, survival, and subversiveness. Nevertheless, La Llorona's roots in strong indigenous warrior women are relegated to a symbolic value in the marketplace by being consumed by a recolonisation via

9   See Santos on the links to the sirens of Greek mythology and other Mexican Goddesses linked to bodies of water (2017: 83–4).

persistent misogyny, sexism, racism, and classism over time and across geographical borders. The film *Las Lloronas* (Villarreal, 2004) depicts La Llorona as a curse placed on women, not as punishment for infanticide, not as a family curse, and not even for ignoring hegemonic gender roles, class, and racial lines; the curse is proposed instead as an intersectional inheritance of the struggles that many women have faced in the past and continue to face today. Colonial and patriarchal discourse have used La Llorona as the archetype of the evil, mad, murderous woman that is the product of dominant discourses of intersectional feminism and colonialism in the cultural marketplace. La Llorona may still be an undead figure consuming children and wayward men, but she is also consumed by some contemporary transmedial cultural artefacts such as television, film, and media. It is a critique that La Llorona's roots in indigenous mythology have been refigured under Spanish colonisation and then recolonised by its consumerisation in certain cultural products of the twentieth and twenty-first centuries. Despite the instances in transmedial representation within which La Llorona's legend is weakened, her wail continues to disrupt hegemonic codes to avoid being silenced, ignored, forgotten – consumed.

Iain Robert Smith

Go Goa Gone (Raj and D. K., 2013)

'[T]he history of the zombie is one of continual transport, translation and transformation, since it emerged from within the nexus of the transatlantic slave trade and colonial occupation' (2015: 190–1), writes Roger Luckhurst in his authoritative study of the zombie motif across literature and culture. One of the most illuminating illustrations of the tensions underpinning these processes of cross-cultural adaptation and exchange comes in Raj and D. K.'s *Go Goa Gone* (2013), a Bollywood film that was hailed on its release as India's first ever zombie-comedy (Sharma 2013). Midway through the film, three male friends, Hardik, Luv and Bunny, attempt to work out exactly what kind of undead creature it is that has been attacking them on an island off the coast of Goa:

> HARDIK: I know what they are.
> BUNNY: What? Evil-Deads?
> HARDIK: They are Zombies!
> LUV: Zombies? But we only have ghosts and spirits in India. Where did Zombies come from?
> HARDIK: Globalisation! These foreigners have screwed us! First, they brought HIV. Now, Zombies!

It is significant that this framing of the zombie as an unwelcome foreign incursion into India is compared here to the introduction of HIV, especially given what Stacey Abbott notes is an increased emphasis upon 'the relationship between virology and the undead' in the contemporary zombie film (2016: 92). This exchange in *Go Goa Gone* links fears of viral contagion with more nativist fears of cultural contamination through processes of globalisation, while also highlighting the near absence of the zombie figure within Indian culture. Although there have been a handful of South Asian zombie films that have appeared in the last fifteen years – other examples including *Zibahkhana* ('Hell's Ground', 2007), *Rise of the Zombie* (2013) and *Miruthan* ('Zombie', 2016) – the zombie film is still a relative novelty within the context of South Asian cinema. Hardik's complaint that the 'foreigners have screwed us' by bringing zombies to Goa therefore also functions as a self-aware allusion to the way in which globalisation has itself introduced the zombie to Indian cinema. Over the last two decades, there have been numerous similar claims of the 'first' zombie film to be produced in various national cinematic traditions – from *Juan of the Dead* (2010) in Cuba through to *Zombie 108* (2012) in Taiwan – and it is evident that the figure of the zombie has spread memetically (Smith 2016), transforming and adapting to these various contexts as it travels.

As a result, Roger Luckhurst explains, 'the zombie has become a truly global figure – and arguably the central Gothic figure for globalization itself' (2015: 8), and I would argue that *Go Goa Gone* is a particularly resonant text with which to explore these issues. The film follows a trio of male friends who travel to Goa as an escape from their office jobs in Mumbai and end up on an isolated island at a rave organised by the Russian mafia. We discover that the Russians were using this rave to test out a new drug, D2RF, that inadvertently turns the partygoers into flesh-hungry zombies, and the film therefore evokes fears and anxieties around the impact of foreign influences within Goa, and in India more generally.

The implicit commentary here on the threat of globalisation also links with a wider critique of consumerism and neoliberalism within the film, perhaps unsurprisingly given the ways in which the post-Romero zombie figure has often been used to satirise consumer culture in films ranging from *Dawn*

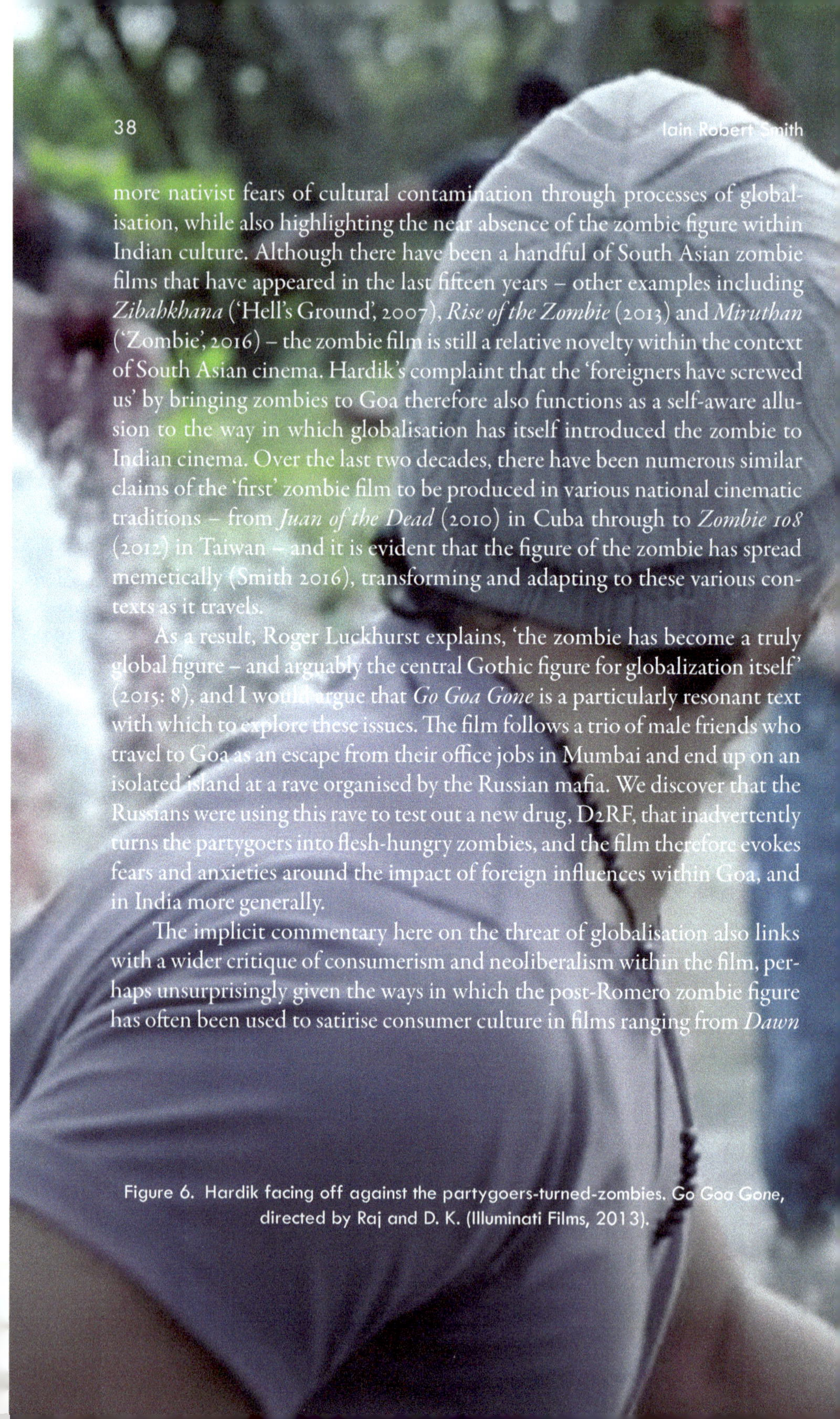

Figure 6. Hardik facing off against the partygoers-turned-zombies. *Go Goa Gone*, directed by Raj and D. K. (Illuminati Films, 2013).

of the Dead (1978) to *Train to Busan* (2016). As Agnieszka Soltysik Monnet notes, the cultural metaphor of the zombie has 'signified a wide range of political and social meanings: slavery, occupation, exploited labour, consumerism, postmodernism, and conformity, among others' (2015: 143). Within *Go Goa Gone*, the deliberate parallels made between the zombie and the alienated office worker under neoliberalism – referenced most explicitly through the poster of Steve Jobs in the office where the three male protagonists work – also links the film to the kinds of satire of capitalism and worklife drudgery present in other contemporary zombie comedies such as *Shaun of the Dead* (2004).

Indeed, while *Go Goa Gone* may express various underlying fears of cultural contamination from foreign influences, the film itself is filled with intertextual allusions to *Shaun of the Dead* and other international zombie films. Most notably, the film has Luv recreate the moment where Shaun (Simon Pegg) leads his group in imitating the clunky, staggering movements of zombies in order to blend in with them and avoid being attacked on their way to the Winchester. When Hardik challenges Luv on what he sees as a ridiculous plan, Luv responds that he came up with the idea because 'I saw it in a movie, okay'. This brief overt reference to *Shaun of the Dead* is accompanied by numerous other similarities with Edgar Wright's film. Both films attempt to combine the conventions of the slacker comedy with those of the zombie genre, and both grapple with the friendship dynamics between men who are in a state of extended adolescence and who therefore initially appear ill-equipped to survive in a zombie apocalypse.

Go Goa Gone also plays self-consciously with Bollywood tropes, such as in a sequence late in the film where Hardik is attempting to escape from his former love interest Ariana, who has now become a zombie. His dodging of her zombie attacks within a forest inadvertently recreates one of the classic song and dance routines associated with Bollywood in which lovers dance

Figure 7. The three protagonists battling zombies with improvised weapons. *Go Goa Gone*, directed by Raj and D. K. (Illuminati Films, 2013).

Figure 8. Parodying the Bollywood trope of lovers dancing around trees. *Go Goa Gone*, directed by Raj and D. K. (Illuminati Films, 2013).

flirtatiously with each other around trees. This form of song sequence, popularised by Dev Anand and Sadhana in the sequence 'Abhi Na Jao' from *Hum Dono* (1961), often revolves around a lover coyly avoiding their partner's advances, and so this zombie variation is playfully evoking and parodying that archetypal aspect of Bollywood aesthetics.

Moreover, this parody is also self-consciously highlighting the differences between *Go Goa Gone* and what is implied to be a more typical Bollywood masala film.[1] While Roger Luckhurst has argued that 'Bollywood genre expectations exerted far more influence than Romero rules' (2015: 187) on *Go Goa Gone*, it is notable that the film is part of a trend within post-millennial Bollywood cinema that is deliberately shifting away from the dominant masala film style. *Go Goa Gone* is 105 minutes in length, which is considerably shorter than the standard three-hour Hindi feature, and it does not feature any of the song and dance sequences typically associated with Bollywood. As Meheli Sen has observed, the film largely dispenses with the generic trappings of the masala form and is 'self-consciously more "global"' in its narrative and stylistic idiom. Furthermore, Sen notes that the integration of the zombie figure into Bollywood is particularly challenging given that 'the Hindi film has to undergo a process of formal disassembly in order to make room for the zombie – the creature, it appears, cannot simply slouch into Bollywood with any degree of ease' (2017: 142). In other words, the conventions of the zombie horror film cannot easily be combined with the dominant Bollywood masala form – not least the use of song and dance sequences – and so Raj and D. K. have had to strip back many of these elements in order to introduce the zombie into Indian cinema.

Go Goa Gone not only rejects many of the aesthetic elements of the Bollywood masala form to make room for the zombie but also deliberately evokes earlier examples of Indian horror cinema in order to more clearly distinguish itself from them. The film opens with Luv and Hardik watching the song sequence 'Golimaar' from the Telugu-language film *Donga* (1985), in which star Chiranjeevi recreates the zombie dance from Michael Jackson's iconic music video for 'Thriller'. The two protagonists sit slack-jawed watching Chiranjeevi performing Jackson's elaborate dance moves, while they themselves eat pizza and get increasingly stoned. Treating this earlier appearance of the zombie figure within Indian cinema largely as a form of kitsch entertainment for knowing, educated urban youth audiences, the opening is reminiscent of the references to the 1980s disco musical *Disco Dancer* (1982) within the

---

[1] The Bollywood masala film (named after the mixture of spices) describes the combination of numerous genres such as action, romance, thriller, musical, family drama and comedy into a single film. Pioneered within 1970s Bollywood hits such as *Sholay* (1975) and *Amar Akbar Anthony* (1977), this mixing of genres came to dominate South Asian cinema in subsequent decades and is largely perceived as an industrial strategy to appeal to a wide range of audiences.

contemporary black comedy *Delhi Belly* (2011). Both *Go Goa Gone* and *Delhi Belly* evoke a certain amount of nostalgia for the earlier Bollywood film style that is being gestured towards, but they also attempt to highlight the aesthetic differences between these examples of 'cheesy' 1980s Bollywood cinema and their own status as new Bollywood titles that exemplify a shift away from the kinds of Bollywood aesthetics that had come to be perceived as 'zany, extravagant, [and] kitschy' (Levich 2002: 48).

This relates to a wider trend within post-millennial Bollywood cinema in that a significant proportion of contemporary Hindi filmmakers such as Anurag Kashyap and Vikramaditya Motwane are shifting away from the dominant masala form and challenging expectations around film length, song sequences and genre-mixing that have typified the Bollywood film style for the last fifty years. While these filmmakers are still primarily working within the Bollywood system rather than in art or parallel cinema traditions, they have nevertheless adopted formal influences from other national cinemas, and they have rejected many of those elements that previously made Bollywood so distinctive as a form of international popular cinema. This contemporary shift is often read as a rejection of traditional Bollywood aesthetics and an adoption of what is perceived to be a more global form of filmmaking. For Meheli Sen, the post-millennial Indian horror film as exemplified by *Go Goa Gone* is therefore 'precisely the kind of Hindi film that seeks to be anything but' (2017: 135). As she explains, this kind of 'millennial supernatural film is "Hindi film" only insofar as its immediate context determines, and that, too, with a degree of sheepishness and reluctance that is unmistakable' (2017: 136). To some extent, therefore, *Go Goa Gone* is less of an attempt to adapt and localise the zombie film genre to conform to Bollywood's formal conventions than an attempt to dispose of those very Bollywood conventions themselves.

These tensions around Bollywood aesthetics are also partly explained by broader shifts in film exhibition and distribution within India and across the diaspora. *Go Goa Gone* is part of a move within post-millennial Bollywood cinema for films that are aimed at the relatively affluent, English-speaking middle-class audience of the multiplexes. It is no coincidence that *Dil Chahta Hai* (2001), the film that is often positioned as the pioneering work within that shift in Bollywood conventions, similarly features three male friends on a road trip and represents what Ranjani Mazumdar has called the 'lifestyle mythology of the urban elite' (2007: 147). There is a clear lineage from *Dil Chahta Hai* through films like *Delhi Belly* into *Go Goa Gone* with their focus on young male friends who are drawn from the educated, English-speaking, urban middle classes and who lead relatively affluent and cosmopolitan lifestyles in comparison to their parents' generation. Whereas earlier cycles of Indian horror cinema, such as those produced by the Ramsay Brothers in the 1980s, were often associated with lower-class rural audiences, it is notable that contemporary Indian horror films such as *Go Goa Gone* have been aimed principally at middle-class metropolitan youth audiences. As Amit R. Baishya explains, the majority of these 'new horror films are screened in multiplexes, which are housed in relatively opulent consumption spaces, such as shopping malls' and they 'cater largely to the metropolitan, bourgeois spectator' (2016: 114).

Go Goa Gone is therefore representative not only of the global circulation and influence of the zombie figure but also of the transnational impact of neoliberal globalisation more broadly. The film may evoke anxieties about the threat of cultural contamination and foreign influence within India, but this acts in tension with the ways in which the film has itself largely dispensed with the Bollywood masala form and has adopted a self-consciously 'global' aesthetic designed to appeal to cosmopolitan, metropolitan audiences. Ultimately, as this film indicates, the global flows of the undead zombie figure within twenty-first-century cinema have much to tell us not only about the transnational circulation of popular culture in an increasingly interconnected world, but also about the broader impacts of globalisation on contemporary society.

John R. Ziegler

Wakening (Danis Goulet, 2013)

The 2013 dystopian sci-fi/horror short film *Wakening*, by Cree/Métis filmmaker Danis Goulet, follows a solitary female figure as she enters the lair of a creature that she has tracked down in a ruined urban landscape under armed occupation. This protagonist is Goulet's reimagining of the traditional Cree trickster Weesageechak, and the creature that Weesageechak has located embodies a second traditional figure, the monstrous weetigo.[1] In the encounter between these characters, *Wakening* shifts the weetigo from its established role in Cree culture as a cannibalistic threat to Indigenous persons to a force of resistance against both diegetic 'occupiers' and the dominant-culture narratives within and counter to which the film stands. Goulet's weetigo thereby resists erasure of Indigenous culture while simultaneously challenging settler culture's dominance within and beyond the sci-fi/horror genre of cinema.

The wendigo, windigo or weetigo (among other variants) appears in the belief system of the Algonquian peoples, North America's largest culture group (Smallman 2014: 266–74).[2] Appearing primarily 'in Anishinaabe (Ojibwe) and Nehiyaw (Cree) stories' (Remy-Kovach 2018: 1), the weetigo is traditionally a type of sacred spirit known as a manitou and most commonly represented as possessed of an insatiable cannibalistic appetite and the ability to transform people into cannibals themselves (Dillon 2014: 196–203).[3] It may also

---

1   Because Cree was originally an unwritten language, there are a number of variant spellings for both of these names. I take my spellings here from the film's credits.
2   Because of my primary focus on *Wakening*, I use the film's term weetigo exclusively throughout, including when referring to works that use other terms.
3   At least one scholar asserts that not all weetigos are cannibals and that the term could also refer to a broader propensity for harmful behaviour (Smallman 2014: 2024).

appear emaciated no matter how much it eats (DeSanti 2015: 188). This 'spirit of winter' often has a heart of ice and first appeared in Algonquian tales as a powerful cannibal giant (Smallman 2014: 203, 304). In older stories, weetigos might also comprise whole families (583). By the early twentieth century, in at least some areas, weetigos had come to be understood as evil spirits that could assume various forms (1064). They might 'be purely monstrous' or spirits possessing human bodies (Remy-Kovach 2018: 1).

Historically, Algonquian narratives have associated the weetigo with conceptions of family and fears of its collapse, fears of starvation, and the devastating effects of imperialism. Shawn Smallman argues that weetigo myths often focused on women's behaviour and roles (2014: loc. 385, 504), and he connects women's transformative power to the transformation intrinsic to weetigo tales. Perhaps this is why kettles sometimes feature in destroying weetigos and why the Cree believed that menstrual blood or menstruating women could resist or repel weetigos (707–46). The weetigo's insatiable appetite and consumption of human flesh also reflected the anxiety for 'the peoples of the boreal forest', including the Cree, that '[g]iven that populations of key game animals could be cyclical, every family could expect to pass through periods of famine' (530).

As early as the nineteenth century, the Cree also associated the weetigo with Europeans and their goods (Smallman 2014: 1030, 1048), which were linked to scarcity, displacement and disease. Grace Dillon neatly sums up this symbolic connection: 'Imperialism is cannibalism, the consumption of one people by another' (2014: 219). Additionally, Indigenous women may have at times labelled Indigenous men who 'collaborated' with missionaries as weetigos (Smallman 2014: 1898). While accounts of weetigo encounters persisted into at least the mid-twentieth century, the second half of the century saw the weetigo largely metamorphose into a metaphor, and contemporary Indigenous works equate the spirit with colonial traumas 'such as residential schools, sexual abuse, and cultural loss', as well as the dominant, settler 'culture of extraction and environmental destruction' (684, 3049, 1128).

Algonquian representations of the weetigo have diversified; but for Indigenous artists, it remains primarily a symbol of 'the danger of greed, capitalism, and Western excess', while in the settler imaginary, it symbolises 'evil, wilderness, and madness' (493, 1124). *Wakening* bridges these two symbologies, or rather it converts the latter into the former, and in doing so counters a long-standing settler film tradition. The weetigo and its permutations have most often appeared cinematically in non-Indigenous works, from the silent film *The Lure of the Windigo* (1914) to *Pet Sematary* (2019). In many such films, the weetigo functions as merely a variation on the standard horror movie monster (DeSanti 2015: 186). Danika Medak-Saltzman situates such uses as part of a practice by mainstream films that arrogates 'traditional Indigenous teaching stories' without regard for accuracy (2017: 141). She writes:

> For example, the repeated use of Windigo as a simple synonym for cannibal across popular culture renders this figure, in these cases, devoid of the implicit and explicit critique of, and important warnings about, overconsumption, greed, selfishness, and the dangers of over/self-indulgence that I understand to be inextricable from most actual Windigo stories. (2017: 141)

Additionally, such use frequently 'excuses Western capitalist expansion and cultural appropriation' (Dillon 2014: 219). In horror films, this justification routinely intersects with the representation of Indigenous culture as 'excessive' and 'forever rising up to haunt White domains and bodies', as seen in horror's sacred Indian (burial) ground trope (Coleman 2011: 149).

Indigenous filmmakers, in contrast, employ the weetigo to critique dominant settler culture. According to Kerstin Knopf, Indigenous filmmaking decolonises cinema by 'quoting, discussing, and subverting [...] colonialist images of Indigeneity' and 'projecting [...] self-determined images' (2008: 7). If settler cinema has co-opted the weetigo as a substitute for werewolves or backwoods cannibal families, then with *Wakening* Danis Goulet undertakes a decolonising counter-appropriation of the figure, positioning the weetigo as a force for resisting the 'occupiers'. This resistance occurs on multiple planes and extends both within and beyond the world of the film. Lee Schweninger argues for cinematic 'self-representation as a form of resistance' (2013: 3); and for Dallas Hunt, *Wakening* both 'enact[s] "visual sovereignty"' through Indigenous self-representation and raises 'uncomfortable [...] questions around the perpetuity of ongoing settler colonialism' and the uncritical consumption of 'Indigenous representational imaginaries' (2018: 83). These disruptive decolonising effects are anchored in Goulet's reimagining of the weetigo.

Goulet's film, as Allison Mackey has noted, assists in 'recuperating modes of knowledge' that dominant-culture narratives have suppressed or

Figure 9. Reclaiming space. Weesageechak slows at graffiti-writing. *Wakening*, directed by Danis Goulet (ViDDYWELL FiLMS, 2013).

'overwritten' (2018: 536). In keeping with such return of the suppressed, one of the first images in the film is the words 'THIS IS INDIAN LAND' spray-painted in an alleyway. Graffiti-writing is one method by which marginalised people can exert a claim on and in shared spaces, and its appearance here introduces the film's concern with decolonising dominant praxis and knowledge systems. *Wakening* was filmed in Toronto, a name which derives from the Indigenous word 'Tkaronto' and thus points to the land's long-contested history (see Howard and Bobiwash 2012).

Following the shot of the graffiti-writing, *Wakening* extends its critique of the expropriation of Indigenous land and the displacement of Indigenous people. As one of the central characters, Weesageechak (Sarah Podemski), evades passing troops, the camera shows a devastated cityscape while part of an announcement from a public address system fades in, saying that anyone

> claiming to be citizens or intermarried with a citizen family shall be deemed to be lawfully in possession of any land in such townships or tracts unless he or she has been or shall be located for the same by the order of the Superintendent General of Citizens' Affairs, and any such person or persons assuming possession of any lands of that description shall be dealt with as illegally in [...]. (*Wakening*, 2013)

The settler government imposes control over land (and thereby people) through the legal system and a department the name of which both echoes Canada's now-replaced Department of Indian Affairs and Northern Development and hints at ongoing xenophobic debates over political personhood. Additionally, the land being regulated appears apocalyptically ravaged. Viewed in one way, the film's apocalyptic future is already the Indigenous present (Monani 2016: 204). At the same time, Mackey posits that this apocalypse may also offer a welcome hope for renewal (2018: 533–4).

This possibility of renewal is inextricably bound with the reimagining of Weesageechak and the weetigo, 'prominent figures in Cree (and other North American Indigenous) cosmologies. Weesageechak can shift shapes and is a transformative figure' (Hunt 2018: 81). That such a figure here assumes the shape of an armed Cree woman both draws attention to the importance of women in weetigo narrative and acts as a corrective to the dominant cinematic tradition of the Celluloid Maiden, a term used by M. Elise Marubbio to refer to a young Indigenous woman character who assists and/or loves a white man before, consequently, dying (Mayer 2015: 2). The reimagining of the weetigo itself is less obvious but equally significant. It functions as the film's central, embodied symbol not only of environmental apocalypse and dispossession but also of the mainstream elision of Indigenous narratives and artists. Extratextually, the casting of the weetigo (Gail Maurice) and Weesageechak strengthens the emphasis on Indigenous representation 'not only behind the camera, but in front of it, not only with Cree characters but Indigenous women to play them' (Hunt 2018: 81).

Weesageechak faces off against the weetigo 'innumerable times in Cree traditional stories' (Monani 2016: 2). In *Wakening*, the encounter occurs in an abandoned theatre. It is difficult to say definitively whether the building is a playhouse or a movie theatre, but the imagery certainly engages with the cinema. In the lobby, the glass in the doors has been papered over, primarily with newspaper, suggesting not only a barrier between the interior/weetigo and the wider outside world but also that media helps to create this containment. In one shot, the edge of an empty shopping cart points simultaneously to the lack of resources in this dystopia and to the capitalist practices that led there. In another shot, the beam of Weesageechak's flashlight rests on a carved grotesque over a doorway, a non-Indigenous emblem marking the theatre as place of settler mythology. When Weesageechak reaches the door to the theatre proper, she lays down her bow, signalling a departure from the earlier model of battling the monster.

Inside the theatre space, a large hole in one wall admits a shaft of light that evokes that of a movie projector, both a complement and a contrast to Weesageechak's flashlight. A third light source appears on a tree that grows inside the theatre: a lantern whose significance is ambiguous, much as the indoor tree itself invokes both apocalyptic breakdown and potential for renewal. The lantern may as easily signify a path forward as it may function as a lure for the weetigo's victims. A woman tied to her seat explains, 'It eats us, one by one'. She continues, 'The seats were full. We're the only ones left', evoking overhunting by colonisers, the decimation of Indigenous populations, and the threat of starvation thought to contribute to weetigo narratives. The elk-skulled weetigo itself, speaking in Cree, explains: 'The forests are all dead … I use this palace to lure humans to my belly'. Monani views the use of Cree, forbidden by colonial powers, as a decolonising tactic (2016: 9), and Hunt sees it as part of 'an attempt to transfer' Cree language and knowledge (2018: 81), but these speech acts also occur within a space coded as enacting the very cultural elision that they resist.

Figure 10. The weetigo illuminated in the theatre. *Wakening*, directed by Danis Goulet (ViDDYWELL FiLMS, 2013).

The word palace in the subtitle translation brings to mind the phrase 'movie palace', a place historically exclusionary towards Indigenous cultures, and Weesageechak confirms the symbolically freighted erasure of the weetigo. She announces that 'The occupiers, they tricked you, weetigo. This is no palace. This is your prison'. She also comments on the creature's reduced place in cultural consciousness: 'Long ago, your hunger was feared throughout the land, but no more'. If we read this erasure as pertaining particularly to cinema, then the weetigo's threat, 'I will eat your eyes', becomes also a threat to spectatorship. Weesageechak closes the exchange by emphasising, 'The occupiers are more feared than you are, weetigo' and switches to Cree to yell, 'You are forgotten!' Given that Weesageechak seeks to free the weetigo from its prison and its obsolescence, it can be seen here as forgotten, not only as a variation of cinematic monster and, more broadly, a symbol for Indigenous voices in film but also, in relation to dystopia, as what Dillon calls 'a metaphor for excess' that 'encourages moderation' (2014: 203). That *Wakening* situates the weetigo not merely as a cannibal monster becomes apparent in the film's final confrontation: Weesageechak flees to the lobby, where she aims her bow at two gun-wielding occupiers who block access to the outside world. However, it is not Weesageechak's weapon but the weetigo, symbol of Indigenous narrative tradition, that kills them. Then, as we hear a snatch of the earlier announcement replaying, this makes possible movement into and through the outside world and further resistance to the occupiers. The doors are suffused with light, lending a doubleness to the symbolic valence of the indoor light sources in the same way that the weetigo itself achieves a doubleness as monster and hero. The cannibal violence that usually affects its own people is turned outward, against the occupiers. Simultaneously, the weetigo's escape represents dissemination of an Indigenous narrative and cultural point of view, a corrective irruption of the past into the filmic present and future.

In *Wakening*, then, the weetigo undermines the boundary between representation (inside the theatre) and reality (outside the theatre) as part of working to decolonise the still predominantly white sci-fi/horror film genre and its use of Indigenous monsters, particularly the wendigo/windigo/weetigo. In doing so, the weetigo enacts what Sarah Juliet Lauro calls in her discussion of zombie narratives a 'counteroccupation of mythical space' (2015: 597). Lauro argues that the zombie myth reinforces that 'the occupier himself is colonized by the experience of colonialism' (342), and the weetigo, Othered both as a monster and as the embodiment of an Indigenous narrative and filmic tradition, reverses its confinement and initiates a potential counter-occupation not only within the film's diegetic world but also of the audience and film culture outside it. When the weetigo crosses the boundary of the theatre doors, it will also cross and so unsettle the boundary between film or performance and life, and it will trade its small, literally captive audience for one without clear limits. *Wakening* sets loose into its world and ours a creature in which traditional narrative and a new Indigenous sci-fi/horror cinema intersect in a powerful figure of resistance, remembrance and reappropriation.

Naomi Simone Borwein

Killer Native (Bjorn Stewart, 2019)

Australian Aboriginal Undead

The Centres for Disease Control and Prevention (CDC 2021) produced a tongue-in-cheek guide to the Zombie Apocalypse, updated in 2021 during the pandemic, as a representation of global horror realism and the blurred lines between fictions of contamination and reality. In Australia, horrors of apocalyptic climate conditions heightened by the impact of COVID-19 are fed by destructive floods and images of marsupials roasting in out-of-control bushfires. Contemporary Aboriginal Horror films increasingly connect cataclysmic social, cultural and climatic events to colonial settler devastations of the eighteenth century – for example, first contact, ghost ships and white ghouls. The 2019 short *Killer Native*, from Noble Savage Productions, is written and directed by Bjorn Stewart of the Kuku-Yalanji (Northern Queensland) and the Wemba-Wemba (New South Wales) groups (Stewart 2014). *Killer Native* is part of a visual anthology of Indigenous horror tales entitled *Dark Place* (2019), which comprises five film shorts that end with Stewart's zombification piece. This chapter offers an examination of the twenty-first-century Aboriginal zombie in Stewart's Splatstick film short. Tracing the contagion process, his modern Indigenous Australian 'undead' figure becomes a critique of hybridised conventions of a global variant within an Aboriginal world view.

The Aboriginal zombie in *Killer Native* stands as a derivation or reimagining of earlier Antipodean zombies in Australian Horror films – where Indigenous figures are mythified, marketised, zombified or whitewashed – and sits in the broad tradition of *The Zombie Brigade* (1988), *Cargo* (novel 2013 and film 2018), *Wyrmwood* (2014) and *Little Monsters* (2019). *Killer Native* is being extended to a full-length film, *Invasion of the Killer Natives* (2019), funded by Screen Australia; the title implies a focus on Aboriginal Futurism and Sci-fi that is more acceptable in Australia than in the wider Horror genre. Stewart's tale or snapshot of indighorror in *Killer Native* mixes 'popularised non-Indigenous' views of Dreaming, such as those seen in Bruce Chatwin's 1987 novel *The Songlines* and the Australian horror flick *The Dreaming* (1988) (Gay'wu Group of Women 2019: 273–4) with his own ideas, partly inspired by Jordan Peele's *Get Out* (Gbogbo 2019). A cohort of terms that define Dreamtime, Dreaming or songlines represent foundational Aboriginal understandings of Country, oral mythology and metaphysics, history and tradition (Gay'wu Group of Women 2019: 273–4; Knudsen 2004: 5, 241). As will be seen, Stewart's overt use of the Dreaming, Totemism and moiety (a term connoting identity underlying ancestry and lineage) adds an epistemological and ontological lens as an agentic web to the hybrid and often globalised zombie figure, which enables this modern Aboriginal variant of the zombie, spirit or ghoul to be delineated.

Dark Place is marketed as a visual anthology of tales of Indigenous Australian horror. Recalling standard anthologies of Australian horror fiction as much as cinema, *Dark Place* is an embodiment of white terror, paratextually inverting the ubiquitous metaphor of fear in Australia, exemplified by titles like *Macabre: Journey through Australia's Darkest Fears* (2010), into a critique of that nightmarish space of shadow Country, where the nature of walkabout and walking dead collide. *Dark Place* becomes part of a dialogue on Aboriginal horror in the Australian context and extends a missing or nascent Aboriginal zombie discourse; Alan McKee notes that 'there is no blackfella tradition of zombies and vampires' (1997: 201), though the undead have simulacra in the oral tradition. The first published and circulated tales of Indigenous horror are split between horror realities and legends, found in oral and written myths of the Aborigines (Unaipon 2006) and later percolating into horror magazines like *Terror Australis* (1988–92), and short stories anthologised in volumes of the Australian Horror Writers Association. By concluding the anthology *Dark Place* with a zombie film, Stewart's form of undeadness punctuates the speculative excess of the contemporary Australian and global moment.

Consider the modern Aboriginal zombie in *Killer Native*. Inside a cabin an unknown white male settler is frantically burning parchment. Outside blue light emanates from the ground. An Aboriginal woman covered with pustules, and draped with a possum-fur shawl, enters the cabin and kills the man by disembowelling him with her bare hands, implicitly fusing White Australia rhetoric of the horror of the outback to Aboriginality and the myth of Terra Nullius

Killer Native (2019)

Figure 11. Movie poster. *Dark Place*, directed by Kodie Bedford et al. (Screen Australia, 2019).

Figure 12. Movie poster. *Killer Native*, directed by Bjorn Stewart (Noble Savage Productions, 2019).

(empty land). Standard Horror font flashes across the screen, reinscribing this sinister vision of a female ghoul as a culturally specific hybrid played by Natasha Wanganeen, a Ngarrindjeri, Narungga, Kaurna and Noongar woman (Slessor and Boisvert 2020). Stewart's glib reflection on the mistranslation of an Aboriginal way of knowing evokes songlines, moiety and Totemism, showcasing a brand of zombie that is sentient. To achieve this effect, Stewart sets up an inversion of identity and agency of the Aboriginal characters in contrast to the buffoonery of the primitive white settlers; the male settler, Thomas (Charlie Garber), and his pregnant wife, Sally (Lily Sullivan), are represented as absurd and inept. Such jocularity recalls the Indigenous humour tradition, which is a form of resistance enabling cultural survival (Duncan 2014: 99). However, the film also resonates with the aesthetics of *Black Adder* and a touch of class commentary, as in the UK film *Revolt of the Zombies* (1936) and the Australian mockumentary style of the 2021 zombie-hunter piece, *Incident Report*. Placing *Killer Native* in relation to Abe Forsythe's 2019 film *Little Monsters* (another Splatstick) produced by Screen Australia, highlights how the Othered migrant lens in Australian apocalyptic zombie films overshadows the early colonial-Aboriginal context with a contemporary New South Wales (NSW) setting and geopolitical issues surrounding immigration. A more ethical engagement with Aboriginality in *Cargo* (2018) actively draws on Indigenous expertise. Alternatively, Stewart extends the gore-comedy subgenre through his own modern Aboriginal lens on zombification.

Early in *Killer Native*, Dreaming and identity are introduced as a way of understanding contamination. When the Aboriginal character (Blackfella) played by Clarence Ryan says, 'my name is a complex web of things' and Thomas retorts, 'I'll call you Billy' (Stewart 2019), Stewart makes the white settlers' epistemological understanding of naming practices – bound to ideas of ownership, identity and the Commons – absurd and horrific. Moiety (as part of naming practice, heredity and identity) and Dreaming co-evolve with zombification. The introduction of Dreaming metaphysics is then conspicuously linked to an outback colonial horror context. An Aboriginal male with a possum-fur shawl, his moiety, is caught by Thomas and Sally and tied up. The clash of colonial and Aboriginal meaning is played out on screen, incorporating the slapstick humour Stewart is known for in the Australian Broadcasting Company (ABC) series *Black Comedy*. The audience later learns that the fire attracts zombies – 'Put that fire out now. It draws her to them!' – as a 'spirit' rushes towards them through the bush (Stewart 2019). What might to Jeffrey Jerome Cohen (2017) be a standard zombie ecology laced with monstrosity, or to Fred Botting (2013) one tinctured by marketisation and economy, is a celluloid zombification of the filmic environment of *Killer Native*, where Stewart portrays the complex effects of a foreign agent infecting the Dreaming. Songlines or Dreaming do not have a one-to-one translation. For instance, in Yolŋu Matha 'the term songspirals' recognises 'understandings of ongoing co-becoming and interweaving through song' (Gay'wu Group of Women 2019: 273–4). The Wemba-Wemba, Stewart's group, have a similar understanding of Dreaming, which they call Yemurraki (Clarke 2003: 382). The film showcases perpetual re- and co-becoming of undeadness.

Furthermore, *Killer Native* actively engages with colonial monstrosity. Settler utopia is repeatedly ruptured. As foreshadowing, Thomas yells 'my land', pounding a stick into the ground and finding a human skull (Stewart 2019). The settler couple's utopian vision of the Thames is projected onto a tributary of the polluted Murray–Darling rivers, recalling pieces from early subgenres of Australian horror like Peter Weir's 1975 film *Picnic at Hanging Rock* or Henry Lawson's 1892 short story 'The Bush Undertaker'. The land is made inherently dystopic through artefacts of the mise en scène. Like a mirroring of the battlefield of Dreamtime creation, 'Billy' leads them to that dark place the settlers once perceived as the horrors of Terra Nullius in Terra Incognita.

Superficially following a classic Horror set-up, where the victim is lead blindly to their fate, the Blackfella leads the whites through the bush to the abattoiresque cabin of horrors, which is prefigured in the first scene. But the Aboriginal moiety is introduced during this journey as a plot device, and as part of the mechanism of zombification, whereby zombie identity is trussed to the totemic and animistic systems of the Dreaming. For instance, the Aborigine greets the possum moiety sitting on a tree branch as a friend. It immediately attacks Thomas, anticipating his contamination and demise. Then Dreaming is layered over this horror plot through nomenclature. A conventional Western greeting, 'What's your name?', elicits 'I have many names, each one as important as the other. It's a complex web of things to identify the kind of man I am, my relationship to the world' (Stewart 2019), somatic, cyclic and oral, and emphasising orthogonal world views (of the written and progressive). Evoking myopic and racist representations of Aboriginality in White Australia,

Thomas states, 'I'm not learning a bloody dictionary of names. I'll call you Billy. Yah Billy Black'.[1] The Aborigine states, 'That's not my name' (Stewart 2019). This exchange plays on Indigenous nicknaming practices used to caricature the colonial settlers in, for example, the Warlpiri (Nicholls 1995: 144). A recurrent reference to naming conventions in the film is connected to the many variations on the Aboriginal zombie figure, visually highlighted by the 'spirit woman' violently entering, and interjected into, the mise en scène. The spectacle is suggestive of the way Country, as a unified whole, and an identity, becomes contaminated, implicating twenty-first-century Aboriginal 'undeadness'.

Pictorialism offers a counter-narrative for this brand of Aboriginal zombification. The settlers find a leatherbound book left by the cabin's last inhabitant, an indigenisation of widespread tropes of the remote cabin and cursed tome, for example, Sami Raimi's *Evil Dead* (1981). The pages create a step-by-step guide to Stewart's form of zombification:

> *Page one and two*: artistic illustrations of the berry sprig,
> *Page three and four*: three Aborigines sitting around a fire, sun to the right top, and dead white guy (labelled 'me') with an arrow,
> *Page five and six:* green bottle with a skull and a label reading 'SMALL POX' in capital letters,
> *Page seven and eight*: smiling stick man holding smallpox bottle over dead stick figure aboriginals grey-faced and no fire,
> *Page nine and ten:* Transformation into vengeful grey-faced ghouls; the third stick drawing looks like a zombie, arms outstretched in a classic posture; sun gasping, in the sky to the right is part of the whole system of knowing. (*Killer Native*)

Destroyed in the fireplace by Thomas, the guidebook to the transformative process incorporates artefacts and outcomes of settler–Aboriginal conflict – the medicinal berry sprig, colonial contamination and the evolution of disease (smallpox) – and is reminiscent of the historic slaughter of Aborigines, for example, the Myall Creek Massacre. Once the zombie gene enters the totemic system – imagery recalling D. Bruno Starrs' discussion of Aboriginal vampirism (2014) – the entire living somatic system becomes corrupted, where Aboriginality, Aboriginal zombies and Country create a different category of sentient undead in contrast to a plethora of global alternatives, such

---

1   Symbolic of the mistranslation of Aboriginal language systems, the *Kuku Yalanji* have been thoroughly studied by anthropologists and ethnographers.

as in *iZombie* (2015–19), that are placed in an orthogonal epistemological framework.

Aboriginal zombie aesthetics are a product of the medium. The trailer resembles a classic Horror film with high-contrast, suspenseful music, Cut-Tos and Black-Outs, fast-paced like a shuttered image utilising the photographic skills of the Hungarian László Baranyai. *Killer Native* applies a strong contemporary Aboriginal auteur perspective and voice. The musical score by the Australian composer Jed Palmer layers crackling fire, didgeridoos, bell birds and kookaburras (both moieties), and other sounds of the outback with pianos and violins. Strange blue light at night mirrors the effects of nocturnal vision, in contrast to the glowing orange-red sky of conventional outback horrorscapes, where the undead traditionally roam (Allen 2014: 70). Liminal aspects of the audiovisual landscape (as signs and signifiers of identity) accent the zombification process and produce a multifoliate reimagining of standard horror-terror-fear paradigms.

The moiety, which can be anything in nature, illustrates a key feature of Stewart's zombification process. The possum moiety is a talisman, a 'fundamental backbone' for certain clans '[t]he possum string [...] It guides them back when they die, using the deep name of the clan. With this burrkun, I'm going back to the River of Stars, to my spiritual land' (Gay'wu Group of Women 2019: 134, 157). The possum shawl in *Killer Native* represents a fraying of the original totemic system, by colonial-catalysed monstrosity, and actions against the ancestry and lineage of the moiety. To explicate this concept, each person in a marriage has a moiety of one of their parents, but the parents cannot have the same moiety. The Aboriginal characters wear possum shawls, but only one can have the possum as a moiety, which stays with them for life. People take spouses from outside their moiety, so both Aboriginals would not be wearing the possum cloak. If two Aborigines are out hunting, one can kill his own moiety and give it to the other Aborigine (Lawlor 1991: 282–4). In the context of the film, Stewart's use of the possum implies a contract of violence between the Aboriginal male and the already zombified female, and again highlights the corruption of the totemic system by outside contagions.

For comparison, consider the ingestion of marsupials in *Little Monsters*. A slow-moving zombie, a US military officer, has quills embedded in its face after eating an echidna (a moiety). Tied to zombie legends of Australian

Killer Native (2019)

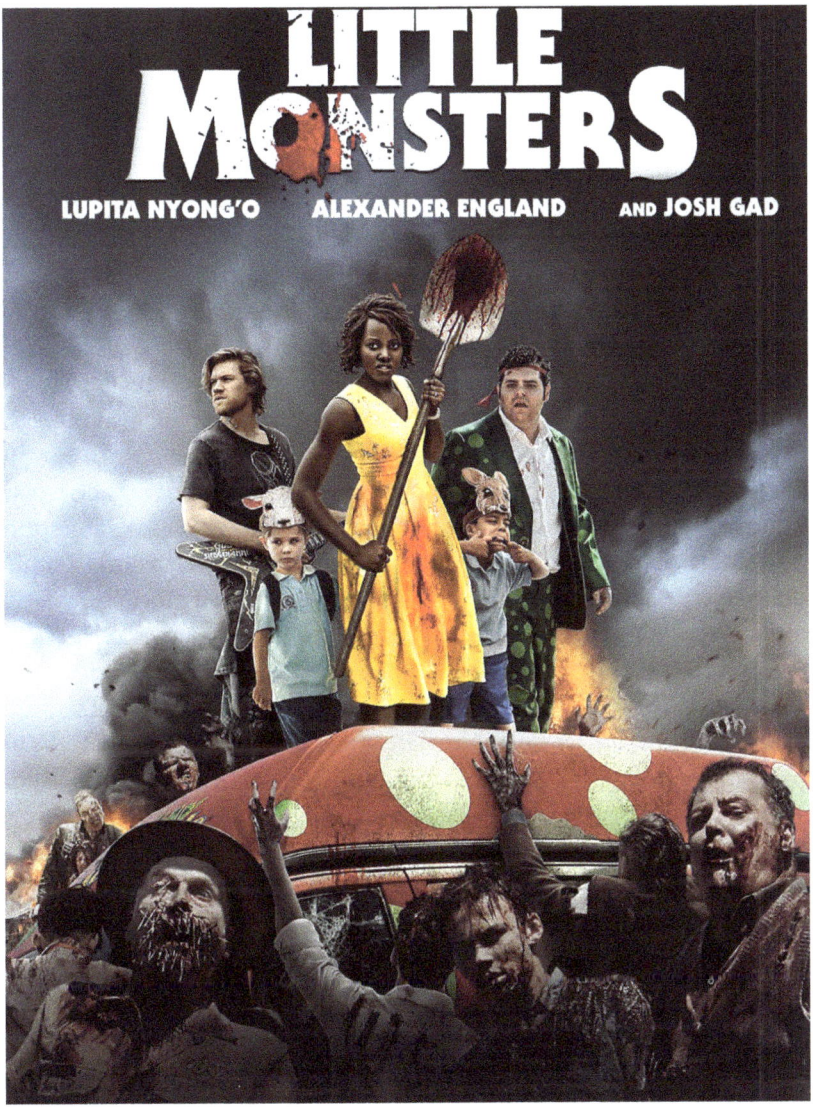

Figure 13. DVD cover. *Little Monsters*, directed by Abe Forsythe (Screen Australia, 2019).

military history (Connor 2010), 'slow zombies' in *Little Monsters* are farcical expressions of the variations of mouldering figures in the mainstream, flesh weeping away from the bone, ravenous, mechanised; they are inadvertently impacted by markers of Aboriginal culture, like echidna quills. A moiety has been consumed by an American zombie, but the possum is never cannibalised in *Killer Native*; it is Billy's moiety, and the piece follows his metamorphosis.

Consider the zombie woman of *Killer Native* in contrast to her husband, 'Billy', whom she (or their community) infects. She is alive and undead, as part of Aboriginal epistemology, and suggests oral myths of fire women seen in David Unaipon's 1930 *Legendary Tales of the Australian Aborigines* or Alexis Wright's 2006 *Carpentaria*. However, unlike in classic white Australia outback horror, here bushfire offers a unique renewal of life; fire brings life and death, and death is a process of transition and transformation into new life, or new undeadness. This complicates the symbolism of Thomas destroying the zombie guidebook in a fireplace. Billy compliments his zombie-bride, highlighting her agency and identity. Fire glows in the background, illuminating the faces of Sally and Billy, as he describes his community getting sick and their attempts to treat it with 'bush medicine': 'When they turn ... it got worse ... skin boiled. They went insane' (Stewart 2019). Signposting his transformation, Billy scratches his neck pustules.[2] Giving a humanising narrative to the female zombie, he states that 'she didn't always look like that, she was beautiful'. Described variously as a spirit and devil in the film, an Aboriginal zombie in press releases, and a 'ghoul', in the casting list, Billy's discourse on the complex web of names links to his oral account of the process of zombification tied to demonic naming practices. Ghoul is a broader label than zombie; it is an evil spirit that consumes dead bodies. Not quite a zombie, she has agency and consciousness: 'my wife she still loves me' (Stewart 2019). Part of this multilevel dialogue on colonialism and zombification engages with universalist rhetoric about primitive societies and cannibalism, proliferated by scholars like Claude Lévi-Strauss, Emile Durkheim and Michel Foucault. As a gory take on colonial horror and autophagic natives, the ghoul rips the baby from Sally's stomach with her bare hands. The ghoul's eyes flicker with life, as

---

2   A cross-cultural parody. Consider the pointed scene where the white woman stabs the Aboriginal female zombie. Thomas and Sally have their faces sprayed with black fluid; it is reminiscent of blackface. As the fluid drains off their faces, they look like zombies.

she says 'baby' before biting into it (Stewart 2019). The remains are roasted on a spit over an open campfire. The image reinforces a complex metaphor of rebirth through fire that spans the film, while offering a radicalisation and subversion through parody of pervasive stereotypes of Aboriginality.

The film ends with the impact of Stewart's hybrid form of zombification, understood through the white settler, Thomas, who is infected by the ghoul at the cabin, and Billy. The implication is that Billy has been in the process of zombification throughout *Killer Native*. The final bonfire scene and the book outlining the smallpox zombification are intertexts. The Aborigine stands by a campfire at night with his ghoul-bride and enters the end-stages of transformation, throwing on the possum cloak. In Aboriginal tradition, marriages take place at midnight; 'the fire is symbolic' of the binding nature of marriage (Unaipon 2006: 82), here a zombie unification. In the sunlight, Thomas, infected, sits on a log by the river and shoots himself in the throat. A piece of his bloody flesh splatters a flower and sprig, symbolic of the contamination process. These images bind modern Aboriginal identity and zombification to settler action. The film cuts to black. This final juxtaposition of the impact of zombification on the two men (the white man dead, the Aborigine in a process of renewal with Country) is a pointed expression of a new undeadness in the metaphysical context of modern Aboriginal Australian zombie identity.

The mainstream zombie has no direct translation nor historic tradition in Aboriginal Australia. A ghoulish gestalt, it feeds on underlying Dreaming metaphysics and engages with global derivations of the undead figure. In *Killer Native*, the Aboriginal zombie suggests continuous co-becoming and interweaving between figures and Country – between Dreaming and Dreamtime – and the contamination process ironically follows that same path.

Katarzyna Ancuta

Seoul Station (Sang-ho Yeon, 2016)

Following the release of *Train to Busan* (Yeon, 2016), you could be forgiven for thinking that zombies have suddenly turned Korean. In recent years, South Korean films and television dramas have successfully cornered the zombie market, as evident from productions like *Rampant* (Kim, 2016), *Peninsula* (Yeon, 2020), *#Alive* (Cho, 2020) and, even more so, the television series *Kingdom* (Kim and Park, 2019–present), *All of Us Are Dead* (Lee and Kim, 2022), or *Happiness* (Ahn, 2021), all of which have generated an immense global fan base. This is not to say there were no Korean zombie films made before that. Released in 1980, *Goeshi* (Kang), a loose adaptation of *The Living Dead at Manchester Morgue* (Grau, 1974), is usually considered the first Korean zombie film, although until quite recently it has been mostly forgotten. The interest in zombies spiked in twenty-first-century Korea, with several zombie-themed features and segments in horror anthologies making limited impact, but it is safe to say the global recognition of Korean zombies owes much to the unique brand of zombie social realist drama which has become a directorial trademark of Sang-ho Yeon.

While Yeon's *Train to Busan* and its sequel *Peninsula* have both generated a healthy profit and garnered critical attention, the first film in the trilogy, *Seoul Station* (2016), remains relatively unknown. Released the same year as *Train to Busan*, *Seoul Station*'s limited reception owes much to it being an animated feature. Given its theme, the animation is generally considered a prequel to *Train to Busan* despite the fact that there is no continuity between the two. Unlike *Train to Busan*, which focuses on the rise of the selfless hero and his subsequent sacrifice for the greater good, *Seoul Station* offers a more pessimistic take on the zombie dystopia, depicting a world beyond redemption that ends up imploding upon itself. *Seoul Station* presents a bleak scenario of a zombie outbreak where there are no survivors. While the consistent zombie iconography positions it as part of the *Train to Busan* trilogy, the film has much in common with Yeon's earlier animated features *The King of Pigs* (2011) and *The Fake* (2013) in terms of both its distinctive style of animation and its concern with social problems: all three films deliver stark realistic portrayals of systemic poverty, violence and bullying in modern-day Korea while taking a jab at the country's education system, organised religion or, in the case of *Seoul Station*, the state's inadequate welfare policies and inability to reduce homelessness. The effect is striking; the films' combination of disturbing imagery, tragic plots and relentless social critique drives the message home with the subtlety of a bulldozer.

Seoul Station sets out its theme very early in the film. The opening sequence welcomes us with a dreamy shot of a technicolour sunset against which the first zombie appears. The film's zombie zero is an elderly, shabbily dressed man easily identified from his appearance as a homeless person. He is shown staggering across the square leading to Seoul's main train station, a pivotal landmark associated as much with the city's busy lifestyle as with its homeless population. The man's neck is bleeding, probably from a bite, although the cause of his wound is never revealed. The opening dialogue of the film records a random conversation between two men in the square on the need to introduce a universal welfare system in Korea. One of these progressives offers to help the old man but is quickly repelled by the 'homeless stench'. Clearly, his ideals do not measure up to reality. As the wounded man enters the underground passage leading to the station, the design of the film becomes clear: we are shown that in neoliberal Korea there is not much difference between the homeless and zombies.

Linnie Blake has observed that, in recent years, the zombie has become 'the monster of choice for a generation tired of a decade of governmental facilitation of the anti-democratic impulses of neoliberal corporatism' (2015: 28) and, indeed, the zombies in *Seoul Station* fit well into this category. The titular Seoul Station, from where the outbreak spreads throughout the city, has become something of a symbol of the shortcomings of Korean neoliberalism. Built in 1925 by the Japanese colonial regime, the station remains one of the busiest spots in the capital, functioning as a transportation hub, a commercial centre and a significant civic space. Until the 1990s, the square adjoining the station was a frequent site of mass political rallies, but its image changed drastically in the years following the 1997 Asian financial crisis. In accepting a bailout by the International Monetary Fund in 1997, the Korean government agreed to restructure the country's economy in line with liberal free market practices. This led to the bankruptcies of large companies and banks, a massive spike in unemployment and a rapid increase in the homeless population in the country. Seoul train station and its adjoining square became the largest homeless congregation in the city. In the winter of 1998, it was estimated there were around 4,000 homeless people living in the station (Song 2009: 29).

Since the station's homeless people were highly visible and therefore a potential spark that could ignite civil unrest, the government decided to tackle homelessness under the newly established welfare state developed in accordance with the logic of neoliberal governance. The homeless policy adopted under President Dae-jung Kim's administration made a distinction between the 'deserving homeless' (*nosukcha*), who were deemed employable and therefore worthy of state-provided benefits, and the 'undeserving, rootless homeless' (*purangin*). Whereas the first group was said to exhibit a 'desire to work' and an 'intention to be rehabilitated', *purangin*-type homelessness was treated as a choice or an inability to adjust to living in society, which effectively stripped this group of their rights as citizens (Song 2009: 41). By focusing on short-term homelessness caused by an external economic crisis, the policy disregarded larger social issues, such as inadequate housing, mental health care, and domestic and sexual violence, which are typically seen as major factors contributing to long-term homelessness (Song 2009: 39). Although the central government eventually recognised all homeless people as permanent welfare subjects, the financial burden of dealing with the issue was passed on to municipal governments and the budget was kept to a minimum. This means that the problem of homelessness in Korea has never been treated systematically (Song 2011: 977–8). In 2016, when the film was released, the government reported more than 11,000 homeless people in the country and most of the related news items carried pictures taken at Seoul Station (Bak 2017).

Seoul Station foregrounds the notion of home/homelessness, setting up the zombie as the homeless person's uncanny double. The film makes a claim that the living and undead homeless masses are indistinguishable: they look and smell alike (see Figure 13a). When the zombies lay siege to a police station, the officers report that 'the homeless are attacking civilians'.

In another scene, a rampaging zombie is eventually revealed to be a mentally unstable homeless woman. Both the zombies and the homeless people in the film represent the externalised Other threatening to disrupt lives of ordinary citizens. Both expose the failings and unpreparedness of the authorities to deal with a crisis, from lack of shelters and general inefficiency of security guards and police officers, to easily overwhelmed medical services and escalating abuse of power by the state.

Home is the central notion in the Freudian unheimlich, where dread is generated by the merging of 'the homelike' with 'unhomeliness'. Kathleen Arnold argues that, in a world where home is commonly seen as a 'precondition for freedom' and a 'symbol of self and self-identity' (2004: 58), the homeless are perceived as uncanny because they are simultaneously similar to and different from the housed (62). Just like the homeless, zombies have no home. They are said to be devoid of self-identity and free will, unhuman and yet unmistakably human-like. From within the safety of one's home, the two groups look disturbingly alike and they generate the same fear.

Maria Kaika reminds us that 'there can be no homelessness without an economic, political and social process that produces "the home" as a commodity' (2004: 273). In the film, images of homeless people sleeping under billboards advertising expensive property development projects mingle with those of zombies rampaging through apartments feeding on renters and homeowners. Just like the homeless, zombies are expected to roam the world outside, separated from the safety of the home space: some of the most frightening scenes in zombie films are those in which the undead threaten the integrity of the home. In *Seoul Station*, having a home one can return to is what ultimately distinguishes humans from zombies. Without a place to call home, the homeless are already on the brink of becoming the undead. Overwhelmed by the situation, Hye-Sun, the film's main protagonist, cries that she wants to go home. Her homeless companion responds, 'Home? I want to go home too. But I don't have one!' Homelessness weighs heavily against the human right to life.

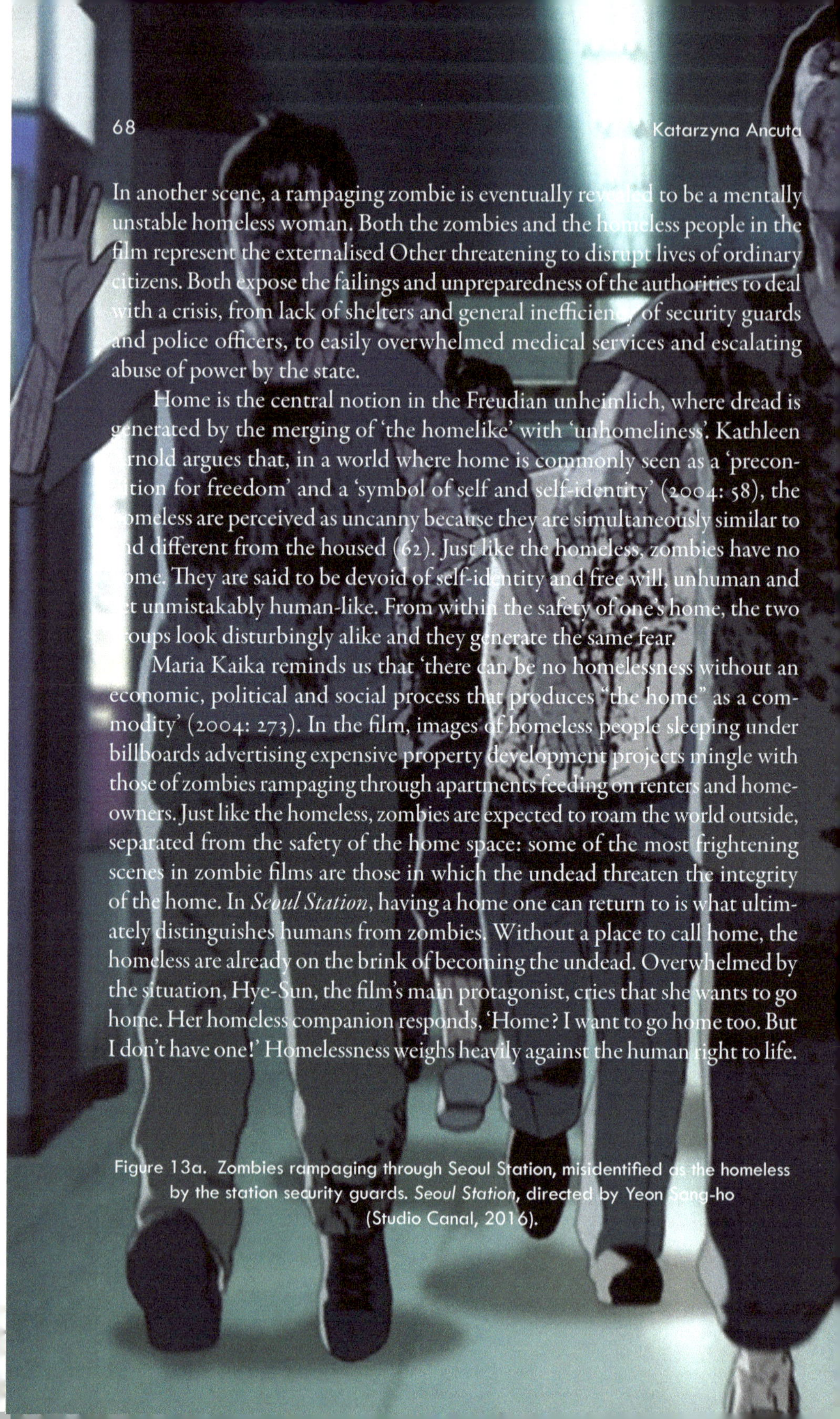

Figure 13a. Zombies rampaging through Seoul Station, misidentified as the homeless by the station security guards. *Seoul Station*, directed by Yeon Sang-ho (Studio Canal, 2016).

Home plays a central part in Hye-Sun's journey from human to zombie. A teenage runaway and sex-trade survivor, Hye-Sun discovers that her reluctant-to-work boyfriend, Ki-Woong, intends to prostitute her to pay the rent. Following an argument with him, she finds herself among the homeless people at Seoul Station when the outbreak begins. A glimmer of hope appears when a middle-aged man, Suk-Kyu, contacts Ki-Woong, identifying himself as Hye-Sun's father. The two men defy the authorities and zombies searching for her, but when the three of them are finally reunited at an empty luxurious apartment showroom, it is revealed that Suk-Kyu is not a concerned father looking for his daughter but rather Hye-Sun's former pimp hoping to reclaim his 'property'. The man kills Ki-Woong and attacks Hye-Sun, attempting to rape her. It is then we realise the girl has already been bitten, as she transforms and turns on her attacker (see Figure 13b). Though it may be tempting to conclude that Hye-Sun has finally found agency in (un)death, her vacant expression and automated movements suggest otherwise.

Hye-Sun's quest for a home – both as a safe space and a family she can rely on – ultimately proves a failure. Portrayed as a vulnerable teenager, a victim of organised crime, sexual violence and domestic abuse, she lives a life that is highly precarious: she is effectively homeless and alone. Hye-Sun's identity is reduced to that of a body: a broken body of an abused teenager, a morally transgressive body of a prostitute, a socially disruptive body of a homeless person and an infected body of a zombie, different faces of the uncanny Other. Throughout the film she is shown passing through a number of unhomely spaces: a temporary accommodation, an internet café, a homeless camp at the station, a police holding cell and an apartment showroom. The luxurious apartment where her human life ends is the ultimate uncanny space. Although it is designed to perfectly mimic a home, it will never become one, as it is not meant to be lived in. Trapped inside, zombie-Hye-Sun seems to have found her 'forever home', but it is destined to remain unhomely.

Mun-Young Chung has argued that although they are clearly modelled on Western cinematic sources, Korean zombies have managed to retain some distinctiveness in the way they combine humanity with the uniquely Korean concept of *han*. Notoriously difficult to translate, *han* is frequently explained as an emotional concept entailing a 'mixture of frustration and sorrow due to feelings of isolation' (Shim cited in Chung 2017: 3), 'a sense of unresolved resentment against injustices suffered' (Hyung cited in Chung 2017: 4), and a feeling of self-pity, helplessness and an urge for revenge (Chung 2017: 4). While in *Seoul Station* the *han* seems to be more directly applicable to the homeless rather than zombies, the fact that the two are linked complicates the issue. Presented as vulnerable, the homeless are the first to fall prey to zombies; from this perspective, zombies are just one more calamity that befalls them and aggravates their dire situation. The homeless-turned-zombies then attack unsuspecting citizens, but it is difficult to see this as an act of vindication, since by then they have become creatures devoid of rationality and consciousness. The fact that both the zombies and uninfected civilians are subject to the same state suppression (the militarised police scorched earth tactics leaving no room for survivors) once again sends the *han* levels rising.

Sung-Ae Lee has argued that zombie narratives have become a convenient vehicle for expressing the social impact of Korea's traumatic history and cultural wounds inflicted on the nation as the result of Japanese colonialisation, the Korean War and four decades of military dictatorship (2019: 150–1). The scenes portraying clashes between zombies, civilians and the riot police/military bear uncanny resemblance to media representations of the brutal suppression of labour movement protests and anti-regime demonstrations, such as the 1980 Gwangju Uprising. Ironically, such a hard stance is supported by some citizens in the film, provided they do not find themselves on the wrong side of the barricade. Trapped in a blocked alley, one civilian blames the zombie outbreak on the communists and demands to be rescued because he is a 'good' man who 'dedicated his life to this country', a clear reference to the distinction between deserving and undeserving citizens. His plea meets with an immediate riposte from Hye-Sun's homeless companion: 'I'm the same too! I made sacrifices for this country! So how did I end up this way? Know why? This country doesn't care about us! But we worked ourselves to death, you fools!' His complaints reiterate that homelessness means not only the inability to own a home but also exclusion from the larger 'home' of the nation. Enraged by a sense of injustice (*han* again), the man climbs the barricade only to be shot dead by the police when he is misidentified as a zombie. We are reminded that the authorities do not discriminate between people and zombies and that once a zombie outbreak is identified as an insurrection they respond with a show of force.

Lee concludes that 'the erasing of the personhood of characters who become infected thus accords with processes of exception which embrace not only zombies but also underclasses, security threats, terrorists, aliens and frequently women' (2019: 153). Zombies, homeless people and frustrated citizens protesting in the streets are seen as equal dangers to the state, their positioning outside the home, even temporarily, making them always potentially 'unhomely'. Unsurprisingly, it is difficult to conclude that in such contexts it is the zombie that represents the ultimate threat, as the undead seem more like a symptom of an underlying condition than the root of the problem. *Seoul Station* is less concerned with the man vs. monster conflict the zombie genre typically implies and more focused on exposing the neoliberal state's contempt for humanity in general and injustice that demands retribution. Classic Korean horror films teach us that a *han*-driven ghost will never fail to take vengeance on the wrongdoers, but when injustice becomes systemic, apparently it is time to bring in the zombie hordes.

Figure 13b. A shadow of zombie Hye-Sun devouring Suk-Kyu inside the model apartment. *Seoul Station*, directed by Yeon Sang-ho (Studio Canal, 2016).

Part II

The Undead and Never-ending Present

Dara Downey

The Haunting of Hill House (Mike Flanagan, 2018)

In Episode 9 of Mike Flanagan's 2018 Netflix reimagining of Shirley Jackson's *The Haunting of Hill House* (1959), Poppy Hill (played by Katie Parker), a long-dead resident of the eponymous Hill House who does not feature in Jackson's original novel, tells Olivia Crain (Carla Gugino), the mother of a young family who move in there, about the deaths of both her children from baffling diseases. Poppy recounts how she quickly realised that the horror of their illnesses was 'just a dream', and states, 'Then, I woke up. And they were safe in their beds', implying that all three of them had died and had become ghosts haunting the eponymous Hill House. Feeding the increasingly fragile Olivia a dangerous myth about maternal fears and maternal triumph over those fears, she goes on to insinuate that, by re-enacting Poppy's experiences in the house, Olivia can protect her youngest children, the twins Eleanor (Nell/Nellie) and Luke, from the dangers of the world outside. Poppy asks Olivia to imagine what she would do if the twins were trapped in a bad dream:

> I mean a dream so mean, so scary ... a dream about sick. And sad. And disease. And rot. And loss. And darkness. If they was stuck in that dream, you'd wake 'em [...] and you'd keep 'em just perfect, just like they is, wouldn't you? [...] I got a secret. A way to wake 'em up. A way to keep 'em safe ... (*Hill House*, Episode 9, 2018)

What she is suggesting that Olivia 'save' Luke and Nell from is, essentially, life – its unpredictability, its cruelty, its relentless entropy – by removing life altogether: by killing them. Olivia almost succeeds in following Poppy's plan, but instead fatally poisons Abigail (Olive Alise Abercrombie), the young daughter of the housekeeper Mrs Dudley (Annabeth Gish), before succumbing to Poppy's subsequent proposal: that she attempt to 'wake up' by sacrificing herself within the house and becoming a ghost there too. As I argue in this chapter, Poppy is central to understanding the representation of the malevolent dead in Flanagan's *The Haunting of Hill House* (henceforth *Hill House*).

Dressed as a 1920s flapper, Poppy is the imaginative descendent of Daisy Buchanan in F. Scott Fitzgerald's *The Great Gatsby* (1925). The flapper was a 'sexually aggressive modern girl' who 'would smoke, drink and neck her way through films, wearing revealing clothing and making suggestive remarks while attending wild parties' (Ross 2001: 409). Fundamentally 'irresponsible, uncaring, and unabashedly selfish', the flapper was therefore situated as the polar opposite of the domestic woman (Liming 2015: 105). Along with her imaginative predecessor, Nora Montgomery (Lily Rabe) in *American Horror Story: Murder House* (2011), Poppy manifests these characteristics superficially, primarily through clothing, while simultaneously voicing and embodying ideals associated with early twenty-first-century models of motherhood, such as attachment parenting. By collapsing together the 1920s and the 1990s through the figure of Poppy, the series projects contemporary attitudes back onto the past, transforming the flapper, a figure of female sexual independence and modernity, into a symbol of all-encompassing maternity. In this way, although Flanagan's *Hill House* ostensibly dramatises a horrific colonising of the present by the frightening, demonic past, the exact opposite is in fact what takes place. Instead, it implies that the drive towards the maternal is natural, eternal and unaffected by sociohistorical change or difference. Flanagan's adaptation therefore flattens out the twentieth century, transforming a range of historical moments into ciphers for contemporary notions of family (see Link 2020), effectively recruiting history as a vehicle for heteronormative concepts of femininity and motherhood in particular, with Olivia and her daughter Nell as both the victims and the agents of this process.

Flanagan's series tells the story of the Crain family, who move into Hill House in 1992, are forced out by a series of horrific events and, almost three decades later, find themselves drawn back there one by one, with the action moving between the two timelines as well as straying into the intervening years. The parents, Hugh (Henry Thomas) and Olivia, make their living by 'flipping' houses (buying promising wrecks and transforming them into desirable properties), with Olivia's role as architect perfectly complementing Hugh's more hands-on renovating skills. Olivia divides her time between the current project and designing their 'forever home', which she promises her five children they will build and occupy once the money from Hill House is safely banked. It is this desire for stability and complete aesthetic and financial control over her living space that, as in Jackson's original novel, Hill House exploits in order to subdue the female protagonist to its wishes, convincing Olivia, like Jackson's Eleanor, that Hill House is the only 'forever home' she needs. In this way, the series draws attention to the ways in which domestic ideology promulgates itself, and to the role of the Gothic in this process. As Emily Jane Cohen points out, in its more conservative manifestations, fiction in the Gothic mode, such as that by Ann Radcliffe, might begin by depicting the home as a dangerous, unstable place, but by the denouement,

> its narrative machinery delivered nostalgic consolations to a society that looked to the home for shelter from the dislocation experienced without. [...] 'Do not worry', it assured its readers, 'though all hell break loose, though you be invaded by bandits, impostors and vengeful ancestors, domesticity will prevail. In the end, your house will be your home'. (Cohen 2005: 653; see also DeLamotte 1990)

Flanagan's *Hill House* therefore aligns with the Gothic's simultaneous critique and perpetuation of the middle-class, single-family home's 'institutionalization of capitalist and patriarchal relations and values (among them, monogamy, heterosexuality, and consumerism)' (Sobchack 1996: 144). From Radcliffe's work to recent films such as *Winchester* (2018), many Gothic texts perform this operation by situating their narratives in a distant past onto which are projected contemporary values and forms of subjectivity. On the one hand, fiction such as the Gothic that employs historical settings contains 'subversive potential', in that it troubles our sense of 'the normative experience of the everyday and the contemporary world' but on the other, can 'close down difference' and often 'works conservatively to promote universalising tendencies' (de Groot 2010: 4).

Flanagan's *Hill House*, as Jessica R. McCort (2020: 230) notes astutely, should be understood as produced during and by the current age marked by anti-feminist sentiment and loss of rights for women in the United States, an age in which 'myths' around motherhood as women's destiny are in the ascendant. For McCort, the series 'depends upon cultural anxieties regarding working mothers, absentee and over-present mothers, and helicopter parenting for the strength of its metaphors' (231; see also Carruthers 2020). Within this context, the series also represents an assertion of heteronormative familial patterns at a time when marriage equality and reproductive choice are under serious threat in America. It is arguably for this reason that, after building up the fear and tension for nine episodes in which we are repeatedly told by numerous characters that the ghoul-haunted house is particularly attractive to, and therefore fatal for, those who identify as female, the final episode of the series executes an abrupt reversal, transforming the nightmare house into a dream 'forever home' from which the world-weary dead need never depart. Hugh sacrifices himself to be with Olivia, and the house allows the younger members of the family to leave. When they do so, they return to their own homes, cast off their unresolved traumas, repair their own broken familial relationships, and pair off into suitably monogamous, largely heterosexual couples.

This, combined with the decision of Hugh and eldest son Stephen to ensure that the house remains in the Crain family name, means that the house will now have a steady stream of willing victims, as it is implied that all of the family members, as well as the housekeepers, the Dudleys, will return to Hill House to die and become ghosts, never needing to part from one another again. Whereas the 'Murder House' in *American Horror Story* remains on the market, functioning as a stark symbol for the economic as well as the emotional toll that homeownership takes on those who enter the system, Hill House will never be threatened by new owners, and the production of a subsequent generation guarantees that the house's food supply will not run dry. Sinister as this may sound, as Rachel Syme (2018) points out, tonally, the series 'ends on a practically sunny note: An acoustic guitar plays, and the family unit is restored to safety'. For Janette Laredo, '[t]his changes Jackson's message of fragmentation and loneliness to one of unity and communion', and, while 'Jackson's novel leaves you queasy, uncertain about the world', by contrast, 'Flanagan's show attempts to leave you with a gooey heart and the warm assurance of human connection' (2020: n.p.). The final episode suggests that even haunted houses can be happy homes, once the inhabitants learn to accept their own traumatic pasts, implying by extension that the dread built up in previous episodes was the result of nothing more than a misunderstanding. Indeed, the right attitude can apparently transform a 'hungry' demonic structure into the perfect haven from financial and psychological instability and pain.

Consequently, in contrast to Jackson's original, 'the television series ostensibly finds hope in the heteronormative model of marriage and childbearing, giving striking dominance to the transcendent power of unified families and the process of maturing into adulthood' (Roach 2020: n.p.). The series as a whole can therefore be read as a movement away from what Jack Halberstam refers to as 'queer time': 'a term for those specific models of temporality that emerge within postmodernism once one leaves the temporal frames of bourgeois reproduction and family, longevity, risk/safety and inheritance' (2005: 2). Halberstam acknowledges the dominance and power of more normative forms of temporality, including a drive towards heterosexual marriage and reproduction, which bulldoze through those who attempt to resist (2005: 4; see also Roach). Elizabeth Freeman's term for this 'ambivalent or failed subjection to these temporal and structural norms' is 'chrononormativity', which she defines as 'causality, sequence, forward-moving agency, and so on' (2010: xxi; see also Garber 1992: 64). Nell (Victoria Pedretti) and middle daughter Theo (Kate Siegel) – a child psychologist who lives in her sister Shirley's guest house, to which she brings a string of female lovers, and a psychometrist who sees people's dark secrets and occasionally futures by touching them, a 'gift' inherited from her maternal grandmother, whose gloves Olivia gives Theo so she can protect herself from intrusive thoughts – 'exhibit queerly temporal ways of living, and as a result they have the most to fear from societal expectations that seek to realign them with dominant life trajectories' (Roach 2020: n.p.). In Theo's case, the house (and the series) succeeds: she is ultimately 'saved' by her eventual commitment to Trish, whom she meets in a bar and who actively pursues a relationship, despite Theo's reluctance. Theo is therefore made less 'queer' and less supernatural simultaneously, as she casts off her gloves and engages in 'homebuilding and monogamy' by the end of the final episode (Roach 2020: n.p.).

However, it is arguably Nell, around whose death and funeral much of the action of the series revolves, who is most instrumental in the shift from Halberstam's queer temporality to Freeman's chrononormativity. As a child, Nell has difficulty sleeping because she is haunted by a terrifying ghost she calls 'the Bent-Neck Lady', who hovers over her, long hair and nightdress draped over the young Nell, and whom none of the other family members can see. As an adult, over twenty years later, Nell still sees the Bent-Neck Lady at key moments in her life, and she suffers from a debilitating sleep paralysis that only abates when she meets and marries a sleep technologist named Arthur Vance (Jordane Christie). During her marriage, she is safe from the spectre of the Bent-Neck Lady; this stint as a married woman is, as Roach (2020) observes, the point in her story when Nell fits most comfortably into traditional familial models (see also Carruthers 2020). Arthur's sudden death is, consequently, attended by the return of the Bent-Neck Lady, a convergence of traumatic events that pushes Nell into serious mental illness and, ultimately, her death in Hill House. The house transforms her into a ghost, and she appears to her parents, siblings and younger self at unexpected moments both before and after her biological death, in the 1990s and 2010s. For Roach, this indicates that, '[e]ven in death', Nell 'must inhabit spaces that create a temporal paradox, a queer destabilizing force that haunts and violently disrupts the linearity of the narrative' (2020: n.p.).

Specifically, as revealed in Episode 5, 'The Bent-Neck Lady', the ghost haunting Nell's childhood is herself. Here, the series suggests that Nell's short, troubled life has been blighted, not by any haunting force in Hill House, but simply by her own pre-remembered trauma, and that she is driven to commit suicide in the house, not by the house or even really by the ghost of her mother, but by the horror of living with the foreknowledge that she commits suicide. Like Poppy's, then, the specificity of Nell's past has been erased. Poppy Hill is rendered an anachronism, a mouthpiece for the next century's parenting norms, and by extension for the house's insatiable desire to trap women within its illusive idyllic domesticity. In Nell's case, it is suggested that the house has played no role whatever: that she herself, and nothing external, has been the problem all along. The house claims her as its own by convincing her (and the audience) that it has done nothing of the sort, and that she only has herself to blame for her death and eternal unrest.

Consequently, visually and emotionally stunning as the revelation of the Bent-Neck Lady's identity is, it nonetheless serves as a turning point towards normativity, suggesting that Nell has merely been haunted by herself all along, and by her resistance to the call of the house. Giving in translates her from haunted and grieving to belonging and convincing others to belong: in the final episodes, she lures her siblings into the Red Room, the heart of the house, apparently locked when they were children, but in fact serving as a sort of Room of Requirement for each of them, giving them exactly what they wanted in order to bind them to the house. The Nell that we see in the final episode in particular is notably happier and calmer than she has been in life, having apparently accepted the role of the Bent-Neck Lady, a permanent fixture in the house (see Alexander 2020). It is therefore unsurprising that Episode 5, which focuses on Nell's funeral, also features flashbacks to her wedding. She is removed into the safe spaces of marriage and death simultaneously, and her appearances to her family, out of sequence with linear time, are intended to do the same to them – to bring them first together and then to the house, which 'exploits her and her desires', offering her 'an overly idyllic future' via a vision of her dead husband and her reunited family when she arrives (Kaufler 2020: n.p.). Convincing her that the world inside the house is literally heaven, it then recruits her to pass the message on, and it succeeds; Hill House will remain in Crain hands for as long as there are Crain heirs and it can continue to absorb them one by one in death.

As Tricia Lootens states, Jackson's *Hill House* is 'a horror story about the ways in which people, especially women, are destroyed by the nuclear family, sexual repression, and romantic notions of feminine self-sacrifice' (2005: 152). The same can be said of Flanagan's, except that it is difficult not to see the series as suggesting that this sacrifice is a positive thing. Offering what Fredric Jameson sees as a depthless veneer of 'pastness' (1991: 19) and of chronological distortion, it nonetheless moves inexorably towards stasis and linearity, with everyone safely dead or safely married off, at which point Hill House is somehow exorcised of demons, both literal and psychological, and is transformed from a devouring monster to a haven in a heartless world, a forever home – that is, a grave.

Tyler Unsell

The Girl with All the Gifts (Colm McCarthy, 2016)

> Sergeant Eddie Parks: It's over. It's all over.
> Melanie: It's not over. It just doesn't belong to you anymore. (*The Girl with All the Gifts*, 2016)
>
> There's no such thing as neutral education. Education either functions as an instrument to bring about conformity or freedom. (Freire 2014: 34)

Horror movies have always been ripe areas for pedagogical development. We know our students are very interested in genre literature and film. We also know that the transgressive nature of horror makes it a perfect vehicle to teach critical thinking. Placing students in horror-based thought experiments allows students to become their own final boys and girls. *The Girl with All the Gifts* takes everything one step further. What if our students become the horror? We often use the metaphor of students as zombies. At least in popular culture, our classrooms are full of children who seem bored, tired, unemotional and, most importantly, unengaged. They are, by all accounts, zombies. The zombie students of *The Girl with All the Gifts* give us one possible solution to our educational concerns. If teachers can learn to raise their students from the dead, we can fix our educational system before it is too late. It is our choice. Our children can be either our enemies or our future. Apotheosis or Apocalypse: it is our choice.[1]

---

[1] The question Apotheosis or Apocalypse was first posed by Chuck Wendig in his fantastic nature attacks novel *Invasive* (2016).

The Girl with All the Gifts

M. R. Carey was a well-known comic writer and artist at DC Comics before he wrote the young adult novel *The Girl with All the Gifts* (2014) – and its subsequent prequel *The Boy on the Bridge* (2017) – which was adapted for big-screen release in 2016. A number of details were changed for the adaptation, but the core of the plot remained the same. Melanie (Sennia Nanua) is a student at the Beacon military facility. She is part of a cadre of students who retain their mental capacity despite the fact that they crave human flesh. They are, in essence, smart zombies.

Ms Justineau (Gemma Arterton) acts as their teacher, teaching them in what looks very similar to a pandemic classroom setting. Each student is strapped to a chair where Justineau lectures to them (mostly about Greek myths and tragedies). When Justineau is not teaching, the children are used as experimental subjects by Dr Caldwell (Glenn Close), a scientist hell-bent on finding a cure to the zombie disease. Sergeant Parks (Paddy Considine) is a cold and calculating soldier who is charged with protecting the humans from their potentially dangerous students.

Early in the film, Beacon gets overrun by feral zombies. Melanie escapes from Dr Caldwell just before she vivisects her. Melanie saves Justineau but, in the process, also eats human flesh for the first time (thankfully, not Justineau's). The surviving group of humans, including Parks, Justineau and Caldwell, decide to head into the city and allow Melanie to accompany them. While in the city, the group find other zombie children who have maintained their ability for rational thought.

The climax comes when Caldwell tries to kill Melanie again only after revealing that there is no cure for the fungus that caused the zombie apocalypse. Melanie releases millions of the zombie spores, and Justineau wakes up in a hazmat facility where she is protected from the now airborne fungal disease. The movie ends with her teaching the zombie children in a fashion very similar to the opening of the movie, but this time she is the one who is trapped.

Figure 14. Melanie's learning environment changes immensely throughout the film. *The Girl with All the Gifts*, directed by Colm McCarthy (BFI Film Fund, 2016).

Pedagogy of the Oppressed

Generally speaking, until the middle of the twentieth century, traditional models of education were mostly teacher-centred. The onus was on the students to adjust to the teacher lecturing, and academic achievement was narrowly defined by standardised assessments. Classrooms looked the same. Students were expected to act the same way. Most importantly, students were expected to *learn* the same way. Learning was seen as uniform and often defined by its coldness and austerity. The 1960s gave rise to a number of educational reforms, including a critique of the traditional system. This 'critical pedagogy' was best exemplified by Paulo Freire's seminal work, *The Pedagogy of the Oppressed*, in which he argues that traditional models of education dehumanise students by creating the banking model. In this model, students were seen as empty vessels until the teacher deposited knowledge into their brains. They were mindless: devoid of function, personality and purpose until the teachers provided them with the knowledge necessary to exist in our society.

Freire's argument ultimately led to a broader Marxist critique of capitalism which was particularly popular during the time in which he wrote.[2] While the *raison d'être* has changed over time, Freire's argument remains solid. Traditional methods of teaching are less concerned with creating independent thinkers and more interested in preserving existing power structures. This, in Freire's view, is the root of oppression, and as a result a critical pedagogy would reaffirm each student's own narrative, creating powerful critical thinkers that view the teacher as a guide rather than the arbiter of wisdom and knowledge.

Justineau as Guide

The single most important relationship in *The Girl with All the Gifts* is that between teacher and pupil. This relationship is complex and often relies on the dialogic approach to education initially touted by Socrates and further articulated by Freire. In the beginning, Melanie is the perfect student, answering questions with the exact answers Justineau is looking for. She is sweet, innocent and entirely non-threatening. It is only later in the scene, when Banks reveals the students' true nature, that we learn exactly what they really are.

As Justineau's role changes, after they escape the compound, so does her role as teacher. Her questions become more open-ended. The answers are not prescribed but rather constructed, and as such education becomes more dialogic. By the end of the film, Melanie makes choices and comes up with answers that threaten the very institutions that Justineau is a part of (if we can call traditional conceptions of humanity an 'institution').

---

2   Freire can certainly be classified as a Marxist, but more because of his predilection for the dialectic and less because of his economic policies (although those are clearly Marxist as well).

Melanie brings on the revolution even while doing her best to protect Justineau from its effects. Yet, it is difficult to find a happy reading of the film from Justineau's point of view. A single tear runs down her face when she realises what has happened and what the next phase of her life may entail. A teacher and believer of critical pedagogy should not be surprised if their students burn down the institutions they have all been critiquing. Freire is very clear: the end goal of the pedagogy of the oppressed is to provide students with enough guidance that they will one day replace these flawed and oppressive institutions with new ones that place a greater value on fairness, equality and justice.

Education as Experience

It is important to note that the bulk of *The Girl with All the Gifts* takes place outside the classroom but that education is readily available and apparent throughout the film. In fact, a great deal of Melanie's growth takes place by personal exploration. It is only through her own exploration that we find the existence of other children similar to her. Her own knowledge and creativity saves the group a number of times, and it is this critical thinking that enables her to remain non-threatening to the group as she learns to feed off animals, specifically house cats.

The juxtaposition of Melanie's early educational setting (a cold military barracks replete with restraints, prison cells and wheelchairs that are converted into student desks) with the outside world (which is full of life, both human and zombie) could not be more stark. Again, *Girl with All the Gifts* provides a blueprint for how education can better serve this brave new world. It is through embracing this freedom of movement and choice that Melanie finds her greater purpose. Borrowing heavily from the Montessori school of education, M. R. Carey again breaks from traditional modes of education by embracing Melanie's exploration. She is at her most confident – her most self-actualised – when she is given a task and allowed to complete it in any fashion she sees fit. I would also argue that the movie works very hard to place Melanie in her greatest peril when she is forced into confined spaces, typically indoors. Moreover, there is a clear link between the cold calculations of those who use and teach science and mathematics and how they treat Melanie. The first engagement we see Melanie make with any curriculum is with Justineau's discussion of Greek mythology, specifically the story of Pandora's box. The study of Greek myths is a regular part of the English curriculum taught in most high schools. It represents a distinctly non-STEM field in this movie, and while the myth was clearly used to draw parallels with Melanie's own situation, it also points out the perils of focusing too much on STEM education while neglecting the arts.[3]

Rejection of False Charity

Freire's pedagogy aims to be transformative. He argues that education should be viewed as a tool of liberation and revolution. Forms of critical pedagogy reject small changes that impact students on an individual level. These small actions are referred to as 'false charity'. Instead, teachers and students should embrace large revolutionary change that seeks to supplant old power structures with new more egalitarian structures. In this way, the 'white saviourism' that tends to flourish in public schools is rejected for large-scale political change. Students and teachers should look for ways that completely reject past traditions and seek to learn from past mistakes and not replicate them. Melanie does exactly this when she sets the fungus on fire at the end of the film. This action spreads the spores worldwide, ensuring that all humans will become infected with the disease. It is not the piecemeal charity that Justineau offers but rather the full-scale change Freire calls for.

Authenticity is critical to Freire's conception of education. This type of authenticity has become a type of fungible currency our students use to

3   The Montessori credo leans heavy into the experiential elements of education: 'Scientific observation then has established that education is not what the teacher gives; education is a natural process spontaneously carried out by the human individual, and is acquired not by listening to words but by experiences upon the environment' (Montessori 1989: 102).

negotiate social transactions. Our students have become hyperaware of adults who have agendas, especially agendas that are existential threats to their own futures. Often, our students reject these antiquated practices outright. Freire argues this is the only way to build true change.

> True generosity consists precisely in fighting to destroy the causes which nourish false charity. False charity constrains the fearful and subdued, the 'rejects of life', to extend their trembling hands. True generosity lies in striving so that these hands – whether of individuals or entire peoples – need be extended less and less in supplication, so that more and more they become human hands which work and, working, transform the world. (Freire 2014: 45)

The Evolution of the Pedagogy of the Undead

Justineau's actions early in the film create the pedagogical tension I discussed above. The army base insists that Justineau refrain from doing things that challenge the traditional model. She is not allowed to get too close (both a physical warning given by Banks and an existential warning given by Caldwell). She is not allowed to treat them with 'too much' respect, love or caring. When she attempts to physically reassure Melanie, she is given a fierce display of how the zombie children could react if she lets her guard down.

The dilemma facing modern educators is how to balance a critical approach to pedagogy while maintaining our own identities and humanity. *The Girl with All the Gifts* answers that question. We teach for a world that will outgrow us. If we give our students enough room to explore and encouragement to think critically about some of the assumptions our society has made, then perhaps this future world will be a better place: a place that values each student's humanity and identity; a world that sees knowledge as experiential as opposed to imparted. We also need to be ready as educators for a world where our students outgrow us. Even when they may come back to visit, these sweet moments of reconnection remind us that these students no longer belong to us. Perhaps it is time for us to embrace that they were never ours to begin with.

Figure 15. Ms Justineau's role as educator shifts throughout the film leaving her trapped while the rest of the students travel freely. *The Girl with All the Gifts*, directed by Colm McCarthy (BFI Film Fund, 2016).

The movie presents us a choice to make about how we think education should look in this ever-changing world. Do we chain our students to their desks in an underground bunker, or do we allow them to experience the world as they are, each student a potential monster or a potential saviour? The reality is equally complex. They are both and neither at the same time. They are the next generation and, frankly, the world belongs to them, not us.

The end of *The Girl with All the Gifts* makes that choice for us. Surrounded by undead children who are rational beings that could be real threats to Justineau, in a world that is just as threatening, the teacher becomes the subject. We get the distinct impression that Justineau may not be happy in this new environment, but there is no doubt that the tables have been turned and she now acts both as teacher and as a historical exhibit to be examined everyday by this new generation.[4] The real question becomes, what choice do

4   Although it does not bode well for Justineau, Freire argues this acceptance of power and agency over reality by students is the only way to create lasting change: 'Teachers

we make as society? Do we hold our students back and shoehorn them into the roles society wants them to play to preserve our own lace in society, or do we trust them enough to create solutions to problems that are increasingly global in nature? Just as parents may have difficulty giving up control to their children, we too find ourselves at a similar crossroads. We can either maintain the status quo and accept the eventual educational and social apocalypse, or we can trust these children and help them build their own apotheosis, even if that means our own roles will change. The choice remains ours, in and out of the classroom.

---

and students (leadership and people), co-intent on reality, are both Subjects, not only in the task of unveiling that reality, and thereby coming to know it critically, but in the task of re-creating that knowledge. As they attain this knowledge of reality through common reflection and action, they discover themselves as its permanent re-creators' (Freire 2014: 69).

Antares Leask

ZOMBIES 2 (Paul Hoen, 2020)

The 2018 Disney Channel film *ZOMBIES* opens with teenager Addison Wells (Meg Donnelly) describing the idyllic planned community of Seabrook. The narrative shifts between Addison and Zed Necrodopolis (Milo Manheim), both excited about their first day of high school. For Addison, it is the first day because it is a human rite of passage. For Zed, it is the first time zombies have been allowed to attend Seabrook High since an accident with a lime soda at the power plant caused half the town to turn into zombies as the 'green haze blew west'. Instead of the west representing a new frontier, Seabrook West becomes a zombie ghetto. 'Ghetto' is a racially charged word, but it describes the way zombies are treated in Seabrook. Before the school was integrated, the zombies had not been allowed to leave their area to enter the town proper. They have a strict curfew and they wear Z-bands, bracelets which electronically control their violent urges. Most stores have 'humans only' signs. These Disney zombies have even gone vegan and eat 'brains', usually cauliflower, from a can.

The *ZOMBIES* films, particularly the second one, echo the view of anti-racist activist Ibram X. Kendi that

> [a]ntiracist ideas are based in the truth that racial groups are equals in all the ways they are different, assimilationist ideas are rooted in the notion that certain racial groups are culturally or behaviorally inferior, and segregationist ideas spring from a belief in genetic racial distinction and fixed hierarchy. (Kendi 2019: 31)

Throughout the films, characters explore these concepts, not along racial lines as we know them, but through the lens of humans, zombies and werewolves, teaching anti-racism to the pre-teen Disney Channel audience and giving their parents gentle, although not very subtle, reminders.

The integration of Seabrook High mirrors historical school integration: the 'normals' are against it, there are separate entrances divided by a fence, security only monitors the zombie entrance, and zombies have segregated classes in the basement. Zed and his friends Eliza (Kylee Russell) and Bonzo (James Godfrey) are disappointed to learn that, as zombies, they won't be allowed to participate in extracurricular activities. Principal Lee (Naomi Snieckus) tells the zombies, with a look of absolute discomfort, 'We are thrilled to be forced to have you here'. If the zombies do leave the basement, there is an alarm to protect the 'normal' students and zombie shelters built into the school infrastructure.

Eliza is the zombie most willing to fight for equal rights (as usual, this burden is placed on a Black/zombie woman), and is even willing to stand up to Seabrook's prized champion cheerleaders, telling Bonzo that 'Humans are bad, but cheerleaders are monsters'. The Seabrook Mighty Shrimp cheerleaders are pretty awful. Led by evil-cheer captain Bucky (Trevor Tordjman), the cheerleaders knowingly play on the stereotypical zombie fear of fire and torment them with flaming spirit sticks. Worse, directly afterward, they perform a musical number about being 'fired up'. For Bucky, the status quo is everything, and the zombies are a threat to the town, the school and cheer. He laments, 'People love cheer and that's what makes me important. I'd hate to see that change'.

Bucky is also Addison's cousin, and their family history is full of anti-zombie prejudice. Addison's father is the police chief for zombie segregation. Getting to know her new classmates, Addison realises, 'are Zombies always so harassed? I had no idea life was like this for them', and 'I'm still learning that zombies aren't what I was taught'. As Beverly Daniel Tatum writes, once 'it [the silence about race] is meaningfully broken, a process of identity development – specifically linked to an understanding of what it means to be White in a race-conscious society – begins to unfold' (Tatum 2017: 186). Addison is the character who shows the most development, moving from fear to learning to growth, which also explains why she is the first to accept the werewolves in the second film.

Addison also has a secret: pure white unruly hair that no one can explain (until the final film comes out in 2022). Bucky, even as family, uses this knowledge, telling her that 'It's best if you don't question things' while gently pulling some of her real hair from beneath her wig. Addison is not sure where she fits in, which will be the main conflict of the second film, and Bucky, as a male human in power, feels no shame in emotionally manipulating her with the threat that works on most teenagers: loss of popularity. Bucky is a clear segregationist, telling Addison, 'You're either pro-cheerleader or pro-zombie. Decide now'.

While the humans of Seabrook dress in similar pastel outfits, the zombies have individualised their government-issued coveralls, which, along with their green hair, presents a visual difference in aesthetic for the zombies. Zed explains, 'It's not so bad on this side of the tracks; we make it work with a little bit of swag'. Similar to American fashion trends, the 'normals' adopt this zombie look as their own, culturally appropriating zombie style and exemplifying Ijeoma Oluo's observation that 'this is not usually the wholesale adoption of an entire culture, but usually just attractive bits and pieces that are taken and used by the dominant culture' (Oluo 2019: 146).

The humans use zombies in other ways as well. When Zed zombies out at a pep rally and tackles the football team, Coach (Jonathan Langdon, a Black actor whose character is never given a name beyond his job description) realises that this zombie, whom he initially cut from the football team on grounds of zombie-ness alone, can be useful. This zombie can help Coach, and the school, achieve their athletic dreams; he can be their 'good zombie'. The benefits for Zed are multiple: he's always dreamed of playing football like his dad did before zombification, he can use his prowess on the field to leverage for greater zombie rights at school, and it legitimises his budding feelings for Addison. (Who could object to a football star/cheerleader romance?)

Paul Hoen, the director of *ZOMBIES* (2018), shows Addison and Zed's human/zombie differences visually, but also musically. During their duets, Addison sings the melody while Zed raps his lyrics. This provides an aural division between their styles of expression and is an ever-present reminder for the audience of their own potentially racial musical expectations. Choreographer Jennifer Weber also made sure that the humans, zombies and werewolves move differently, commenting:

> The cheerleaders move in perfect unison nailing lots of tosses, jumps and quick formation changes. The Zombies have their own unique hip hop style. They are the ultimate dance crew, mixing old school locking and more contemporary hip hop. In contrast,

the Werewolves have a more freestyle club inspired vibe that incorporates house and breaking. (Ferri 2020)

The filmmakers made an effort for the different groups to look, sing and dance differently, an anti-racist choice to celebrate the strengths of each group. While the treatment of zombies by humans clearly mirrors American racial tensions, Hoen uses actors of all races as both 'normals' and zombies. Nevertheless, Seabrook is literally a vanilla town. The town ice cream parlour only serves vanilla. The symbolism is a bit heavy-handed.

The first film focuses on Addison and Zed exploring how they can be together as themselves. Addison tells him, 'We're changing ourselves when what we need to change is everyone else'. Zed wins the Homecoming game, playing for the first time without his zombie performance enhancement, but the cheerleaders, who have discovered his trick, manipulate the Z-bands so that Zed, Eliza and Bonzo zombie out in front of the horrified crowd. Zed is tased and led away in handcuffs – the Seabrook police, seeing a zombie as dangerous, immediately tase first and ask questions later – and subsequently Zed, Eliza and Bonzo spend time in containment. This is a clear parallel to racist police in our world with segregationist ideas, although the film's racist (humanist?) cop is portrayed by a Black actor. Addison gives a rousing speech to the crowd as they turn their back on Zed, reminding them 'He was your monster', using Dr Kendi's definition of an anti-racist idea as 'any idea that suggests the racial groups are equals in all their apparent differences – that there is nothing right or wrong with any racial group' (Kendi 2019: 20). Addison, sure of her cheerleader popularity and that the crowd will follow her no matter what, then rips off her wig to reveal her unusual hair, only to be booed off the field. Her white saviour narrative fails once she aligns herself visually with those who are different. At this point in the series, Addison, Zed and Eliza make the same argument as Tatum in that 'We all must be able to embrace who we are in terms of our racial and cultural heritage, not in terms of assumed superiority or inferiority but as an integral part of our daily experience in which we can take pride' (Tatum 2017: 200), but Seabrook society is not listening.

As the serious conversations about race begin in Seabrook, and Bucky's paranoia about his waning popularity causes the cheer team to self-destruct right before the championships, Addison finds community with the zombies because 'zombies celebrate their differences'. The zombies and humans cheer together in a rousing reprisal of 'Fired Up' and bring the Seabrook community together. Racism is seemingly solved ... until the sequel.

The second film explores zombie assimilation. No longer celebrating their differences, the zombies just want to be like everyone else. Kendi describes assimilationist ideas as 'racist ideas. Assimilationists can position any racial group as the superior standard that another racial group should be measuring themselves against' (Kendi 2019: 29). In the case of *ZOMBIES 2*, Zed has positioned humans as superior to zombies and humanity as a goal to be fervently pursued.

This film also opens with Addison and Zed exploring Seabrook history, this time the legend that the first settlers found 'wild beasts with sharp claws'. Once they had conquered them, the humans discovered (and stole) the Moonstone, from which the werewolves derive life, health and power. In typical human colonist fashion, the settlers used the Moonstone in their power plant, with no regard to native needs or customs. If this plot sounds familiar, it is because it is not that far from the plot of *Frozen 2* (Buck and Lee 2019).

At the start of the film, everyone is in their typical roles, with Bucky reluctantly allowing zombies on the cheer squad. Addison and Zed sing a duet about 'teaming up to make progress', but Bucky complains, 'I'm not anti-change, I'm just pro-keeping things the way they are' and Eliza worries, 'Making progress, that sounds great, but what's the price we have to pay?' Bucky originally introduces the werewolves as an urban legend to scare rookies, but when the werewolves actually re-emerge in Seabrook, the town reinstates the anti-monster laws, once again lumping Others together. The town, which had learned to accept differences, as evidenced by Coach opening a Fro-Yo stand with multiple options – new flavours such as Cauliflower Brain Mocha Crunch – easily and immediately falls back into its segregationist ways.

The other plot of the film revolves around the planned demolition of the Seabrook Power Plant, which, as Eliza points out, is 'important to zombie heritage', and, as it turns out, is important to werewolf heritage as well. Willa Lykensen (Chandler Kinney) is the head werewolf but also represents the trope of the angry black woman, something Disney has already explored in *Descendants 2* (Ortega, 2017) with the pirate Uma. Willa and the werewolves cause havoc at Seabrook High, and she confronts the humans about the lies in their history books concerning vicious werewolves, pointing out that the settlers attacked first and stole the werewolves' Moonstone.

Although Wyatt (Pearce Joza), one of the lead werewolves, believes that Addison's white hair means she is the Head Alpha who will lead the werewolves to the Moonstone, she clearly is not, because her name does not start with a 'W' like the other werewolves (nor does it have a 'Z' in it like the zombie names). At the end of the second film, something shoots through the sky and her mystical hair glows, insinuating that the third film will reveal that she is an alien; but does it cheapen her character arc if the white human 'normal' fighting for zombie and werewolf justice isn't actually normal?

Wyatt's focus on Addison is upsetting to Zed's male ego, but also to Willa and her role as pack leader. She sings, 'I'm the alpha; I'm the leader; I'm the one to trust', again reminiscent of Uma in *Descendants 2*. Apart from the human/werewolf difference, visually, Wyatt's push to install Addison as pack leader is a white man trying to use a white woman to usurp Black female power. Addison isn't sure what to do with all the attention, but since her hair has made her feel like an outsider, she is grateful to have the chance to finally feel like she belongs. She admires the werewolves and the fact that they are 'unique but you have unity; you know who you're supposed to be'. Through dancing with the werewolves, her appearance also radically changes as she tries to assimilate to werewolf culture. Tatum explains that 'sometimes the emergence of an oppositional identity can be quite dramatic as the young person tries on a new persona almost overnight' (Tatum 2017: 144). Addison's appropriation of werewolf style upsets her family and friends and is her third visual change on her anti-racist journey.

Zed, meanwhile, is trying to work within the system to become president of the student body in order to re-abolish the anti-monster laws. To defeat Bucky, Zed needs the werewolf vote and is frustrated by their anti-racism, complaining, 'Werewolves! They're not interested in fitting in'. Zed is assimilating too well: his friends point out that he has whitewashed his own image on his campaign posters to look more human. Bucky takes this to the other extreme, changing Zed's posters before the big debate to feature an exaggerated zombie self with the slogan 'Zed 4 Prez, you for dinner?' Of course, these are both tactics used by modern politicians for assimilationist and segregationist purposes. Zed zombiesplains and tries to help the werewolves fit in as the zombies have, but Willa is willing to fight assimilation, singing, 'Why should we change? / They should be like us / Yeah, he may eat brains, but he's got no guts'. Wyatt, on the other hand, tries to remind the zombies of their life before assimilation, saying, 'Imagine how alive you'd feel if you didn't have to tamp it down, could be your true selves'. Zed's struggle with his own self-worth as a zombie causes him to try to preserve Addison's humanity as well. When the werewolves give Addison a Moonstone necklace – the final test of her potential werewolf-ness – Zed steals it, telling Eliza, 'I have to protect her'.

Part of the werewolf mythos is that because of their distance from the hidden Moonstone, the elder werewolves cannot travel: the young have to do everything and represent the pack. This new generation of werewolves, convinced that the Moonstone is underneath the soon-to-be-demolished power plant, attempt to end the destruction. Zed's father, in his prominent position as foreman, and Addison's father, still in his police role, stop the werewolves. With the werewolves restrained, the humans and zombies come in to finish their fight – and their song and dance.

Ibram X. Kendi writes of demonstrations such as this that

> the most effective demonstrations [...] help people find the antiracist power within. The antiracist power within is the ability to view my own racism in the mirror of my past and present, view my own antiracism in the mirror of my future, view my own racial groups as equal to other racial groups, view the world of racial inequity as abnormal, view my own power to resist and overtake racist power and policy. (Kendi 2019: 215)

In joining the demonstration late, Zed finally understands the damage his assimilation has caused both zombies and werewolves. Tatum writes that understanding and accepting racial identity is 'uncomfortable and even frightening', but 'it is also liberating, opening doors to new communities, creating possibilities for more authentic connections with people of color, and, in the process, strengthening the coalitions necessary for genuine social change' (Tatum 2017: 208). Zed has been so focused on the human/zombie dichotomy and his own personal rise to power that he has ignored the plight of the werewolves, missing the point of community building. As Ijeoma Oluo notes, 'our social justice efforts often self-segregate in this way as well. Intersectionality requires that we break free from these divides and reach out to people we have not reached out to in the past' (Oluo 2019: 79). Zed learns what Addison has been trying to tell him all along: that all voices deserve to be heard and respected.

In the end, the power plant is demolished, but the Moonstone is rescued through a collaboration between humans, zombies and werewolves. Zed realises the error of his anti-anti-racist ways, saying, 'I was wrong about werewolves. You have every right to fight for who you are'. He also comes to terms with his unwillingness for Addison to be a part of something else, that 'I couldn't accept that you might be a monster because I can't accept that I am one'. Through this reflection, Zed is able to move past his assimilationist ideas and toward becoming an anti-racist.

The *ZOMBIES* franchise has many important lessons for pre-teen Disney Channel viewers: Milo Manheim, who plays Zed, reiterates the anti-racist ideas of the film that 'I want [viewers] to understand that being unique is awesome. Doing what you love to do is how you can become truly happy, and you have to give everyone a chance. We don't have to all be the same way' (Deitchman 2018). Despite this cheery outlook, the musical ending puts the onus of social change on the youth alone – the 'declaration of our new generation'. While the message could have been more impactful if the adults in the film also embraced anti-racist ideas, it is a hopeful message that youth can change the world, and Disney Channel viewers struggling with tough questions of identity can explore these issues with zombies, werewolves and, coming soon, aliens.

Natalie Wilson

Deadgirl (Marcel Sarmiento and Gadi Harel, 2008)

Focus on the undead is often directed at monstrous figures, zombies and vampires prime among them, but the undead can also be thought of in terms of ideologies and practices. In what follows, I will focus on rape culture as one such undead ideology by examining the 2008 film *Deadgirl*. First, a bit on rape culture itself.

Conceptually, rape culture encompasses the range of violence that results within contexts that glorify power, aggression and ownership. Patriarchy is one such context. Patriarchy normalises 'a continuum of threatened violence that ranges from sexual remarks to sexual touching to rape itself', as argued in *Transforming a Rape Culture* (Buchwald, Fletcher and Roth 2005: xi). This 'ideology of rape', as Susan Brownmiller deems it, makes sexual violence seem a natural – or at least to-be-expected – part of culture (1975: 2). *Deadgirl* enacts a similar naturalisation of rape. Rather than naming toxic masculinity as the 'patient zero' of rape culture, the film constructs the female body as irresistible, and, by extension, as 'asking for it'.[1]

Written by Trent Haaga and directed by Marcel Sarmiento and Gadi Harel, *Deadgirl* revolves around a pair of high school friends, JT (Noah Segan) and Rickie (Shiloh Fernandez), who find a naked female chained to a gurney in an abandoned asylum. JT wants to keep this 'Deadgirl' (Jenny Spain), as a 'personal sex object' but Rickie is not so sure. Rickie's reticence is framed as stemming in part from his unrequited desire for Joann (Candice King), a

---

1   Significantly, Kate Harding's book-length analysis of contemporary rape culture is titled *Asking for It* (2015), a naming that invokes a key contention 'justifying' rape, namely, that women are 'asking for it' whether or not they consent.

girl he has been smitten with ever since their elementary school kiss. JT, on the other hand, wants to make Deadgirl his 'sex slave' and sequesters himself away in the asylum, eventually recruiting several other males to join him in his rapist pursuits. Presenting the sexual assault perpetuated by the male characters as a logical consequence of the patriarchal world they inhabit, the film courts sympathy for the teenage males at its centre, casting them as victims of the 'real man' ethos of white-blooded machismo as it plays out in American high school culture. By monsterising the only two female characters to speak of – Joann and Deadgirl – the film places the blame for rape culture on the supposed irresistibility of the female body and its overwhelming impact on heterosexual males. As cogently argued by Justin Lowe in his *Hollywood Reporter* review, the film's 'virulently misogynistic storytelling essentially condones and even revels in the characters' violent objectification of women without offering any revealing perspectives on the young men's depravity' (2008). Not only does the film revel in objectifying females, it also eroticises sexual violence, presenting the female body as only of import in terms of its ability to 'serve' heterosexual males.

Such objectification is on display from the opening moments of the film as Rickie gazes hungrily at Joann as she plays catch with her boyfriend on the front lawn of their Southern California high school. 'What are you staring at?', she asks him as she is retrieving a missed catch, her annoyance giving way to a coquettish smile, as if she is honoured to be the object of Rickie's gaze. As she walks back to her boyfriend Johnny, the camera focuses in on her backside, her tight red shorts suggesting she is 'asking for' such hungry looks. JT approaches and pronounces Joann a waste of Rickie's time, proposing they cut class and 'go to the nuthouse'.[2] As they make their way there, JT berates Rickie about Joann. 'You should have fucked her when you were nine when you had the chance, boy!', he scolds. His comments here foreshadow what

---

2   It is worth noting the widespread tendency to represent females as crazy, mentally unstable and in need of medical intervention, something prevalent in the horror genre. In *Deadgirl* specifically, JT's naming of the asylum as a 'nuthouse' nods to the 'nutty females' of the film, Joann, Deadgirl and the woman whom JT and Wheeler attempt to abduct. These women variously imperil the males of the film via their 'crazy' refutations of male desire (Joann), their polluting potential (Deadgirl) and their violence (the intended abductee). All belong, according to the logic of the film in 'the nuthouse'.

follows, namely, JT capitalising on the 'fuckable chance' posed by the female body they soon discover within the walls of the derelict asylum.

When they find Deadgirl, she is chained to a gurney and shrouded in plastic. Staring down at her longingly, as if she is too good to be true, JT marvels, 'She's like someone in a magazine ... I could spend all day looking at that body'. Pulling down the plastic covering her, JT touches her breast, encouraging Rickie to do the same. Angered by Rickie's refusal, JT punches him and tells him to leave. Not long after, JT finds Rickie and begs him to go back to the asylum so he can show him something 'real important' – in short, that the woman they found seems unable to die. As he explains it, 'She woke up. She started to struggle. She didn't scream ... She just sort of growled. And tried to bite like a wild fucking dog ... I hit her just enough to make her stop ... She just kept gnashing at me with those teeth. So, I hit her again and it felt good'. That hitting her 'felt good' reveals JT's proclivity for enjoying violence. That he goes on to try and kill her multiple times reveals he would prefer a dead 'sex object' to a live one. Rickie, not sharing JT's enthusiasm for what he deems 'hot pussy ... straight out of porn', avers, 'I'm not fucking touching her man'. Notably, Rickie does not voice any objections to JT's suggestions that they rape her; instead, he fears going to jail. 'I got to think about this', he tells JT, apparently weighing up the pros and cons of making Deadgirl their 'sex slave'. As if to sway his friend's decision, JT instructs Rickie to watch as he puts his hand between Deadgirl's legs. In response, her back arches and her head thrashes about, the implication being she is sexually aroused. Such indications of arousal convey 'she wants it', an animating premise of rape culture and one that is sometimes used in the real world to refute rape allegations.

In the next scene, Rickie is back at school, drawing a sexy zombie figure in his notebook before again watching Joann from a distance. His friend Wheeler (Eric Podnar) approaches, scolding, 'Are you thinking about Joann Skinner again ... You better watch it with those eyeballs'. This emphasis on the male gaze continues throughout the film, an emphasis that never condemns males for looking. After arriving back home after school in the scene that follows, Rickie heads to his bedroom for some masturbatory fantasising. Positioned within his gaze, we watch as he pictures Joann dappled in sunlight, smiling at him flirtatiously. She bends down and disappears outside the frame. The camera adopts a heterosexual male gaze, scanning the female body, homing in on the eyes, mouth, breasts and butt. After Joann completes a fantasy blow job, she re-emerges into the frame, her glossy lips seemingly glazed with semen. Joann's face then gives way to Deadgirl's. She, like Joann, is represented as sexy and full of desire, a depiction that alternates with images of her gnashing mouth, a clear nod to her castrating potential. Pulled from his wet-dream reveries as a result, Rickie hurriedly heads back to the asylum.

When he arrives, Deadgirl's gurney is moving back and forth rhythmically as Wheeler rapes her. Angered by his presence, Rickie berates JT for breaking their promise to keep Deadgirl a secret. Significantly, Rickie does not voice any disapproval regarding Wheeler's actions. JT encourages Rickie to 'go get some', continuing, 'We can call her Joann if you want'. Wheeler then offers, 'If you want, man, we can, like flip her over. We haven't hit her backside yet'. Both of these proposals evoke the swapability suggested by Rickie's earlier fantasy, a representation that continues throughout the film.

Intent on freeing Deadgirl to avoid being punished by the law, Rickie procures some bolt cutters in the next scene and again returns to the asylum. As he stares down at Deadgirl, she gently touches his hand as if to assure him it's safe to cut her free. He cuts the chain securing her arms. Hearing JT and Wheeler's voices, he freezes. Deadgirl grabs Rickie's wrist violently, perhaps a visceral reaction to hearing her rapists return. Rickie hides away and watches as JT jumps up on the gurney and unbuckles his belt. Deadgirl lashes JT across the face, screaming and thrashing as she struggles to break free. Her actions in this segment clarify that she is indeed sentient and does not consent to what is being done to her. Once her arms are restrained, JT rapes her again, saying as he does so, 'you fucking like that, don't you'. Here, JT gives voice to the blame and shame narrative that informs rape culture, namely, that women 'like it' despite claims to the contrary, that they are 'asking for it' whether or not they consent. Wheeler watches from the sidelines, something that nods to sexual assault as providing 'viewing pleasure' for heterosexual males, a message that pervades not only torture porn, but mainstream films and television. As Steve Jones argues in 'Deadgirl and the Sexual Politics of Zombie-Rape', sexual violence 'is representationally acceptable within contemporary popular culture' (2012: 525). So too is representing women as mere bodies, or, as comments from characters and the film's screenwriter suggest, as 'holes'. For instance, Wheeler asks JT, 'How's her hole doin', man?', he replies, 'Unwilling but able', 'unwilling' being a key word here. Noting how she is beginning to stink, JT then sticks a finger in one of her bullet holes, proclaiming, 'It's warm. Wet'. 'That one's mine', he informs Wheeler, 'but there's two more just like it'. In other words, any hole – willing or unwilling – will do.

That much is proved to be the case when Jonny (Andrew DiPalmer) and Dwyer (Noland Gerard Funk) arrive at asylum to affirm if the 'sex slut' Wheeler has been bragging about really exists. 'So, you boys decided to come by, give our girlfriend a ride, huh?', JT asks. Spying Deadgirl, Dwyer inquires 'Why she all tied up and beat up and shit?' 'Because that's the way she likes it ... Ain't either of you seen any pornos before ... That's the way we give it to her. You know, whips and chains and shit', JT replies. In response to Johnny and Dwyer's reticence to 'give it to her', JT scoffs, 'Two red-blooded all-American studs like you passing on a free pussy?' His manhood on the line, Dwyer encourages Johnny to join in on the 'free pussy'. Johnny declines, explaining, 'I may be horny ... but I got my own sweet pussy waiting for me tonight', a.k.a. his girlfriend Joann. 'Why don't you go for the mouth then?', Rickie suggests, underscoring the fact any hole will do. 'I bet that you haven't had your dick sucked your whole life', Rickie taunts. Though these scenes display the peer pressure components wherein males pressure other males to commit sexual violence, they do not condemn this practice so much as display it as normal, as 'a bit of fun'.

Johnny positions himself to put his penis in Deadgirl's mouth, saying to Deadgirl, 'Come on baby. It's all right. It's not gonna bite you'. When Deadgirl bites him instead, Johnny howls with pain then punches her repeatedly. Dwyer insists they call the cops. 'You're going to go to the cops and tell them what? That you were raping a chick in a mouth, and she bit your dick?', JT taunts. Johnny retorts, 'I wasn't raping her. You said she wanted it ... You said she liked it'. 'Prove it in court', JT replies. 'Prove it when they show photos of her face', JT adds, hinting he may be familiar that allegations of sexual assault are interpreted as more credible when the accuser has physical injuries. Of note in this exchange is the fact these are the only instances any derivative of the word 'rape' is deployed within the diegesis. Moreover, Johnny's insistence that Deadgirl 'wanted it' echoes real-world rape denials, the most common of which are some permutation of 'She didn't say no'. Not saying no is, in fact, as Jones points out, 'a prevalent defense evoked in rape rhetoric in the real world' (2012: 529).

Significantly, screenwriter Trent Haaga also suggests the teens are not raping Deadgirl but rather partaking in necrophilia. He also claims the teens are 'not getting off on torture', that they are merely using Deadgirl 'as a sex object' (Haaga 2009). Not voicing any objections to such 'use', Haaga instead asserts the film critiques toxic masculinity and serves as 'a condemnation of misogyny as opposed to being misogynous'. In this regard, he describes the narrative as encouraging viewers to ask themselves if they are more like JT or Rickie (i.e., whether they are toxic like JT or 'the good guy' like Rickie). Notably, the suggestion here is similar to real-world framings of (white) male perpetrators of sexual violence as good boys, as with Brock Turner, for example.[3] Such males, hegemonic narratives insist, are to be pitied for the damage such allegations cause, while the harm done to female victims and accusers goes largely unacknowledged. As much is true of Haaga's insinuation we should feel sorry for Rickie but not for Deadgirl, whom he compares to 'a blob ... with a bunch of fuck holes' (Haaga 2009).[4] Haaga's explanation of what inspired the film is similarly worrying. 'The core of the story actually came from my unrequited love I had for a girl in high school and the feelings of frustration and helplessness that came with that', he explains in a 2011 videoblog (Haaga 2011). That Haaga is comfortable revealing such details is itself a testament to the undead status of rape culture, a status that is made particularly plain at film's close.[5]

In the final act, Rickie heads to the asylum, machete in hand. He discovers Joann tied up next to Deadgirl. Kidnapped by JT and Wheeler in their pursuit to 'make another', JT tries to convince Rickie of the efficacy of their plan. Freeing Joann, JT warns, will get them sent to jail. This fear of ending up in jail comes up several times in the film. Yet, given how rare it is for rape allegations to result in any sort of prosecution, let alone jail, the frequency

3 See Michael E. Miller, "All-American Swimmer Found Guilty of Sexually Assaulting Unconscious Woman on Stanford Campus", *The Washington Post*, 31 March 2016. <https://www.washingtonpost.com/news/morning-mix/wp/2016/03/31/all-american-swimmer-found-guilty-of-sexually-assaulting-unconscious-woman-on-stanford-campus/>. Accessed 8 October 2021.
4 All quotes from Haaga are from the 2009 Metrodome DVD Release.
5 In my discussion here, my intent is not to present authorial intent as a *sine qua non* for interpreting the film. Rather, it is to illustrate the origins of the story as Haaga describes them as well as to illuminate how his commentary on the film fuels, rather than refutes, rape culture.

with which the teens express fear of prosecution is unfounded. Further, given there is no law against sexual intercourse with a corpse in California, what JT and company do is technically not against the law. As the California Supreme Court stipulated in a 1997 case, 'Rape must be accomplished with a person, not a dead body. It must be accomplished against a person's will. A dead body cannot consent to or protest a rape' (Tyler and Jones 1997).

As much is indicated in the closing segment as a smiling and carefree Rickie heads to the asylum to visit Joann, now undead. In the final shot, we witness Joann's lifeless eyes stare up at the ceiling as Rickie stares down at her. Unlike the opening moments of the film, in which Joann castigated Rickie for staring, she is no longer able to voice any objection; she cannot, as claimed in California law, 'consent to or protest a rape'. Rather, as Joann's last name, Skinner, implies, she is only a sack of female skin, one that Rickie has successfully 'skinned'.

In conclusion, the condoning of rape culture that *Deadgirl* enacts speaks to the construction of females as inherently rapeable, as well as to the notion that 'real men' are ready and willing to commit violence, part of which includes, as Robert Jensen puts it, being 'ready to rape' (2014: 1). Eroticising sexual violence on the one hand and framing the female body as an infectious monster on the other, *Deadgirl* presents its white, male, heterosexual teen rapists as merely acting out the dictates of 'real manhood' their culture promotes. This positioning of the teen villains results in a film that leaves rape culture largely unscathed – that makes rape culture, in effect, undead in the twenty-first century.

Brandon R. Grafius

The Nun (Corin Hardy, 2018)

Religious Undead

It is no secret that the Church, as an institution, has not often been a big fan of horror movies. The Catholic Church led a wave of protests against *The Exorcist* (1973), and the nationwide movement against *Silent Night, Deadly Night* (1985) that got it pulled from theatres after an abbreviated run was spearheaded by evangelical groups. It is easy to find blog posts written by pastors or other religious leaders questioning whether the faithful should watch horror movies at all.

Often, horror movies are not a big fan of the Church either. It is a corrupt institution in *Stigmata* (1999), the guardian of the community's repressed secrets in *The Fog* (1980), and the ideology behind the crazed fundamentalists of any number of films, such as *The Mist* (2008). When pastors or priests show up in horror, they are frequently good-natured but ineffectual, such as the poor pastor in *Hellraiser III: Hell on Earth* (1992) who finds that his religious symbols are worthless against the Cenobites (Cowan 2008: 87–8).

However, there is also a pattern within horror that views the Church as humanity's last bulwark against evil, as the watchdog that keeps a constant vigil so that the rest of humanity can go about our daily lives, oblivious to the cosmic struggle that rages on around us. In recent horror cinema, this is nowhere more apparent than in the *Conjuring* universe. In the first *Conjuring* (2013), Ed and Lorraine Warren (Patrick Wilson and Vera Farmiga) are non-ordained laypeople, ghost hunters who help the Catholic Church out in any way they can and have occasionally been called in to assist with exorcisms in a pinch. While the Church is the butt of some light humour – after Ed successfully performs his emergency exorcism and saves the Perron family from the malicious spirit that has been haunting them, Ed and Lorraine receive a belated message from the Vatican that their request for an exorcism has been approved – the world view of the Church is validated, and its rituals are proven to be effective. There is slightly more ambivalence in *The Curse of La Llorona* (2019), in which the exorcism-saviour is a former priest who left the Church because he found its hierarchy too restrictive. Even here, however, the basic premises on which the Church is built are proven to be true; it is just a question of how effective the Church can be.

The Church as Protector from Evil

Perhaps the most positive portrayal of the Church in *The Conjuring* universe is found in *The Nun* (2018).[1] In this film, the Church is firmly positioned between everyday people and the demonic forces that would do us harm. Most of the film is set in a remote Romanian abbey where a nun recently committed suicide. Father Burke (Demián Bichir) and Sister Irene (Taissa Farmiga), a novitiate who has not yet completed her vows, are sent by the Vatican to investigate. On unravelling the complicated backstory of the abbey, they find an order of nuns who have protected the world against the intrusion of the demonic Valak for centuries; Burke and Irene pick up where the sisters were forced to leave off. Unambiguously, *The Nun* presents the Church as a necessary force for good, even if it is not always recognised as such. In the discourse of *The Nun*, much of the Church's work goes unnoticed, out of sight in places like St. Carta's abbey.

In contrast, the secular world is continually seen as aiding and abetting the demonic forces. The film's backstory is rather silly, but it still makes a clear distinction between the evil that comes into the world through secular means and the religious institutions that work to keep this evil contained. First, we note that the building itself was not originally designed as a monastery; instead, it was built as a castle by a Duke with some questionable hobbies. Apparently, he summoned a demon (Valak the Defiler, first introduced in *The Conjuring 2*), for reasons unknown, but was thwarted by a band of Crusaders who arrived

---

1 For a discussion of how *The Nun* fits into *The Conjuring* universe, see Wiggins (2020: 123–40).

The Nun (2018)

at the right time. The Crusaders had recently claimed a vial of Christ's blood from their conquest of Jerusalem, which they used to capture the demonic presence. This containment system worked until the abbey was damaged in a bombing raid; as a result, the sisters took turns praying in a constant vigil to keep Valak under control.

The film only presents a few brief encounters with the world outside the abbey, but the main impression is that the secular world does not understand the sacrifices the Church is making for them. In the village outside of the abbey, the only person who will travel with Burke and Irene is the delivery man (named Frenchie by the locals because of his foreign origins) who first discovered the dead sister; no one else will go near the place. The villagers understand the abbey as a source of evil and respond by keeping their distance from it. The sacrifices that the nuns have been making – maintaining perpetual prayer to keep Valak under control, as well as Sister Victoria's suicide to keep Valak from using her body as a vessel – have gone unnoticed by the villagers, who are only able to perceive the abbey as a strange and vaguely dangerous place. In the local bar, Frenchie learns that a young girl has recently committed suicide. The bartender is clear about the reason: 'It's that place', he says, 'The abbey. Whatever

Figure 16. Irene and the perpetual prayer of the nuns of St. Carta's abbey. *The Nun*, directed by Corin Hardy (New Line Cinema, 2018).

evil is up there is leaking out'. He then spits on the ground. While he intuits (correctly) that the evil is leaking out, he does not seem to credit the religious order for their work to keep it contained all these years.

As Burke and Irene enter the abbey, they meet the abbess, who promises them a meeting with the convent's nuns in the morning. After a night of supernatural adventures and bumbling around in the dark, Irene finds the sisters taking turns praying in order to keep the evil contained. Irene learns of the monastery's history from Sister Oana, who also shares that the abbey still has the relic containing the blood of Christ, hidden away in the catacombs. Apparently, it is this relic, which was used to seal the breach centuries ago, that combined with the sisters' perpetual prayer to keep Valak confined.

Layers of the Religious Undead

The Nun features three distinct groups of religious undead, each with a different set of significances within the diegetic world of the film. First is Valak, embodied as an undead nun. Second are the nuns of the abbey themselves, revealed as ghostly presences who have continued to pray in order to keep Valak contained. Third is the relic of Christ's blood, which is revealed as a powerful undead presence.

Although Valak takes on the form of a nun, with a motive that Sister Oana (Ingrid Basu) vaguely describes as being to 'deceive' and 'prey on [the nuns'] weaknesses', this is perhaps the least interesting manifestation of the undead in the film. Since the presence is demonic, rather than truly undead, there is little in the way of backstory; Valak is simply evil and responded to the ritual of the castle's Duke centuries ago. However, Valak's enduring haunting of the abbey does reveal the film's understanding of evil: once Valak has been summoned, the demon continues its efforts to enter into the wider world through the abbey. It seems that once evil has identified a weak point – such as the breach created by the Duke – it will not relent, even after centuries of efforts.

The abbey's nuns reveal themselves to be undead as well. When Irena and Burke are initially summoned to the abbey due to the disturbing suicide of

Figure 17. The demonic Valak, disguised as an undead nun. *The Nun*, directed by Corin Hardy (New Line Cinema, 2018).

one of the sisters, they learn that this was actually an act of self-sacrifice: by killing herself, Sister Victoria (Charlotte Hope) has deprived Valak of the body it needs to inhabit in order to leave the abbey and spread its evil to the rest of the world. Victoria demonstrates her commitment to stopping evil, even to the point of what her faith considers to be the most sinful form of death. However, with Victoria, as with the rest of the sisters, this commitment does not stop there. Their undead life of perpetual prayer against Valak demonstrates their devotion to stopping evil. In this, the film implies that they are representative of the Church as a whole.

Interestingly, both the evil undead (Valak's embodiment as a nun) and the good undead (the abbey's nuns) exhibit some of the same characteristics. The film presents both of them as being single-mindedly focused on their mission, either to spread evil or to stop it. In pursuit of this goal, neither is willing to give up on the abbey, even after death. Hundreds of years after the breach was sealed, Valak is quick to force its way through once it is reopened, and the order of nuns, who have stood guard against this evil for centuries, continue to perform their duties, even in death. So, while Valak itself might not be undead, its manifestation as an undead nun seems designed to create a mirror image of the abbey's perpetually praying sisters: just as their undead status allows them to continually work for good, Valak imitates this in its continual pursuit of evil.

Relics and the Power of the Undead

In *The Nun*, Valak's initial attack (presented in the film's backstory) is foiled by a vial of Christ's blood. This same relic saves the abbey centuries later. It serves as a fascinating example of how religious traditions can give enormous power to the dead.

Relics – bones of saints, physical objects that came in contact with holy persons, or even objects associated with Christ – became a common feature of Christianity in the fourth century (Wiśniewski 2019: 3) and are frequently still considered objects of worship within Catholic and Orthodox traditions. These objects were thought to have healing or salvific powers, and believers would undertake pilgrimages to the churches that held them. The historian Bede, in his seventh-century work *The Ecclesiastical History of the English People*, tells the story of Saint Alban and 'a portion of the earth from the place where the blessed martyr's blood has been shed' (Bede 1990: 67), which had the effect of converting unbelievers. Throughout the Middle Ages, most churches claimed their own relic (George 2020: 11). Although they are not typically described as weapons against evil as Christ's blood is in *The Nun*, there are some accounts of relics having the function of protecting a particular city ascribed to them (Wiśniewski 2019: 48–69).

During the Middle Ages, many of the items that became identified as relics were plundered from Islamic lands during the Crusades, a reality to which *The Nun* nods by depicting the abbey's relic as having been gifted by knights returning from battle. Historian Marc Venard (2009: 1–12) notes the prevalence of 'blood relics' in the twelfth and thirteenth centuries, which he discusses in conjunction with the de-emphasis on communion during this time: since the blood was no longer given in communion services, popular religious traditions found another way to experience the salvific powers of Christ's blood. In 1247, King Henry III of England announced that he was in possession of a vial of Christ's blood and that this relic was to be displayed in Westminster Cathedral (Vincent 2001). Instead of being used to fight against

Figure 18. Irene and the relic of Christ's blood. *The Nun*, directed by Corin Hardy (New Line Cinema, 2018).

demonic forces, this relic's primary function was healing and forgiveness of sins for those who made the pilgrimage to visit (and paid their indulgence). While few scholars today believe these relics to be authentic, their impact on believers is undeniable (George 2020: 11–38).

The Nun combines this tradition of the power of relics with the hagiographic tradition of the struggle against demonic forces found in such texts as *The Life of Saint Anthony*, in which the saintly protagonist must stand firm against the powers of evil.[2] In ancient texts, demonic forces were overcome by the moral strength of the protagonist. In *The Nun*, the moral strength of the Church is combined with the power of the relic to defeat Valak (at least temporarily).

The introduction of Christ's blood as a powerful relic brings another layer to the undead of *The Nun*. In addition to Valak's appearance as an undead nun, and the ghostly nuns themselves who provide what aid they can to Irene and Burke, there is also the undead Christ, still living through the power of his blood. In the diegetic world of *The Nun*, evil keeps coming after death, but so does good. Nowhere is this demonstrated more powerfully than in the continual efficacy of Christ's blood.

The Church's Hidden Struggle against Evil

In *The Nun*, St. Carta's abbey has been engaged in a centuries-long struggle against evil, upon which the fate of the world depends. The rest of the world, however, is blissfully unaware of this struggle, with even the nearby village having only a vague sense that something about the abbey is strange. The sisters of the abbey have continued working on the world's behalf, without anyone outside their walls having awareness of their ongoing sacrifices. Similarly, the blood relic proves to be the ultimate power of the abbey, although the sisters have kept it hidden for centuries. Most frequently,

---

2   *The Life of Saint Anthony* is a fourth-century text by Athanasius; a translation can be found in Athanasius 1980. The research on how demons were understood in antiquity is enormous. An overview of recent developments can be found in the essays included in Elm and Hartmann 2019.

historical relics were displayed in local churches to attract pilgrims (and donations); however, Henry III claims to have been keeping the relic in secret, hidden in the London Church of the Holy Sepulchre (Vincent 2001: 3). The King only revealed its existence when the time was right. (The more cynical might amend this to say 'when it was politically convenient'.)

In the world of *The Nun*, and in *The Conjuring* universe as a whole, the forces of evil are ever-present, always vigilant and totally determined. They can only be matched by a force of good that is equally vigilant and determined; however, this force, represented by the Church, operates in secret, leaving the rest of the world blissfully unaware of the battle that is being waged on their behalf. While the Church has frequently been declared dead in our increasingly secular age, *The Conjuring* universe in general, and *The Nun* in particular, instead presents a world where the Church's power endures long after this declared death. Perhaps the Church, itself, is the real undead presence of the film.

Laura R. Kremmel

Saint Maud (Rose Glass, 2019)

Medical Undead

> Illness is the night-side of life, a more onerous citizenship. Everyone who is born holds dual citizenship, in the kingdom of the well and in the kingdom of the sick. Although we all prefer to use only the good passport, sooner or later each of us is obliged, at least for a spell, to identify ourselves as citizens of that other place. (Sontag 1990: 3)

Susan Sontag's well-known long essay, *Illness as Metaphor*, demarcates lived experience into two locations: the sick and the well. Both of these locations exist in the larger locale of the living. The 'other place' becomes even more Other when that illness is terminal and nearing its end; it becomes a place of the undead. In an adaptation of Sontag's kingdoms from the well and the sick to the living, the dead and the undead, I propose that the ways in which terminal illness is understood and treated in the Western world makes it not just the kingdom of the sick but also the kingdom of the undead. Rose Glass's film *Saint Maud* (2019) is a guide through end-of-life care and the experience of carers who are forced to dwell in this land of terminal illness, this land of the undead. By proxy, they become undead themselves, unsupported and unvalued by the land of the living. Because the terrors of terminal illness cause so much discomfort for those who do experience them first-hand, horror and the Gothic are particularly well suited to tell these types of stories.

Illness more broadly is simultaneously an experience of isolation and dependence, leading to both loneliness and unwanted attention. As Arthur W. Frank theorises, it is a state of interruption and 'narrative wreck': the timeline of one's life abruptly halts, diverts into a storm and veers entirely off course (Frank 2013). In addition to the sudden separation from those who are healthy, this confusion isolates the ill from their own sense of self. In *Saint Maud*, Amanda (Jennifer Ehle) has been diagnosed with stage four lymphoma of the spinal cord, and her once rich celebrity life has become one of solitude,

Figure 19. Amanda greets her carer near the end of their lives, a particularly vulnerable moment for them both. *Saint Maud*, directed by Rose Glass (Film4, 2019).

physical therapy, medication, and rest. Despite attempts to rejuvenate her social life, Amanda has been all but forgotten and abandoned in her illness. *Saint Maud*, however, reveals that end-of-life carers share many of the traumas of their patients when the deeply damaged Maud (Morfydd Clark) takes over Amanda's home care. 'You must be the loneliest girl I've ever seen' is one of the last things Amanda says to her carer before death.

The Health Humanities, and Narrative Medicine in particular, have been largely responsible for advocating for illness experiences to be valued, but it is only recently – due in part to the rise in burnout and suicides[1] amongst women healthcare workers during the COVID-19 pandemic – that the mental toll on medical carers has been taken seriously. Patricia Stanley writes of the ill that they 'are separated, in some way, from the healthy. Much of illness's isolation is a result of the social and cultural intolerance of illness, which leads to a construction of illness that identifies an ill person as other' (Stanley 2004: 347). Those who care for the ill are Othered in the same way, stigmatised and undervalued because they care for patients who cannot be saved, who no longer have

---

[1] According to US statistics, 'Female nurses are 70% more likely to die from suicide than female doctors and around twice as likely to do so as the general female population' (Ford 2021); 22% of US nurses are considering leaving their careers (Berlin et al. 2021).

a future in living society. *Saint Maud* calls attention to the liminal space of end-of-life care – an undead space – and its psychological impacts on both the palliative care nurse and her dying patient. It might be more accurate to say they become unliving.

Undead, Waiting for Death

This form of undeath is less about the supernatural – though the supernatural is a constant motivation for Maud – and more about the cultural practice of relegating the dying and those who care for them to the social, political, and economic dark corners, excluded from everyday life. Yet, the sick have not yet entered memorialisation and mourning, after which they are welcomed back into society through memory and narrative. They – and the carers who are notoriously unsupported and underpaid by their institutions – are undead. *Saint Maud* is just one of several horror films that depicts private carers as the undead. *I Am the Pretty Thing That Lives in the House* (2016) also features a lonely nurse caring for a dying independent woman, both completely cut off from the world of the living as they wait for death to arrive. As in *Saint Maud*, death comes for them both. Before those final moments, however, both patient and carer vacillate in that undead state, going through the motions of living while preparing the body and mind for the end, the carer following (or sometimes preceding) her charge into death.

Saint Maud opens with Maud's rebirth into the undead out of workplace trauma. In this scene, Maud cowers in a dark hospital corner, away from a dead patient on a table above, dripping blood from an injury we later learn she caused.[2] The entire scene could take place underground, its eerie darkness and artificial lighting, the sound of the dripping, and the overhead shots all suggesting the space of a crypt or tomb. Most importantly, she is alone in this experience except for the dead man, and it is clear that part of her enters

---

2   In performing what looks like CPR, Maud puts her fists through her patient's chest. Glass claims this is based on a true story (Handler 2021)

death with him. This is the moment she leaves her work in the strained hospital environment and discovers religion, the only connection she is able to make after this obvious primal scene. Every future attempt at connection – through caring, socialising or sex – fails because it becomes associated with death in some way.

The undead lack a biopolitical future while at the same time maintaining participation in – even control of – the narratives in which they are found. The audience becomes voyeur to spaces they have likely never seen before, perhaps never even thought of, since the dying and those who care for them are so carefully tucked away out of sight in Western society.[3] In this space, it becomes difficult to tell what is real and what is not. When she experiences God's presence – what Glass calls her 'godgasms' – Maud's body performs lonely supernatural physical contortions that dramatically correspond to Amanda's more subtle lonely progressing decay: two physical female bodies that would produce social repulsion if they were amongst the living (Handler 2021). The dying body is taboo and abject, almost as taboo and abject as the corpse. Yet, carers like Maud must have intimate contact with it, performing some of the acts Amanda no long can. As *Saint Maud* shows,

> Health professionals' bodies are means of perceiving the bodily state of their patients. Embodied knowledge is acquired by not only listening to heart sounds, feeling the swell of a gland, catching the odour of ketones on the breath, or hearing the tremor in a voice; the emotional connection of empathy, sympathy, and compassion are tactile encounters. (Austin et al. 2013: 69)

Scenes in which Maud physically moves Amanda's limbs echo the dancer's previously easy and independent poses.

In addition to the premature entombment to which society has subjected her, Amanda's entry into the undead takes the form of haunting. In a reversal of this traditional horror trope, she is haunted by the ghost of her past living self that surrounds her in the objects of her house: posters of her performances, books she has written, videos of her dancing. Maud uncovers them as though she were sorting through the belongings of the dead, discovering remnants of an earlier historical era. Instead of proving to herself that she is not yet dead,

---

[3] For more on end-of-life care in the Western world, see Gawande 2015.

Saint Maud (2019)

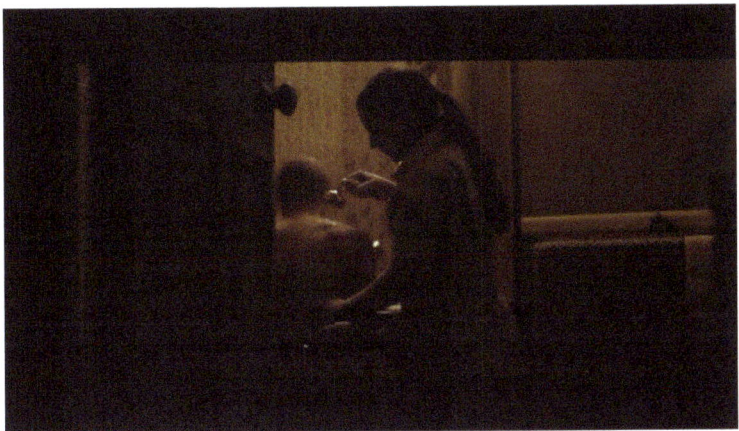

Figure 20. Being a carer entails performing the functions of the failing body in the space of the undead. *Saint Maud*, directed by Rose Glass (Film4, 2019).

Amanda's attempts to revive old habits and old friendships simply prove to her that she is no longer living. Reactions of the few members of the living, seeking to make emotional connections to the undead, further exacerbate the divide between the realms. In the few scenes in which the undead interact with the living, the living simply do not know how to respond. They become floundering intruders into the undead narrative and are even more jarring to an audience that becomes increasingly intimate with the lonely undead.

Previously living, Maud becomes undead via both the underappreciated role of the home carer and the trauma she experienced at the woefully overcrowded and understaffed hospital, where staff are left to care for patients on their own and patient beds routinely line the hallways. As Maud vaguely explains, she was 'spread too thin', a dangerous state for a nurse and her patients without proper physical and emotional support. While Maud's turn from hospital nursing to private care seems like it would alleviate her suffering, especially in independent Amanda's lavish home, trauma cannot be healed by a simple removal of its source, and the lack of human connection that aggravates it continues in this lonely space of the undead.

'How Dull It Is to Be Dying': Coping Mechanisms for the Undead

Amanda vacillates between boredom and pain in her condition. As a dancer, she is no stranger to discomfort, and scenes in which it interferes with her sense of self are rare. More prevalent is evidence of her body decaying: her wheelchair use, constant medication, physical therapy and balding scalp. Yet, what bothers her most is exclusion from her past social life and that she can no longer hold her liquor like she used to. In her boredom and loneliness, she plays along with Maud's coping mechanism – a recent conversion to Christianity – thinking that she might coax the quiet young woman out of her shell.

Recent studies about burnout among healthcare workers describe increased 'compassion fatigue', the labour of unrelenting emotional investment in a wide range of patients without the ability to save them all. Austin compares carers with compassion fatigue to zombies: 'Becoming one of the living dead is a terrible thing to imagine. The bodies of zombies move as if alive, but they are only "residually human" "non-beings" without "compassion, feeling, intelligence, or wit"', and 'like zombies, health professionals with compassion fatigue have to keep on going' (Austin et al. 2013: 81). In being asked to constantly care about others, carers must put others above themselves, instigating a habitual neglect of mental and physical health. Carers cope by either working themselves sick or adopting a protective detachment that negatively impacts patient care. Some, like Maud's successor, have hobbies and distractions that allow them to have healthy lives. Maud does not. Maud's chronic stomach pain indicates burnout compounded by the trauma her body will not forget. Her coping mechanism is possession of her patient rather than detachment, obsessing over Amanda's potential for religious conversion. However, Glass has repeatedly said that the film is about mental illness, not religion.

Because Maud never becomes numb – in fact, her constant self-harm ensures this – I would not compare her to a zombie, although her attempts to convert Amanda resemble zombies or vampires converting the living to their ranks. Dedicating herself to God not only rationalises the systemic neglect and exploitation of nurses, it also precludes her from failed social connections with the living. It gives her permission to become undead. It also provides a system

Figure 21. Maud experiences one of her 'godgasms', typically brought on by a strong connection with her patient or after an act of self-harm. *Saint Maud*, directed by Rose Glass (Film4, 2019).

whereby she can accept pain. Maud's self-harm by burning her hand, picking her scabs and putting nails in her shoes simultaneously reminds her that she is not dead and that her body is disposable, and it becomes the gateway to her own suicide. Thus, the pain itself preserves her place amongst the undead because she continues to need it to feel alive. At the same time, the more Amanda's body begins to resemble a corpse, the more Maud idolises her, envious of the pain her body produces on its own. Her hope of forming a bond with Amanda and her proximity to death by converting her to Christianity, however, is what gets her dismissed: having failed to isolate Amanda from her friends on her birthday, she strikes her patient, reminiscent of the violence of the opening traumatic scene, of the shocking violence that will end the film, and of Maud's ambivalence to life.

Once Undead, Never Living

Neither Amanda nor Maud can return to the world of the living. Feeling abandoned by Amanda and God, Maud's attempts result in a mimicry of life. In one scene, she sits alone in the middle of a bar, surrounded by happy groups of people. She laughs along with them, but they only ostracise her further for trying to intrude. The only connections she manages are brief and sexual, without pleasure. Desperate for connection to either the living or the dead, she experiences her most intense 'godgasm' when she levitates above her kitchen floor, an experience that both physically and spiritually sets her above the world of the living that has abused and rejected her. When God begins speaking to her, she returns to her patient with passports to the kingdom of the dead for them both.

Saint Maud draws attention to the marginalisation of terminal patients and their carers for through the final dismantling of delusions to which Maud has given her life.[4] Amanda's last act is to question everything Maud believes. If the only thing keeping her going as a carer were compensation and support, not from the medical institutions that trained her but from a supernatural entity in a world beyond, then the disappearance of that validation leaves nothing for which to live for. When the devil materialises to mock her, she abandons all medical training and violently stabs her patient before spectacularly taking her own life. While the film purposely makes it unclear whether Maud experiences real supernatural effects or simply suffers delusions, the last moments of the film reveal that Amanda and Maud's deaths are both premature and violent as a result of the systemic mistreatment of the ill and those who care for them whose last days, weeks, or months of living are spent abandoned to the kingdom of the undead.

---

4   For more on carer trauma, see Kremmel, Laura. 'SAINT MAUD: WHO CARES FOR THE CARERS?' Horror Homeroom, 18 February 2021. <http://www.horrorhomeroom.com/saint-maud-who-cares-for-the-carers/>. Accessed 28 October 2021.

Jeffrey Andrew Weinstock

Bubba Ho-tep (Don Coscarelli, 2002)

Don Coscarelli's 2002 American comedy horror film *Bubba Ho-tep*, starring Bruce Campbell and Ossie Davis, inverts the notion of 'undeadness'. While the ostensible antagonist is the eponymous 'Bubba Ho-tep', an undead, soul-sucking, cowboy-boot-wearing Egyptian mummy preying upon the residents of the Shady Rest Retirement Home in East Texas, USA, the true nemeses within the film are time and regret as elderly Sebastian Haff (Campbell), who believes himself to be Elvis Presley, and Jack (Davis), a black man believing himself to be John F. Kennedy, confront not only the eponymous mummy but also the spectres of loneliness, impotence, decrepitude and mortality. Trapped in a liminal space between life and death and remembrance and oblivion, Haff/Presley, Kennedy and the other residents of the retirement home are shown to be the true undead, and the mummy in the end merely a McGuffin. *Bubba Ho-tep*'s particular inversion of undeadness, however, ironically makes clear that this is the general case for all films in which the living do battle with the undead: mummies, vampires, zombies, ghosts and the panoply of supernatural antagonists stalking the pages and frames of modern horror are revealed to be death made present, materialisations of the protagonists' – and audience's – future non-being. It is the human characters and, by extension, the human audience who are the true un-dead, the not-yet- or soon-to-be-dead, beings-toward-death subject to the inexorable predations of time and loss, infirmity and remorse.

But we need to pause here a moment, as this description does an injustice to the film by making it sound oppressively sombre. As I will develop below, *Bubba Ho-tep* does offer a poignant meditation on ageing and mortality; however, the magic of the film is its adroit balancing of these more serious themes with elements of humour, camp and absurdity. Indeed, it is the absurdity of the film that is emphasised in any attempt to summarise it. The predominantly bedridden Haff claims to be the actual Elvis Presley who switched places with Elvis impersonator Haff after separating from his wife, Priscilla, and becoming disenchanted with fame. When Haff died and evidence of the identity swap was lost in a fire, Elvis was stuck as Haff and ended up enfeebled in the retirement home after a broken hip and an ensuing infection. For his part, Ossie Davis's Jack Kennedy claims that, after the assassination attempt in Dallas, he was dyed black by Lyndon Baines Johnson and part of his brain was removed and replaced with sand. It is Jack who diagnoses the existence of a soul-devouring mummy after the deaths of retirement home residents and the discovery of hieroglyphics graffitied in a bathroom stall. Aware that their story will not be believed, Elvis and Jack vow to defend their rest home themselves and donning their chosen costumes – Elvis in his white rhinestone-studded outfit and Jack in his dark suit and tie – confront their undead nemesis, who has adopted a costume of its own: cowboy boots and hat (hence the 'Bubba' part of Bubba Ho-tep). After the mummy kills Jack, Elvis vows to go out fighting and, with the help of a motorised wheelchair, a gasoline-filled garden sprayer and a lighter, manages to defeat the mummy, although he sustains a mortal wound in the process. As the life fades within him, the stars align overhead into hieroglyphs with the subtitle 'All is Well', and Elvis shuffles off this mortal coil with a 'thank you very much'.[1]

Described as possibly 'the most perfect B-movie ever made' (Eddy 2016), the film's light touch and generic hybridity as it interweaves elements of horror, comedy and the Western do not just offset its weightier themes, but are central to their development.[2] Indeed, existential angst is intertwined with carnivalesque ribaldry right from the very start as the film opens with an aged, seemingly bedridden Elvis contemplating a concerning growth on his penis and the aggressive dream he had of lancing it through masturbating while thinking of his ex-wife Priscilla. This fantasy, however, is then succeeded by the admission of his impotence ('Truth was, I hadn't had a hard-on in years')

---

1   On absurdity and silliness in the film, see Weinstock 2015.
2   On generic hybridity in the film and particularly the Western, see Thompson 2012.

and a series of questions mixing the profound with the profane that frame the larger concerns of the film as a whole:

> My God, man. How long have I been here? Am I really awake now, or am I just dreamin' I'm awake? How could my plans have gone so wrong? When the hell are they gonna serve lunch? Considerin' what they serve, why the hell do I care? If Priscilla discovered me alive, would she come and see me? Would we still wanna fuck? Or would we merely have to talk about it? Is there, finally and really, anything to life other than food, shit, and sex? Well, goddamnit. How could I have gone from the 'King of Rock'n'Roll' to this? Old guy in a rest home in East Texas with a growth on his pecker. And what is that growth, man? Cancer? Nobody's talkin'. No one seems to know ... or wants to.

Elvis's opening monologue concisely introduces the film's most important themes, as well as its absurdly comic strategy of engaging them. It questions whether life has any purpose and speaks to the very real fears of ageing, of physical deterioration, of regret, of dependence and being forgotten. The 'King' here is King Lear, contemplating meaning and time; however, these poignant concerns are articulated together with baser questions of the body and its drives, and voiced with a Southern drawl by a man claiming to be Elvis.

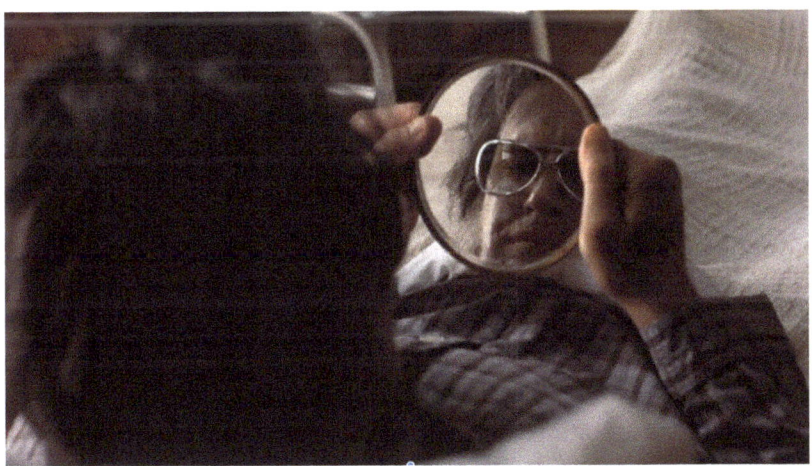

Figure 22. How could I have gone from the 'King of Rock'n'Roll' to this? *Bubba Ho-tep*, directed by Don Coscarelli (Vitagraph Films, 2002).

The theme of ageing and the anxieties associated with it are then amplified by the next several scenes. First, Elvis's roommate, Bull (Harrison Young), sounds his death rattle and gives up the ghost. His body is then retrieved by two funeral home attendants (Daniel Roebuck and Daniel Schweiger) – two Shakespearean clowns – who reprise Elvis's opening monologue in concise form:

> ATTENDANT 1: Makes you wonder, doesn't it? What kind of life this old guy had? What kind of life he had, you know. His kids, his grandkids, his legacy. Look at him now.
>
> ATTENDANT 2: Oh, who gives a shit?

The first attendant's 'Look at him now' encapsulates *Bubba Ho-tep*'s philosophical meditation on mortality as he beholds the corpse and wonders what there was to this man. The second attendant's nihilistic dismissal of those questions makes clear that none of it matters – all will be forgotten in time.

Some, however, are forgotten sooner than others. In the next scene, Elvis awakens to a woman (Heidi Marnhout) in his room going through – and discarding – Bull's things, including a Purple Heart medal for being wounded during military service and old black-and-white photographs such as one of Bull posing in his military uniform with two smiling women. As if in answer to the funeral home attendant's question about what kind of life he led, we concisely learn that this man was a war hero, was once a young, handsome ladies' man and, it turns out, has a daughter named Callie who is now going through his belongings. 'Never seen you here before', says Elvis to the woman. 'I've only been here once before, when I checked him in', she replies. That was three years ago, points out Elvis. 'I was busy', she replies brusquely, later instructing the attending nurse (Ella Joyce) to donate her father's clothes to charity. The exchange with Bull's daughter prompts Elvis to reflect on his own daughter Lisa Marie: 'My own daughter, lost long ago to me. If she knew I lived, would she come and see me? Would she even care?' Then, after having his story of how he came to reside in the rest home dismissed by the women as the ramblings of a confused old man, Elvis is left alone contemplating again, 'In the end, does anything really matter?'

These questions accumulate across the film, as Campbell's Elvis contemplates his youth and the path that led him to his current situation. 'Where'd my youth go?' he wonders. 'Why didn't fame hold off old age and death? Why the hell did I leave the fame in the first place? Do I want it back? Could I have it back? And if I could, would it make any damn difference?' Later, having stumbled across a TV marathon of Elvis films, he reflects on his decisions with regret: 'The bulk of the bad was my own damn fault. [...] If only I'd treated Priscilla right. If I could've told my daughter I loved her. Always the questions. Never the answers. Always the hopes, never the fulfilments'. Presented as voice-overs, Elvis's recurring interrogative monologues reflecting on his decisions and family and contrasting his past vitality with his present decrepit condition emphasise the film's true focus: learning to live before we die. Regardless of whether Shady Rest resident Sebastian Haff is really Elvis or not, the King has been dead for a long time: abandoned, primarily bedridden, impotent and lost in thoughts of what was and what could have been.[3]

Campbell's Elvis is joined to a certain extent in his hunt for meaning by Davis's Jack, who claims to be John F. Kennedy dyed black, to have had part of his brain removed, and then to have been deposited in the rest home. In what can double as a brilliant metaphor for age-related cognitive deterioration, Jack tells Elvis, 'I got a little bag of sand up there now', pointing to his head. 'I'm thinking with sand here', he later tells Elvis. Like Elvis, Jack, too, is preoccupied with the past while contending with his present physical decline and the looming spectre of death. Jack's room (much nicer than Elvis's) is decorated with pictures of Lee Harvey Oswald (JFK's assassin) and Jack Ruby (the man who shot Oswald), and Jack's first response to the mummy's encroachment upon the retirement home is to assume Lyndon Johnson or Fidel Castro has sent someone to finish him off. ('Hey, look, man. President Johnson's dead', Elvis tells Jack. 'Shit. That ain't gonna stop him!' replies Jack.) Like Elvis, Jack's mobility is impaired: where Elvis makes use of a walker, Jack employs a motorised wheelchair. Jack, too, shares in regrets over family and what could have been, although he adopts a more resigned posture. 'We weren't there for our kids when they needed us, were we?' asks Elvis. 'Man, if I could just talk to [Lisa Marie Presley] again, tell her I love her. Try and make things right somehow'. 'No time for regrets, Elvis', responds Jack, 'We were the best fathers we could be under the circumstances'. The talk then turns to

---

3   On masculinity in the film, see Berns and Foronda 2019.

a fonder recollection as Elvis asks Jack about his purported sexual dalliances with Marilyn Monroe. 'That is classified information', replies Jack, 'but, between you and me ... Wow!'

The King vs The King

As the summary above of *Bubba Ho-tep*'s meditations on life, time, ageing and death highlights, the film's true focus is on charting a course between the Scylla of a past that holds a tenacious grip and the Charybdis of a looming future of non-being in order to find meaning in the present. The film's mummy in this respect embodies both the oppressive past and future. What we learn about the mummy is introduced in a mystical moment of connection between it and Elvis as they lock eyes and a rapid montage of images floods Elvis's mind, introducing a suggestive narrative in which – as in the classic 1932 film version of *The Mummy* (directed by Karl Freund) – cursed mummification was the punishment afforded for a forbidden love affair. 'Some mummies get buried without their names, a curse on their sarcophagus', explains Jack, 'Hey, now. Maybe our boy's one of them'. Having been accidentally liberated from his confinement after the theft of his sarcophagus, continues Jack, he now sustains himself by feeding on souls.

In one sense, the mummy is Elvis's doppelgänger, the aged King of Rock'n'Roll from Mississippi confronting an ancient King (or at least member of the royalty) from Egypt. Both Elvis and the mummy are 'cursed' as a consequence of their decisions, and both are things of the past that plod slowly through the halls of the rest home. Like Elvis, who was once sustained by the adoration of his fans, the mummy feeds on the souls of the living. As the film makes clear from the very start, Elvis, like the mummy, is a member of the living dead, conscious and awkwardly ambulatory but not truly alive. But the mummy in another sense is also a bleak vision of Elvis's future. It is not just the spectre of death made manifest in the dark halls of the retirement home, but the materialisation of being forgotten, of having one's name erased, of dying lost and alone.

It is this nihilistic picture of death as a continuation of the slow fading away he has been performing for years culminating in oblivion that propels Elvis into action. 'In the movies', he explains, 'I always played heroic types, but when the stage lights went out, it was time for drugs and stupidity and the coveting of women'. In contrast, continues Elvis, 'Now it's time. Time to be a little of what I'd always fantasized of being: a hero'. Having made his resolution, he extends a challenge to Jack: 'Ask not what your rest home can do for you ... ask what you can do for your rest home'. When Jack asks for clarification, Elvis responds with determination in one of the film's iconic lines: 'You know what I'm getting at, Mr President. We're gonna kill us a mummy'.

Elvis's decision to defend his retirement home from the mummy is an ironic resurrection enacted by embracing being-toward-death. It is, on the one hand, the determination to act rather than passively await one's end. In this, it is also a refusal to allow the past – his past, the embodiment of the past in the form of the mummy – to control the present and dictate the future. On the other hand, it is also a selfless act. 'What do I really have left in life but this place?' asks Elvis. 'It ain't much of a home, but it's all I got', he continues. 'Well, goddamn it. I'll be damned if I let some boring graffiti-writing, soul-sucking son of a bitch in oversize cowboy boots take my friends' souls and shit 'em down the visitors' toilet!' Elvis, who had regretted the various ways he had let people down, revolves here to make amends by defending others, and embracing the prospect of his own death in the service of his rest home is the incantation that brings him back from the dead. In finding a purpose, he also recovers the present, which allows him to live despite the vortex of the past and pressing weight of the future.

The resolution made, Elvis and Jack reassert their preferred identities – Elvis in his white, rhinestone-studded suit and cape, Jack in a dapper dark suit – and set forth, in one of the film's most memorable scenes, to do battle. Moving in slow motion, the scene is set to the Western twang of Brian Tyler's soundtrack, the piece called 'The Hero's Hallway' – two grim-faced cowboys headed to their last gunfight.

Jack falls in the battle, but Elvis's resolve never falters. 'It's time for A-C-T-I-O-N!' he exclaims, as, now occupying Jack's motorised wheelchair, he crashes into the mummy, and both take flight over an embankment. Mortally wounded, Elvis nevertheless summons the strength to douse the mummy

Figure 23. The Hero's Hallway. *Bubba Ho-tep*, directed by Don Coscarelli (Vitagraph Films, 2002).

with gasoline and set it aflame, pronouncing, 'Your soul-sucking days are over, amigo!' The unnatural threat of the past having been thwarted, the stars then align overhead for the dying Elvis, first in hieroglyphs and then with their translation, 'All is Well'. Selfless action has given Elvis a purpose and the strength both to put the past to rest and to confront his now imminent death on his own terms.

In the end, *Bubba Ho-tep* is a film about letting neither the past nor the future, neither one's regrets nor the inevitable good-night to come, deprive one of a present. To do so, implies the film, is to become undead, not fully alive, a creature lost in and to time: to be 'Haff' a man. This is, of course, a serious message, but the sheer absurdity of the film – its preposterous premise, its camp elements, its silly effects, the straight-faced delivery of ridiculous lines and so on – does not just offset the potential heavy-handedness of such a moral, but effectively nuances it to suggest that part of being alive is not to take ourselves too seriously and to appreciate life's comic moments. In place of words of power, laughter, finally, is the film's defence against evil and its tool of resurrection. To the extent that we allow our past to overwhelm us or the future threat of death paralyse us, we are undead. *Bubba Ho-tep*'s formula for

Figure 24. All is Well. *Bubba Ho-tep*, directed by Don Coscarelli (Vitagraph Films, 2002).

fighting the undead is purposeful A-C-T-I-O-N with the welfare of others in mind, a sense of humour and, one might add, the gratitude expressed in the film's final line: 'Thank you. Thank you very much'. If one can speak it like Elvis, so much the better.

Gina Wisker

Relic (Natalie Erika James, 2020)

The living whose faculties are fading still exist among us, confused with and sometimes treated as the undead, as revenants wandering, lost, back into their old homes, their own changed bodies, their families, confused about who and where they are and what they have been doing. *Relic* (2020) is an example at times of salvation Gothic, from which spirits of the dead reappear suddenly like entombed, holed-up ghosts. *Relic* is also about dark inheritances, trauma, place, family and cultural histories. It is Australian Gothic in its setting and in the ways in which it reveals the ostensibly familiar and ordinary to be utterly unknowable. It is also women's Gothic, concentrating on family, mothers, inheritance and the decaying female body, embodied in the decaying house, itself a familiar horror location in European and American Gothic. The inheritances in this film run deep in hidden cultural histories of violence neatened into an imported, translated normality, and in its focus on the matriarchal home, the female family triad and the terrifying inheritance of family, cultural illness. It disturbs everything held as manageable, knowable and safe, like the family is safe.

The film might indeed be about a grandmother who is (like) a ghost, or might instead, as more popularly seen, be about a grandmother who, suffering from a form of dementia, strangely changed and yet sometimes very like her old self, appears as a revenant in her body, her home and family, a relic of herself. Gran, Edna (Robyn Nevin), is an elderly widow living alone in a remote house, and the film starts as she has been missing a while. Kay (Emily Mortimer) is her somewhat distanced daughter, and when Edna goes missing, Kay and her daughter Sam (Bella Heathcote) rush to sort things out and find her, returning to the family house, the grandmother's house, after a long absence, re-entering the Gothic, sullenly decrepit family home, finding the maternal house emptied out of Gran, with no clues as to where she has suddenly gone or why. The house sits on the outskirts of a vast wood, which is systematically searched like a crime scene for the old woman, but such ordered responses produce nothing.

The film draws on several Gothic legacies: the damned house, its façade a face, and its hinted indictment of a problematic national and settler history, with its incestuous brother and sister in Poe's 'The Fall of the House of Usher' (1839) a clear influence. So, too, is Australian Gothic, of which *Relic*, like *The Babadook* (2014) before it, is a fine example. In Australian Gothic, the very unfamiliar, disturbingly strange lands and creatures and the traumatic histories of invasion and settlement are covered up and neatened over with farms, cities and comfortable, well-managed homes. However, the unknown has often been mistranslated, and the traumatic histories of transportation and violence for criminals and settlers alike, and of the accompanying Aboriginal genocide, are inherited guilt. As Steve Bruhm notes, 'the Gothic itself is a narrative of trauma' (Bruhm 2006: 268). Considering Gothic works by colonial and postcolonial Australian women writers, Roger Luckhurst, notes that ghosts in women's stories are 'signals of atrocities, marking sites of an *untold* violence, a traumatic past whose traces remain to attest to the lack of testimony [or] memorialising narrative' (1996: 247 emphasis in original). Turcotte characterises Australia as a 'world of reversals', 'darkness' and 'monsters' populated by all that is not 'us' (1998: 10). Like Edna in her house, like a changed place or person, it seems familiar, 'us', but is not. In terms of its unexpected otherness, Australia is a rich Gothic location. In previous work I noted how 'Australia constructs and represents itself in literature and film as necessarily Gothic, replete with hidden, misrepresented and misunderstood histories and a consistent concern with guilt, identity, contradictions and confusions, producing a range of haunted lives, inherited and recent memories, and a hauntology of invaded or erased spaces and diverse pasts' (Wisker 2020). Defining and characterising Australian Gothic, Ken Gelder (Gelder and Weaver 2007) identifies settler guilt at the displacement and genocide of Aboriginal people in an untamed context where dark memories return. He also talks of the abandoned hut as a symbol of the inability to understand or tame the difference, the wilderness. One such abandoned hut with its unexplained dark history is on Grandmother Edna's property, linking the ostensibly domestic normal with the inexplicable otherness of the Gothicised world outside the house, but also inside it in Edna's damaged mind, and in the shape-shifting corridors and rooms of the house itself. The hidden secrets are not just of her deterioration but hint at an unspoken colonial settler past of haunting darkness and guilt. Jessica Gildersleeve (2020) sees in the Australian Gothic 'a sense of shame or guilt about the consequences of Australia's colonial origins as well as the significance of its early mythologies'. Contemporary Australian Gothic can be seen to build beyond trauma, becoming 'a site for political resistance and for social and cultural disruption' (Gildersleeve 2020). Confusing difference – misreadings of the seemingly everyday – dominate in this family history horror, which draws on the guilty histories, the traumatic past of an ostensibly settled land and community, or family normalities which are often disturbingly other; everything is not as it appears. It is also very much a horror tale of family trauma drawing on *The Haunting of Hill House* (Jackson 1959) in the disorientation of place and in the haunted house to which you bring your own problems and hauntings and in particular to which you might bring your guilt about your relationship with mother(s). It blends Australian Gothic, haunted house horror, trauma and family.

Edna had been hiding things, hoarding, and there are explanatory labels stuck as visible reminders for someone navigating a house which they know too well but sometimes might slip away from them, like lost words. They set about tidying the house with the absent mother/grandmother ever in their minds until suddenly she returns, without explanation or excuse, finding her daughter and granddaughter moving things around, cleaning, ordering and packing away, as if she had left permanently or died. In one sense, Edna is the same: neatly managing the dishes, dictating and organising what people can do in the house, and annoyed at questions about her behaviour and absence. In another sense, she is totally different: dishevelled, mean, forgetful and contrary.

Responses to the re-entry or intrusion of Grandmother Edna to her rambling home set on the outskirts of Melbourne in writer-director Natalie Erika James' debut film have overwhelmingly been personal, identifying and recognising the sad despair we feel when a loved one deteriorates. Particularly disturbing is when this deterioration is a creeping result of an inherited family illness. We see our own ageing and dissolution enacted in theirs, foreseeing ourselves as revenants in our own defamiliarised bodies and homes, stuck without plan or choice in the uncanniness of the aged self, undead but neither zombie nor vampire, just old, damaged, without choice or accident, a reminder to those around us of their own possible futures. The father, ousted, died alone in his cabin under strange circumstances, and in the rambling, shifting old house there is now a family of three women, three generations reunited, two of them returned on a quest to discover where and why Grandma Edna disappeared, and Edna herself returning as if nothing has happened and no time has passed, as revenants are wont to do.

Mark Kermode's *Guardian* review sees *Relic* for the horror movie it is – about 'the true terrors' of 'grieving for the loss of someone while they're still alive' – emphasising the disturbing link between the film and its focus on ageing and loss of faculties, here through dementia/Alzheimer's. He notes that the best movies 'tap into wellsprings of emotion already deeply embedded in the viewer's psyche', admitting that *Relic* 'left me a total wreck – overwhelmed and in floods of tears. Yet I'd wager that this spine-tingling, heartbreaking tale of a woman with Alzheimer's becoming lost in the labyrinthine corridors of her mind, and her home, has a universal power that will resonate with anyone, regardless of personal experience'. Although surreal, it is 'absolutely rooted in reality' (Kermode 2020 n.p.). I know precisely what he means, and this personal location is its source of uneasy success. There is nothing more sensitive, hidden, public, personal or painful than family and what you inherit from them, visible or invisible.

Like Kermode, I take the film personally, and it is confusing, sad and alarming in equal measure. As good Gothic should, it upsets complacencies (Botting 2002), peels back the wallpaper pasted over the cracks in fissures in our everyday normal, and as Stephen King (1981: 149) comments, 'The good horror tale will dance its way to the center of your life and find the secret door to the room you believed no one but you knew of'.

When my grandmother became forgetful, we put it down to age. I lived far away and saw her rarely. I couldn't understand why she would, apparently, forget her tablets and be unable to account for her budgie any more. Nor could I understand why eventually she ended up in a home, where I visited her a few times, taking flowers. When my father died, I inherited my mother. Earlier, he had said, 'You know what your mother's like, please look after her'. But I didn't know what my mother was like, and I didn't appreciate what my grandmother was like; I just found them old and confused, sometimes wilful and angry, and always frail. It was more than forgetfulness. It was a complete disconnect between words and things, deep memories and now issues of identity, a disconnect between her body and her mind. My mother was as startled as I was, looking for someone to blame. Every woman in my mum's family died of dementia or Alzheimer's, I'm not sure which. This creeping fear and gradual recognition of the changing habits and strangenesses of others in oneself and oneself in others is about inheritance far more than legacies of rings, watches or money. While the cruel disease attacks the mind, causing personality and behavioural changes, it also destroys the body, and memory is a shaken kaleidoscope, falling into indecipherable patterns of broken glass.

Defamiliarisation of place, behaviour and once-known others is matched by the defamiliarisation of the ageing and/or sick person for those who remain. Terrifying and confusing in equal measure, the everyday and relationships are emptied out with lack and loss. *Relic*, which begins with the absence of the grandmother, refills with her particularly strange, sudden return in the middle of the night. She stands entirely still, facing the door, hidden by her long grey hair, dishevelled and unable to go forwards or backwards.

Is Edna confused? Is she cruel? Or merely represented as evil because confused? She certainly resembles a witch at times, carving the wax of the huge candles into effigies, naked in her hallway after midnight in the moonlight, surrounded only by her hair, and trapping the neighbours' boy with special needs in the increasingly confining walls of the labyrinthine house, shrinking the corridors and ignoring his cries. As Sue Zlosnik and Avril Horner note, the construction, representation and treatment of the ageing woman and the ageing female body in folktale, myth, literature, film and popular culture very regularly and unthinkingly cast her as someone no longer either functional or truly human, and therefore abject, hounded out, locked up and, in extreme historical cases, drowned or burnt at the stake as a witch. Zlosnik and Horner expose the issues of demonisation and othering of older women, seeing 'women's internalisation of masculine values, so the internalisation of societal perspectives on the old can lead to a sense of dislocation and [...] most extreme, existential crisis' (2016: 184). Ageing and decay is unsettling, old hags threaten tenuously preserved 'normality', and while patriarchy might condemn women to be burned at the stake, other women are also lying, throwing the stones or lighting the fire (Carrier 1981; Rosen 2017; Winterson 2012). Aged mothers are perhaps even more terrifying than childless herbalists and, as Carol Margaret Davison identifies, fear and disgust of the mother lurks at the core of much Gothic (Davison 2004: 47–75). Old women are treated comically, satirically or as figures of horror, terror and particularly of disgust. However, the abject turn is often one of terror at the familiar, the close, the versions of self or self to come.

Domesticity in this house is deceptive. Edna gives a ring to her granddaughter, an heirloom indicating continuity, and very soon after accuses her of theft, destabilising the calm. Has she forgotten? Is she merely disorientated? Is her memory going? Or has she hidden for years a mean controlling streak? Behavioural façades dissolve. The management of time collapses, and slippage of the parameters of space leads to the moment when daughter, and then mother, investigating the papered-over corners of the house, wander in the parallel hidden corridors where shared and hidden rooms reinforce and mirror this breakdown, this disorientation of the grandmother's mind.

Kermode characterises the parallels between confusions and disorientations of mind and those embodied in the shape of the house:

> While Kay is haunted by dreams of a cabin riddled with creeping black mould, Sam finds her memories of the benign gran she loves usurped by a more volatile presence, prone to random aggression and plagued by paranoia. Meanwhile, the house itself starts to mirror the contortions of Edna's Alzheimer's-afflicted mind, full of strange turns and unremembered passages that give physical form to her own sense of fear and bewilderment. (2020: n.p.)

Ken Gelder's (Gelder and Weaver 2007) characterising of the abandoned hut as a sign of untamed unknowable otherness links the hut on the edges of the family land, on Gran's property, where the grandfather died and collapsed to bones, insects, dust, with historical settler confidence, the grand but Gothic house itself, and Gran's mind. Each is a sign of attempted settlement and its abandonment, the reinvasion of something earlier than that which is imposed as settled and tamed. Such places reveal a disturbing inability to curb the wild or to manage the unmanageable everyday behaviours, like Gran's straying mind and ways. However, the unknowable hut and the unexplained mistreatment of the neighbour's son are of a piece with the wayward shifting behaviour of the inner walls and corridors. Each hint at and threaten a dissolution back to untameable behaviours, the unknowable, and the ways before grand houses and settler dominance. Places and people maintain 'civilised' fronts while history tells more damaging stories of violence to the Other, denial of difference, and hubris about controlling nature, a transient control over difference and also over the constructed norms of mental stability and family coherence. The house itself seems itself active in preying upon or confusing and entrapping the women. Lonely Edna and the two younger women are all caught in its corridors.

In the house, in time, behaviours slip between the identifiable and categorisable, the everyday and the extremely strange, moving through shrinking and expanding time and space, undermining the everyday cooking, clearing out and the solid solidity of the shape of the walls of the house. The house is like their family minds: fluid, unfixable and constantly being redefined, resolidified in walls and corridors, like the strange rooms, passageways and cupboards behind the main house. While they grow closer, living together, the threesome begin to act out the same dislocated, defamiliarised responses to place, time, identity, fixity and direction that Edna has shown. All three women are trapped in a creeping inevitable inheritance of mental disorder, of dementia/Alzheimer's. *Relic* takes the historical trauma of cultural invasion, translation, erasure, and dark secrets, the defamiliarisation of place, history and people, and the abjection of women and particularly aged women and locates it in this newly tightly interlocked family, disturbingly but comfortably damned in their inevitable cultural and family inheritance.

Part III

Undying Identity

Leah Richards

AHS: Hotel (Ryan Murphy and Brad Falchuk, 2015–2016) and *The Strain* (Guillermo del Toro and Chuck Hogan, 2014–2017)

Undead Children

Well before the twenty-first century, Anne Rice's Lestat and Louis, the original queer vampiric fathers, learned what was problematic about vampire children: their angelic Claudia grows into a woman trapped in a child's body for all time and turns on her blood father Lestat, enacting the childish commonplace of 'I never asked to be born!' Although Claudia possesses adult desires and intellect, her instincts still seem to be those of a child. In the 2010s, two vampiric television series explored this latter characteristic in greater depth, with vampiric children not just acting with the impulses of children but be(com)ing monsters, exhibiting not just the inherent narcissism but also the often-but-not-always-unintentional cruelty of children. Ryan Murphy and Brad Falchuk's *American Horror Story: Hotel* (2015–16) and Guillermo del Toro and Chuck Hogan's *The Strain* (2014–17) bring vampiric children up to date with a vengeance as they become feral, hunting in packs through their respective communities, their origin stories complicated by manifestations of the threats that children face in the real world.

Vampire Children in *AHS: Hotel*

AHS: Hotel is not exclusively or even primarily about vampires or children, although vampiric children are one of the ways the series explores biological and chosen families. The fifth season of the anthology series features a wild array of quirky mortals and supernatural beings who staff and reside in the extremely haunted Hotel Cortez in Los Angeles, which is owned by the Countess, a stylish woman with a viral form of vampirism. Her biological child, Bartholomew, was delivered via attempted abortion and born of a vampire and a human; he is severely deformed, has remained physically unchanged since his birth, and craves blood. The Countess adores Bartholomew and will do anything to protect him, but most of the other characters see him as a monster.

The Countess has other children, all of them pale blonde children whom she has 'saved' from their families, claiming that the children were all neglected, and turned into passively well-behaved video-game-playing vampires who become savage when given a chance to feed on live victims. As she explains to one parent who accuses her of threatening to kill his son, 'I don't kill children, but I could make him a blood relative'. These children are passive unless they are feeding and are easy to control, but one is the missing son of police officer/serial killer John Lowe and paediatrician Dr Alex Lowe. The Countess turns Dr Lowe, who subsequently uses her blood to save a child who is dying of the measles because his mother chose not to vaccinate him, later mimicking the Countess's reasoning: the child, Max, was neglected and needed to be saved. Max returns to school and rapidly infects his classmates with vampirism instead of measles. In opposition to the Countess's well-behaved 'little monsters', these children function as a feral pack, first killing everyone in their school before going home to kill their families and then rampaging through suburban Los Angeles.

Vampire Children in *The Strain*

The Strain is about a plucky team of outsiders trying to save New York City and then the world from a rapidly growing horde of parasite-created vampires known as strigoi and find a cure. At the start of the second season of the series, in order to clarify their role as the heartless adversaries, the strigoi ruling cabal abducts a bus full of blind school children and turns them into a new type of strigoi with hunting and tracking abilities as well as a pack mentality enhanced by a psychic hive mind. These children, the 'Feelers', are turned over to Kelly Goodweather (the wife of the doctor, CDC epidemiologist Ephraim [Eph] Goodweather, leading the resistance) to ... parent? She uses their abilities, non-verbal communication and her psychic bond with them to help her fulfil the in-world strigoi-biological imperative of hunting down and turning her 'dear ones', including her own son, Zach. The Feelers diminish in number and significance through the second season but remain a minor presence for the remainder of the series; they are typically seen protecting and serving Zach, who remains physically unturned, although he and his loyalties reside with the strigoi.

The Anti-Vax Vampire Children in *AHS: Hotel*

Dr Lowe is introduced, well before she is turned, treating Max, who is running a high fever which his WebMD-checking mother is relieved to learn is measles rather than something 'serious'. Dr Lowe is quick to correct the mother's dismissal, stating that the virus, in addition to being dangerous, is 'completely unnecessary'. The mother justifies her choice not to vaccinate her child, contrary to Dr Lowe's advice, as 'what [they] thought was right' given 'all that stuff out there, about how vaccines can lead to autism, how they can actually kill people'. Dr Lowe responds that there are 'plenty of real threats right outside these doors for you to be worried about' and says 'when there is something we can do to make them just a little bit safer, we do it'. Max's mother is both wildly defensive and, even before her son is hospitalised, stunned to learn that there is no treatment for measles beyond treating the fever and waiting.

AHS: Hotel demonstrates the worst-case outcome of a parental decision not to vaccinate through the realistic illness of Max, who is dying, his measles-related pneumonia having turned to antibiotic-resistant staph. He is saved only because Dr Lowe – who has accepted the Countess's offer to remain with her vampire son Holden (the Doctor's unabashedly favoured child) forever – injects her blood into his IV bag, bringing about a truly miraculous recovery. However, his recovery is a horror show juxtaposing *AHS*-style bloodbaths with a reminder about how epidemics spread: after feeding off his parents, he goes to school. His classmate Madeline asks if he is contagious and, after some exchanged kisses that escalate quickly to blood exchange (itself a reminder of adolescent sexuality, a terror in its own right to many parents), we learn that yes, he is indeed contagious, but that the measles virus has mutated. Madeline almost immediately begins to manifest the symptoms of measles, a rash and very high fever, and these symptoms spread quickly through their class, the virus changing from bloodborne (like vampirism) to airborne (like measles).

These symptoms can only be abated by blood-drinking, and children being children and *Lord of the Flies* being only somewhat fictional, the children are ruthless, killing all of the adults at the school. Their attack on the adults within their school, after being exposed to and contracting a mutated form of a preventable childhood illness, leads to another common American Horror Story, the middle school under lockdown. Benefitting from the tendency of adults, especially parents, to see children, especially their own children, as innocent, the feral vampire children are able to manufacture a myth of a masked intruder. They are sent home, where they turn on their families and then reunite as a pack of feral vampires roaming the suburbs.

Again behaving very much like children, with a childlike imperfect sense of consequences, most of the pack regret their actions, particularly killing their own parents. However, Max, the 'patient zero' of the vampire measles, remains unrepentant, suggesting perhaps that mercilessness is an element of the new virus that weakens through transmission (or, alternatively, that he recognises that his parents' decision to not vaccinate him put him at risk of death, thus making them indirectly responsible for their own deaths). Dr Lowe, feeling some responsibility for her blood-progeny, tries to curb their behaviour and get them to the Hotel Cortez, where she imagines they can be controlled. She is initially unsuccessful, but the Countess, wanting to protect her own birth-child and blood-children, insists that she is accountable for the outbreak and the children's actions. To protect herself and Holden, Dr Lowe willingly sacrifices the children, just as the Countess would sacrifice Holden, or any of her vampire children, to protect Bartholomew. Using the death of one of the pack to her advantage, Dr Lowe is able to lure the children back to the Cortez; she locks them in a room with the Countess's former lover Ramona, a vampire who had been betrayed in the midst of a plan to take revenge on the Countess through both her blood-children and Bartholomew. Now more interested in feeding than in payback, Ramona says, 'Mama smells ... appetizers'; although the children's story ends with a fade to black, their fate is certain. Max was created out of something like love, a mother's desire to protect another child, but when he becomes a threat to her own child's safety, Dr Lowe willingly turns him and her grand-progeny over to Ramona, who identifies herself as a devouring mother.

The Feelers in *The Strain*

The strigoi are the product of a parasitic worm that introduces a virus that almost immediately begins to radically change the host's body. Along with the physical changes, the human-turned-strigoi develop heightened senses and a telepathic link to all who share their bloodline but typically lose most of their human capacity for reason, becoming dependent on their Master (in *The Strain*, known as The Master) for direction. This latter trait is, however, not a result of the infection, as the Master can restore reason and free will to an individual should they wish to do so. Kelly Goodweather is one of a very small minority granted this power, shortly after she is infected and at the start of Season 2, when she attains adversary status. She is told by Nazi-turned-strigoi Thomas Eichhorst that, because of her connection to her son, as 'the mother our dear Zach cried for in the night', she is being given an important role, the eventual ability to speak and otherwise pass for human, and 'a new family' with 'unique abilities, sight and perception beyond the visible spectrum'.

Eichhorst introduces Kelly to a newly turned group of children known as 'the Feelers, the children of the night', students from a school for the blind. Kelly appears to assess each child, killing one and reaching out to the others. She introduces them to Zach's scent, and the Feelers, who are doglike in their abilities and their loyalty to Kelly, are able to track him through the background of a few episodes, from Queens to Harlem, the first places where the anti-strigoi resistance had been in hiding. In return, she 'mothers' their residual humanity, for example by singing a lullaby to comfort them after an encounter with the police in Red Hook, Brooklyn.

The Feelers are originally presented as unique and something more than or distinct from human or animal, as well as being different to the adult strigoi. However, as they become more comfortable with their skills and abilities, they become more animalistic, both in reality and in others' perception of them; only Kelly communicates with them. They are recognised as children by humans as well: one character shows sentimentality for the children that the Feelers once were, remarking 'Blind kids. That just ain't right', but then almost immediately shoots and kills several, referring to them as 'little monkeys'. From their first introduction, the Feelers' oral communication sounds insect-like, and they scuttle on all fours, being described at one point as 'the little spider kids ... fast as hell; they can climb anything'. They eventually prove able to track Zach in real time, putting one of their own at risk as a decoy to get him out of a car and into church and scaling the exterior like Bram Stoker's Dracula, 'with considerable speed, just as a lizard moves along a wall'. Many of the Feelers are killed in a shootout at the church, acting as sacrifices in the unsuccessful pursuit of Kelly's birth-child.

As their second-class status is revealed, evidence is found at the Feelers' 'nursery' that Kelly snapped the necks of several – which one character describes as 'culling the herd' – and left others behind. The exact number of Feelers is unclear. However, based on school bus capacity, deliberately vague group shots at the school and on the bus, and the fact that, although Kelly is rarely seen with more than six to eight, she continues to travel with a group even as they are killed, it is likely that there were originally thirty to forty, with several 'culled' almost immediately and others who were left behind killed later; additionally, some are killed in almost every encounter with humans. As these encounters are all part of Kelly's search for Zach (a biological imperative that she is allowed to pursue because it aligns with the Master's wishes), it is clear that the Feelers, though cared for, will all be sacrificed if need be for Kelly to claim her birth-child. It is notable that the children on the bus in the first place were the ones whose parents could not be reached before they evacuated, which to a child might be perceived as being abandoned. To emphasise this privileging of the birth-child, when Kelly finds Zach and attempts to convince him to come with her, a Feeler deliberately takes a bullet to protect her; another later tries, without success, to comfort her after her failure.

The Feelers become less useful, and less present in the narrative once Kelly knows the area that Zach is in; a horde of adult strigoi invade the location the boy is in, and Kelly is able to find her son through her connection to the larger strigoi hive mind. She finally achieves her aim by having a train derailed to allow for his abduction whilst some Feelers are used to create a covering distraction. Season 3 opens with Zach's father Eph, drunk and distraught, attempting to shoot his strigoi son, but this turns out to only be a nightmare; Kelly has not turned him, and never does, although his loyalties ultimately lie with the strigoi and his mother. When his mother is killed, his trauma-related response is to detonate an atomic weapon and bring about a nuclear winter, which creates an ideal environment for the strigoi. The Master continues to groom him for his 'dark potential', and the Feelers become essentially an extension of Zach's plot line.

It is notable that two series as distinct from one another as *AHS: Hotel* and *The Strain* approach child vampires so similarly. The vampire children plot of *The Strain* is significantly less convoluted than that of *AHS: Hotel*, but Zach, Holden and Bartholomew all learn that 'a boy's best friend is his mother', with both narratives foregrounding overprotective-to-the-point-of-obsessive human-birth and vampiric-blood mothers. The fates of the feral vampire children are, in both series, decided by these mothers, who ultimately demonstrate their preference for their birth-children over their blood-children. In both narratives, it is only the undying love of an undead mother that remains constant, and yet it is the quality of that love that simultaneously creates and propagates the monstrous worlds they live in.

Sara Williams

Suspiria (Luca Guadagnino, 2018)

'There's more in that building than what you can see', the terrorised Patricia Hingle (Chloë Grace Moretz) warns a dubious and ill-fated Dr Klemperer (Tilda Swinton) in *Suspiria* (2018). Here, Luca Guadagnino's film and its inspiration, the original *Suspiria* (1977), are viewed through the lens of the maternal gaze to see the Mater mythos as an exploration of undead motherhood, passed down through a maternal oral tradition, which exploits cultural assumptions about the hysterical female body and uses choreography to captivate and consume its desire, the child. Theorised by Alina M. Luna in *Visual Perversity* (2004), the concept of the maternal gaze transforms discourses of motherhood and gaze theory. Psychoanalytic, art and film theories have historically aligned the gaze with masculinity; Jean Clair proclaimed, 'the gaze is the erection of the eye' (in Solomon-Godeau 1991: 229), while Laura Mulvey's seminal work 'Visual Pleasure and Narrative Cinema' exposed the male gaze as objectifying by reaffirming female passivity and victimhood as 'linchpin to the system' (1975: 14). Since Mulvey, Mary Ann Doane (1982), Teresa de Laurentis (1984), Brigid Cherry (1999) and others have conceptualised a female gaze, but Luna's theory is the first to present a maternal gaze as both dominant and damaging. For Luna, the maternal gaze comes from the 'originary space' of the womb and is as objectifying as the male gaze, as it desires to reclaim the child that has fled the womb through birth:

> In the process of having been given birth, the child becomes enmeshed in a perpetual state of indebtedness [...] The mother wears [the mask] that pretends she has no desire to collect on that debt, but the eyes betray her true intention. With the removal of the mask, the nature of the maternal instinct will unfortunately be revealed. (2004: 92, 14)

Figure 25. Pat's (Eva Axén) menstrual death. *Suspiria*, directed by Dario Argento (Seda Spettacoli, 1977).

Luna's concept is unsettling, but in presenting the gaze as a mode for maternal monstrosity it recognises a parity of Sadeian perversion in men and women and exposes how dichotomously viewing the gaze relies on gender essentialism. In Guadagnino's *Suspiria*, we see the devouring maternal gaze of undead Helena Markos (also Tilda Swinton), whose acolytes sacrifice the pupils of the Tanz Dance Academy through dance performances to sustain her, and her destruction by Susie Bannion (Dakota Johnson), who reveals herself as Mater Suspiriorum, the ancient Mother of Sighs, in an abrupt departure from the ending of Dario Argento's original film.[1]

Known as the 'Italian Hitchcock', Argento was notorious for his exploitative directorial gaze. Recalling the abject menstrual trauma of *Carrie* (1976), the excessive gore of his sanguine aesthetic in the original *Suspiria* from 1977 (see Powell 2012: 170) evoked the culturally embedded assumption that women's hysterical bodies are beholden to their chaotic wombs. Considered a 'video nasty' in the UK, Argento's *Suspiria* was significantly cut before it was deemed suitable for release in the US, and it remains uncomfortable viewing.

Argento dismisses accusations of misogyny, declaring 'I like women, especially beautiful ones. [...] I would much prefer to watch them being murdered

---

1   The other Mothers of the mythos are Mater Tenebrarum, Mother of Darkness in New York who appears in *Inferno* (1980), and Mater Lachrymarum, Mother of Tears in Rome whom we meet in *Mother of Tears* (2007).

than an ugly girl or man. I certainly don't have to justify myself to anyone about this' (Jones 1983: 20). His Sadeian directorial gaze is not satisfied with watching murders but demands that others watch too. He expressed disdain for audiences who look away during his films, joking that they should watch with pins under their eyes to stop them not looking, and he realised this in *Opera* (1987) when Betty is captured by an obsessed fan who tapes needles beneath her eyelids and forces her to watch his murders. This vicarious scopophilia through a captive audience defines Argento's directorial gaze as uniquely horrific. As Maitland McDonagh writes, 'what distinguishes [his] nasty imagination is his relentless emphasis on looking long and hard' (2010: 197).

But while Argento's directorial gaze oversees *Suspiria*, its provenance can be traced through the film's co-writer and Argento's then-girlfriend Daria Nicolodi, who as a child was told a story by her grandmother the French pianist Yvonne Müller Loeb Casella, who attended an academy on the Germany/Switzerland border and fled on hearing rumours of witchcraft (see Rayner 2018). Martha Shearer argues that *Suspiria* has multiple authors and that, because Nicolodi's contribution is seen as a threat to the imago of Argento as cult *giallo* auteur, her authorship is either marginalised or she is perceived as a passive artistic muse by fans and film criticism alike (2020: 48–50). Nicolodi has claimed ownership over the Three Mothers mythos and explicitly places it in the context of a Female Gothic literary tradition: '*Suspiria* and *Inferno* the two "fantastic" films that I wrote for Argento […] are I think as good as

Figure 26. Captive audience Betty (Cristina Marsillach). Opera, directed by Dario Argento (Cecchi Gori, 1987).

Frankenstein by Mary Shelley and could only have been thought up by a woman' (Shearer 2020: 55). Nicolodi insisted that 'everything belongs to me in *Suspiria*' and implied that she directed Argento's struggling artistic vision: 'there is a lot of myself, my cultural background and my experience [...] he didn't know which path to take' (Palmerini and Mistretta 1996: 114).

Nicolodi found inspiration for Suzy's pursuit of truth in the *Bluebeard* archetype. Some versions of *Bluebeard* gave the tyrant an ambiguous female accomplice whose role as house/gatekeeper allows her access to forbidden knowledge (see the Brothers Grimm's 'Castle of Murder' and 'The Robber Bridegroom' [both 1812], Jane Austin's *Jane Eyre* [1847] and Daphne du Maurier's *Rebecca* [1938]; see Lovell-Smith 2002), but in *Suspiria* we have a maternal Bluebeard who is not an accomplice but the primary threat to the child. This grants women more agency than Argento intended, which is embodied by Markos's simultaneously omnipotent and invisible gaze, as we only see her when she is stabbed by Suzy (Jessica Harper). For Shearer, this ending 'seems less like the restoration of the symbolic order and more like a simultaneous collapse of meaning and a cathartic moment of artistic production'. It enacts a non-reproductive inheritance as Suzy, the Final Girl in the 1977 film, 'is coming to occupy not the position of the dancer for which she has been training but Markos' position as author/murderer' (56), a perpetuation of undead motherhood which is performed again in Guadagnino's 2018 denouement when Susie becomes Mater Suspiriorum. Nicolodi continued to assert her authorship late into life, tweeting 'I imagined and wrote *Suspiria* and *Inferno* for Mr. Argento' (24 March 2018) and '*Suspiria* 1 was imagined and written by a woman: me' (22 August 2019). *Suspiria* is a mythos created by women about infanticide and matricide, and beneath Argento's misogynistic gore waits an undead matrilineage of maternal monstrosity that Guadagnino articulates.

Donna de Ville has commented on the prevalence of older maternal murderers in Argento's films (2010: 65), and for Erin Harrington *Suspiria* is an example of Hagsploitation, a genre where the postmenopausal body which is hostile to male insemination becomes 'an alternate mode of (re)productive femininity, rather than an end or loss' (2018: 254). Guadagnino explores this idea of female monstrosity as an expression of creative autonomy embodied in dance and choreographed by the maternal gaze of Madam Blanc (also Tilda

Swinton), a parthenogenesis that actively prohibits men; Argento's academy is co-educational, Guadagnino's is not. The cultural mythos of the child-hungry witch was repeated in horror films like *Rosemary's Baby* (1968) and *Don't Look Now* (1973), but there is not a baby in sight in Argento's *Suspiria*, and Guadagnino continues the coven's renunciation of biological reproduction through the act of testing the dancers' urine. If the spectacle of choreography is their sustenance and creative parthenogenesis, for a dancer to 'fall' pregnant would be problematic.

Argento's aesthetic of excess was accused of causing a 'forceful retardation of a narrative drive' (Hutchings 2012: 14), but Marcia Landy has suggested that this chaos 'invites a mode other than narrative', a maternal storytelling sublime where discrete limits of the real and the symbolic 'lost their clarity' (2017: 38, 22). Guadagnino's *Suspiria* unearths narrative threads from this chaos to weave an intricate plot. One such thread is the continuing influence of the male psychiatric gaze on women's bodies in 1977, when the original film was released and when Guadagnino's film is set. Psychiatry appears fleetingly in Argento's version when Suzy talks to former psychiatrist Frank Mandel (Udo Kier) about Markos. In the 2018 film, it is not Susie who seeks answers but Dr Klemperer, Patricia's psychiatrist, who suspects the matrons when she disappears. At the outset, the hallmarks of Freudian/Lacanian hysteria as a manifestation of the Oedipal fear of the devouring mother are ostensibly plotted. Patricia foetally curls up on the couch in Klemperer's office, muttering 'They took my hair. They took my urine. They took my eyes [...] now she can see me [...] she wants to get inside of me, I can feel her [...] they'll hollow me out and eat my cunt on a plate', while he observes and silently diagnoses her words as a constructed mythology. Later, we see him attending a seminar given by Lacan. Patricia's horror is perceived by Klemperer as a delusion, a hysterical symptom to be conquered by analysis, the 'repeated attempt to formulate an answer to the riddle of how a woman becomes a woman' (Verhaeghe 1999: 2). This exposure of male psychiatric blindness towards the female patient has been unceremoniously described as 'the closest *Suspiria* comes to displaying something useful' (Jones 2018).

Rejecting the Freudian/Lacanian focus on the singular hysterical female body, Guadagnino explores mass hysteria through dance – described by Kélina Gotman as 'the site where bodies become public, infecting audiences,

Figure 27. Klemperer (Tilda Swinton) analysing Patricia (Chlöe Grace Moretz). *Suspiria*, directed by Luca Guadagnino (Amazon Studios, 2018).

including with erratic and spontaneous gestures' – and specifically through choreomania, which 'stands for this complex of medicalized, anthropologized ideas about a disorderly social body that [...] affects those around it' (Gotman 2018: xiv). Historically, episodes of mass dance and choreomania have been viewed through a colonial lens of infection and sociopolitically as an expression of freedom of movement. Dance as a mode of women's religiosity was demonised in the Reverend Jonathan Townley Crane's Methodist tract 'An Essay on Dancing' (1849) as 'ceremonies of the savage and the semi-civilized' (Reckson 2020: 91), while the 1518 Dancing Plague of Strasbourg was initiated, according to Paracelsus, when Frau Troffea 'turned stubborn' against her abusive husband (Gotman 2018: 77). In the 2019 *Suspiria*, Susie, who was raised in a strict Mennonite household – a culture where dancing is often prohibited – chose to study dance in Germany as a rebellious act. Her participation in *Volk*, the coven's attempted sacrifice ritual, embodies choreomania as defined by Gotman: 'a hyperbolic, feminine, and queer sort of expansive gesturality spilling beyond the individual body into public space' (2018: 6). This collective power catalyses tensions of political unrest and historical guilt, demonstrated by the film's backdrop of *Vergangenheitsbewältigung* ('overcoming the past') and Klemperer's historic spectatorship of the Nazis' rise to power. As Madame

Figure 28. Susie (Dakota Johnson) dancing *Volk*. *Suspiria*, directed by Luca Guadagnino (Amazon Studios, 2018).

Blanc tells Susie, 'movement is never mute', and Monica Castillo writes how Damien Jalet's arrangement of *Volk* 'taps into the otherworldly choreography of an austere era, unlocking a physical expression that is entirely absent from the original' (2018).

Unlike Argento's Suzy, who appears lost and vulnerable when she arrives in Freiberg, Susie sees leaving her childhood home for Berlin as an act of completion: 'That includes me now. I live in Berlin'. While Guadagnino portrays divided Berlin in the throes of the *Deutsche Herbst* ('German Autumn', see Jones 2018), which is reflected in the coven's political tensions between the Markosites and Blancites, Susie feels (re)united and sheds the mantle of guilt placed upon her by her biological mother, who condemned her childhood dreams of dancing in Berlin and on her deathbed calls her 'my sin [...] what I smeared on the world'. In Berlin, Susie awakens from a nightmare about her mother by screaming 'I know who I am', and disowning her mother's inheritance of reproductive guilt, she pursues the maternal gaze of Madame Blanc at the Academy, a mirrored *mise en abyme* inside which she is infinitely observed by Blanc and, most crucially, herself.

Blanc's developing instinct to nurture and protect Susie's talent is her downfall, and during the climactic Sabbath in the *Mütterhaus* Markos declares

Figure 29. The studio's *mise en abyme* capturing Susie. *Suspiria*, directed by Luca Guadagnino (Amazon Studios, 2018).

'we all know what you want [...] we have been on two sides of this for too long now' and decapitates her. Witnessing this, Susie envisions her biological mother's death and parthenogenetically becomes Mater Suspiriorum. Through her rematriation and (re)birth, we see Susie-as-Mater Suspiriorum has been watching the dissenting coven, and her arrival has restored order to the matriarchy. She summons Death and destroys the tyrannical Markos, who had proclaimed 'death to any other mother!', tears herself open to birth Mater Suspiriorum while declaring 'I am mother', and grants a peaceful death to Olga (Elena Fokina), Patricia and Sara (Mia), who were tortured by the coven. Susie has pursued the maternal gaze to the point she has embodied it. As Luna writes, 'it is easier to rid oneself of her child than it is for the child to rid [herself] of [her] mother' (2004: 102).

If we understand the *Suspiria* mythology as a female-authored matrilineage passed down to Nicolodi through the storytelling of her grandmother, retold by male directors but not originated by them, we view both films as an articulation of the maternal gaze, its desire to reclaim the child, the child's reaction and, in Susie's case, their reciprocity. Susie's pursuit of the maternal gaze through dance is the ultimate act of rebellion against the symbolic order, as

Figure 30. Susie's (re)birth as Mater Suspiriorum: 'I am mother'. *Suspiria*, directed by Luca Guadagnino (Amazon Studios, 2018).

for Luna this is the realisation of 'existence lacking merit and consequence' (2018: 98). Through choreomania, the Mater mythology eschews phallocentric constructs of creative (re)production, where men's artistic output is triumphant while women's is either compared to their childbearing abilities or it is the death of them, as exemplified by Vicky in *The Red Shoes* (1948) and Nina in *Black Swan* (2010). Instead, *Suspiria* demands we see relationships between motherhood, hysteria and creativity differently, not as lack or death but as continuing through the undead reproduction of Madame Blanc's and Susie-as-Mater Suspiriorum's gaze. Women are not vessels for creativity but its manifestation and, for Guadagnino, Susie's (re)birth shows 'the power of the witches [and] the capacity of women to find strength of being united [...] and completely refusing to be victimized' (Anderson 2018). Argento's Suzy is the genre's typical Final Girl, but Susie is an evolution of this trope because she actively pursues and embodies the threat to her and 'is often the source of the horror in *Suspiria*' (Righetti 2018).

Guadagnino's *Suspiria* has received criticism for being a laborious 'pseudoacademic gumbo of psychoanalysis' which falls short of the 'genre's visceral expectations' (Leader 2018). Argento stated that 'it did not excite me' (in Squires 2019), and this boredom betrays the fragility of a gaze dependent on titillation, something Guadagnino rejects through his excavation of motherhood so deeply embedded in the Mater mythos. For him, the original 'is about how you behave in the relationship between mother and daughter and what happens when the balance of power is swapped', and he wanted this to resonate as 'a relentless experience that's going to go deep into your skin' (Anderson 2018). Reperceiving the hysterical maternal body through choreography rather than excessive sanguinity, Guadagnino's *Suspiria* resurrects Nicolodi's authorial vision previously overshadowed by Argento's notoriety. For the maternal gaze in *Suspiria*, the dancing body is a volatile site/sight of rebellion where movement is a pre-symbolic language that calls to the true mother, and the portrayal of undead motherhood rejects the prescriptive psychoanalytic gaze that sees the maternal body as a hysterical site of lack and frustrated desire. As Susie-as-Mater Suspiriorum tells the emasculated Klemperer when she compels a seizure in him to erase his memories of 'all the women of your undoing', 'We need guilt, Doctor. And shame. But not yours'.

Valerie Estelle Frankel

Game of Thrones (David Benioff, 2011–2019)

Undead Masculinity

As characters chant, 'What is dead will never die', the undead of *Game of Thrones* present an eight-season epic shrouded in mystery. The massive army of wights leads the ice side of the fire and ice conflict and, as established clearly in the show (more murkily in George R. R. Martin's books), they are transformed humans: the hungry dead feasting on the living, as seen in folklore worldwide. Most are walking soulless bodies with no trace of personality, though their generals are intelligent and seem to possess memories of before. Opposing them are Melisandre and her fellow fire priests, who raise dead warriors with their fire magic to combat these ice forces. With this, the series presents opposing visions of the undead: ravening zombie hordes and also the more nuanced central hero and villain.

In the first episode, Old Nan (Annette Tierney), transmitter of the old legends, sets up the show's central conflict as the Northerners warn that 'winter is coming'. She tells Bran Stark (Isaac Hempstead Wright), the future seer for the forces of good:

> Oh, my sweet summer child. What do you know about fear? Fear is for the winter when the snows fall a hundred feet deep. Fear is for the long nights when the sun hides for years, and children are born and live and die, all in darkness. That is the time for fear, my little lord; when the white walkers move through the woods [...] They swept through cities and kingdoms, riding their dead horses, hunting with their packs of pale spiders big as hounds. (Season 1, Episode 1, 2011)

Of course, this time is soon coming again, with the world needing a new hero. Melisandre the red priestess indicates the same. Her belief system is rooted in opposing the threat from the North, as she insists on burning her enemies and worships fire as saviour. 'Make no mistake, good sers and valiant brothers, the war we've come to fight is no petty squabble over lands and honours. Ours is a war for life itself, and should we fail the world dies with us', Melisandre insists in the novels (Martin 2000: 884). She is an exaggeratedly feminine instigator, seducing the king and anointing him as her hero, and birthing shadow creatures in the dead of night. As she beguiles King Stannis into serving her cause, and insists he is the fire hero Azor Ahai reborn, she tells his loyal warrior Davos:

> The war has been waged since time began, and before it is done, all men must choose where they will stand. On one side is R'hllor, the Lord of Light, the Heart of Fire, the God of Flame and Shadow. Against him stands the Great Other whose name may not be spoken, the Lord of Darkness, the Soul of Ice, the God of Night and Terror [...] It is death we choose, or life. Darkness, or light. (Martin 2000: 288)

Neither god is shown in the television series, and the books, with two more to release, have not yet reached this point.

Little more is known of the nebulous enemy of Westeros. The wights begin the first book, emphasising that this will be a story of monsters and magic. The first of them attacks a group of rangers. 'Tall, it was, and gaunt and hard as old bones, with flesh pale as milk. Its armour seemed to change colour as it moved; here it was white as new-fallen snow, there black as shadow, everywhere dappled with the deep grey-green of the trees' (Martin 1996: 8–9).

Old Nan tells Bran that the Others 'hunted the maids through frozen forests and fed their dead servants on the flesh of human children' (Martin 1996: 240). This suggests they eat the human babies. However, in his northern stronghold, the amoral Craster gives his baby boys to the Others to turn into wights – the show reveals the transformation, and the book suggests it – as one of his daughter-wives insists a new baby will go to Craster's other sons. As she adds ominously, 'The white cold's rising out there, crow. I can feel it in my bones. These poor old bones don't lie. They'll be here soon, the sons' (Martin 2000: 505). These scenes at Craster's Keep shockingly reveal that these are not just monsters but former humans.

Melisandre takes the role of fire avatar and seductress as in Book and Season 2 she drains the energy of her king and lover Stannis (Stephen Dillane), to create a murderous wraith. As she notes, 'Shadows only live when given birth by light, and the king's fires burn so low I dare not draw off any more to make another son. It might well kill him' (Martin 2000: 385). Early on, this emphasises how her magic comes from the living to create unnatural creatures powered by her will. Both fire and ice are birthing unnatural children as weapons, perverting the natural birth process and gender roles. Filled with fire as she is, she is clearly an avatar of her god. As she thinks, 'The fire was inside her, an agony, an ecstasy, filling her, searing her, transforming her' (Martin 2011: 408). The show startlingly reveals her as ancient, her life unnaturally prolonged so she can aid the forces of good.

The war for the throne of Westeros has many heroes, but Jon Snow is the viewpoint character for what appears the deepest conflict of the story, the war of ice and fire. He has a miraculous, secretive parentage and grows up marginalised and hidden, like so many epic heroes. Up in the North, he discovers that the petty war of the Seven Kingdoms is pointless when the ice wights threaten to kill them all. When he becomes Night Commander, Melisandre gradually shifts her loyalty from Stannis to him, flirting and toying with him as her new prey. As she thinks in a single chapter from her point of view, 'I pray for a glimpse of Azor Ahai and R'hllor shows me only Snow' (Martin 2011: 408). In this scene, she still seems oblivious to Jon's importance, but readers have already been made aware.

Jon allies with the local Wildlings, a massively unpopular decision that Jon insists will give their side soldiers while depriving the wights of new recruits. This and other rebellions against the Black Brothers' code lead them to conspire and stab him to death. This imagery, rather like Julius Caesar's death, is framed as dishonourable and cowardly, a break in social order but also against their personal oaths. Their brotherhood is based in loyalty and hierarchy, but the traitors shatter it all.

The published books stop here, but in the show, Melisandre (Carise van Houten) frantically rides up and magically revives Jon (Kit Harrington).

In epic fashion, he becomes the reborn hero who has gained deep wisdom from his journey through death and return. In fact, with his new insight, he quits his post, noting that he only swore to hold it until his death. He spends Season 6 reclaiming his ancestral home of Winterfell and being proclaimed King in the North. He is a moral and merciful leader, having gained a mature

Figure 31. Melisandre brings Jon Snow back from the dead. *Game of Thrones*, Season 6, Episode 1, directed by Jeremy Podeswa (HBO, 2016).

wisdom many other lords never display in the series. As such, he models a very particular kind of masculine heroism and growth.

Jon's return is foreshadowed in the life of Lord Beric Dondarrion (David Michael Scott), who in Season and Book 1 is a frivolous tourney knight, before he is sent to apprehend Ser Gregor Clegane for his atrocities. The villain kills him in battle, and his friend, the drunken red priest Thoros of Myr (Paul Kaye), accidentally resurrects him. Fighting for the common people, Lord Beric returns in Season 3, having formed a Robin-Hood-style resistance group known as the Brotherhood Without Banners, committed to justice for commoners rather than the feudal system in which the capricious leaders prey on the weak. According to Martin in an interview, Beric is not technically alive at this point and is a wight created by the red priests:

> Poor Beric Dondarrion, who was set up as the foreshadowing of all this, every time he's a little less Beric. His memories are fading, he's got all these scars, he's becoming more and more physically hideous, because he's not a living human being anymore. His heart isn't

beating, his blood isn't flowing in his veins, he's a wight, but a wight animated by fire instead of by ice, now we're getting back to the whole fire and ice thing. (D'Addario 2017)

In the books, Beric dies after the Red Wedding, in order to transfer his powers to a character who becomes Lady Stoneheart (whom Martin in the same interview identifies as another inhuman echo of their former self). Beric's and Lady Stoneheart's status provokes the question: is Jon also an inhuman fire wight, or did Melisandre's expertise or her god's need for Jon to fight the Night King restore him more completely? Melisandre is one of the strongest of her order, and being at the magical Wall gives her more power (Martin 2011: 411), Still, is this enough to bring Jon fully back, and how does that affect the type of masculinity he performs in the series?

It should be noted that, when less than human, Beric devotes himself to justice for all, with his new self giving up his showy tournaments and driven to protect the common folk. Does this sort of resurrection make a hero more connected with the big picture (and more 'humane') or with the fire god's mission? It is unclear. Alongside Beric is Lady Stoneheart, whom Martin describes as being an answer to Tolkien's Gandalf, and who returns from death in a very similar manner.

> It always felt a little bit like a cheat to me. And as I got older and considered it more, it also seemed to me that death doesn't make you more powerful. That's, in some ways, me talking to Tolkien in the dialog, saying, 'Yeah, if someone comes back from being dead, especially if they suffer a violent, traumatic death, they're not going to come back as nice as ever'. (D'Addario 2017)

Lady Stoneheart is another of Martin's cruel unnatural mothers, like Cersei, Lysa or Melisandre, and undeath only makes this more so. Beric begins as kinder, but is shown to be clearly losing his humanity and his control over the undead masculinity within him, over time.

However, Jon does not show this sort of damage. Post-resurrection, his loyalties and desires are roughly the same as before. He falls in love and defends his friends and family with a full emotional range. The show never brings up the question, except in the final episode, when Jon, asked if there is life after death, can only say, 'Not that I've seen' (Season 8, Episode 6, 2019). The books, which have Jon as a viewpoint character with extensive inner monologue, would clarify this. Still, Jon's fully human status, torn between loyalties, drives the series finale and thus remains a vital part of himself.

Just as Jon Snow is the story's great hero – the figure that is in control of his masculinity – it has a great villain: not just the many tyrants, torturers and warlords seeking power, but the magical epic villain the Night King, who manifests excessive undead masculinity. Many fans wondered from the start whether a war of good fire and evil ice was more complicated than it appeared – whether, perhaps, both natural forces needed to be balanced. In fact, the complication arrived in Season 6, with the Night King's origin story.

As revealed in flashbacks in 'The Door' (2016), the elflike Children of the Forest captured one of the primitive First Men and pressed a dragonglass dagger into his chest, turning him into the first of the White Walkers. He and his fellow warriors were made to defend the Children, as pawns in their fight with the new human invaders. In this relationship, the Children of the Wood were the powerful ones, using intellect and magic to compensate for their spindly frames. Under attack from invaders, they decided to create an army, sacrificing the First Men's free will and humanity to accomplish their goals. The White Walkers become craggy monsters exiled from their people and stranded in the ice, a case of honour being corrupted by innocence so that they become the worst kind of violent barbaric males. The ancient war called the Long Night occurred when they turned on their creators and their former brothers (Season 6, Episode 5, 2016). In Season 1 they are presented as the ravening violent horde behind a calculating leader, but this twist shows how the forces of good sacrificed the noble warriors and created their own enemy.

Bran explains that the Night King (Richard Brake) has become a force of complete destruction, warring on all the forces of life – unbridled masculine dominance. Now he wants, in Bran's words, 'An endless night. He wants to erase this world' (Season 8, Episode 2, 2019). More specifically, he seeks vengeance on the Three-Eyed Ravens, seers who work with the Children of the Forest, as their powers represent all he wants to destroy. The Night King smirks as he invades the caves to slaughter them all, emphasising that he takes pleasure in the personal side of the conflict.

Another ice wight with personality is Coldhands. In the books, this undead former ranger saves the everyman hero Sam and then Bran and has not clearly been identified. In the show, he reveals himself as Jon and Bran's

Figure 32. The Night King. *Game of Thrones*, Season 6, Episode 5, directed by Jack Bender (HBO, 2016).

lost uncle Benjen (Joseph Mawle) and adds, 'I led a ranging party deep into the North to find White Walkers. They found us. A White Walker stabbed me in the gut with a sword of ice. Left me there to die. To turn. The Children found me. Stopped the walker's magic from taking hold'. This was done by plunging a shard of dragonglass into his heart (Season 6, Episode 6, 2016). This transformation emphasises his origin as a special case reengineered by the Children's magic. It has also left him independent, untethered to the violent masculinity represented by the Night King, loyal to his family and determined that Bran resist the Night King. It is unclear how much he is required to serve the Children, as he is last seen defending both them and Bran.

Jon Snow ends Season 6 insisting the Night King is their true enemy, as he is the storm (Season 6, Episode 10, 2016). This dehumanises the Night King and the wights, casting them as the 'winter' that has been threatened as the enemy from the beginning: an unstoppable, unrestrained masculinity, seen as a natural (or rather, unnatural) killer of humanity in the series that consumes everything. Further, killing a White Walker kills any and all wights it raised, and so killing the Night King will destroy every such monster under his command. It leads ravening, destructive hordes, until they can all be ended, seeing such forms of destructive masculinity radiating from a source whose influence can be abruptly curtailed.

Season 7 has Jon trying to convince the last factions fighting for the throne that the real battle is in the North, even as the Night King's army invades Westeros. In Season 8, it reaches Jon's defences at Winterfell. Thanks to its unreasoning hatred of any Three-Eyed Raven, Bran serves as bait in their great battle. Small, selfish heroes Theon (Alfie Allen) and Arya (Maisie Williams) defend him, the former on a long redemption arc and the latter skilled from training and the need for revenge. As such, both represent complicated, messy humanity defending the unworldly seer (rather than Jon Snow, the prophesised chosen one and reborn warrior of fire, as the story appears to set up). This counters and deconstructs the image of the warrior hero as saviour. With her small stab, Arya slays the Night King and, with him, all his creatures. Furthermore, Beric has just died saving Arya, and Melisandre states that he thus fulfilled his purpose to the Lord of Light (Season 8, Episode 3, 2019). After the battle, Melisandre dies, insisting her own task is fulfilled. Thus, all the undead find peace.

The Night King's defeat by a lone assassin in the forest, rather than in single combat with Jon, somewhat echoes *Lord of the Rings*, in which the legendary king fights the war. However, Frodo, Sam and Gollum's tiny act destroys all Sauron has wrought; it is the humane mess of humanity that kills abhorrent masculinity and not 'honourable' men. With the war of ice and fire abruptly concluded, Jon leads his forces south to battle beside Queen Daenerys (Emilia Clarke) for the throne of Westeros. He insists he is loyal, but she remains fearful the people will choose him if they learn his parentage as her nephew and the rightful king. Her paranoid selfishness alerts viewers that she is a corrupted ruler (as are the majority of the series' dominant women, but that would be another chapter). After losses, Daenerys lets her rage take over, savagely attacking her enemies but also murdering civilians and then surrendered soldiers. When a frighteningly totalitarian speech follows, in which Daenerys plans to conquer the world, Jon sorrowfully ends the threat by killing her, willingly sacrificing himself to save the world yet again. Their people, sick of selfish rulers, elect an underdog to the kingship: Bran. He sentences Jon to exile once again amongst the Black Brothers, whom he will presumably rule

(Season 8, Episode 6, 2019). Unlike Melisandre, Jon still has a purpose, healing the kingdoms after he fought to defend them.

Contrasting with the traditional heroic epics, this series appoints the humble, crippled, intellectual Bran and Tyrion (Peter Dinklage) as its leaders, condemning the powerful warriors to death in many cases, with exile for Jon. Female rulers, whether wielding strength (Daenerys), magic (Melisandre) or guile (Cersei), lose their power, leaving Sansa (Sophie Turner) and Brienne (Gwendoline Christie) leading beside gentler, kinder men. However, the series also emphasises the victimised nature of the terrifying hordes of the undead, seeing them as victims of the very same violent masculinity they embody, and revealing that war turns everyone into monsters. These monsters, meanwhile, give up – are forced to relinquish – their humanity to become killers. Thus, they are contrasted with living, loving Jon, who may be undead, but as a good leader is far more than a zombie. Yet, as seen in Bran's banishing of his 'brother', he knows that even honourable men who are equally exiled from the mess of humanity will eventually become the violent, destructive force they most abhor.

Madeleine Mackenzie

Dorohedoro (Q Hayashida, 2000–2018)

Over the decades, as zombies have become an entertainment mainstay, so too have they become an empty signifier: an undead mass that can take multiple shapes to perform 'multiple and simultaneous allegorical roles' (Lizzardi 2013: 103). When read queerly, zombies generally become a signifier of liminality. If *Frankenstein* (Shelley 1818) is included in generalisations about zombies, as encouraged in Xavier Aldana Reyes's undead overview 'Promethean Myths of the Twenty-First Century' (2018), we can find a wide body of work exploring this notion of the zombie as inherently liminal. Across this work, the consistent argument is that zombies are queer because they lie outside the normal binary of life and death (Gardner 2020; Halberstam 1995; Moore 2016; Mora 2013; Oswald 2013; Simonsen 2016; Stryker 1996; Zigarovich 2018); that to perform a queer reading of a narrative regarding undeath is to read undeath as no man-or-woman's land, and to do otherwise is a 'conservative' approach (Zigarovich 2018: 260). Q Hayashida's cult classic seinen horror manga *Dorohedoro* (2000–18) presents an alternative. By naturalising the state of undeath as an unstoppable fate within a binary biological system, *Dorohedoro* offers a new angle on the relationship between queerness and undeath, where characters fight to avoid a binarising form of zombification.

Dorohedoro is set between two fantasy worlds: the world of the sorcerers and the world of the humans ('the Hole'). When a sorcerer dies, they are sent to hell as either a devil or condemned spirit. When a human dies, they become a zombie. This binary system could variably signify class, nationality or gender; what matters is a sustained power imbalance between two categories. Though some analogies are made with a divide between rich and poor or American and Japanese, the most consistent analogy is with a divide between men and women. Many significant characters within *Dorohedoro* fight for the right to transition from one to the other in these allegorical binaries or to exist between them. The main antagonists embody the extreme version of each binary: the devil Chidaruma, who rules hell, and the collective consciousness of the zombies, Hole, which wants to usurp him.[1] Somewhere in the middle is the protagonist, Caiman, a human who died trying to become a sorcerer and found himself in a liminal position between human, sorcerer and zombie. By interpreting the binary of *Dorohedoro* and the conflict between Caiman and Hole as a gender allegory – an interpretation supported by key generic and iconographic elements of the story – *Dorohedoro* becomes the story of an undead trans-masculine hero asserting his subjectivity as the unstoppable feminine forces of undead nature attempt to objectify him. Caiman's struggle to live in spite of Hole's hold on his body resists attempts to read undeath as inherently neutral. Through analysis of *Dorohedoro*'s secondary human–sorcerer gender system, the gendering of Caiman and Hole, and the conflict between them, this manga presents an opportunity for undeath to be de-essentialised and opened to new forms of queer reading.

Before discussing how concepts and characters are gendered in *Dorohedoro*, I offer a few words on the manga's broader relationship to gender. Like *Frankenstein*, *Dorohedoro* is written by a woman for a presumed audience of men. Manga genres are based on the age and gender of their intended audience rather than their subject matter; as 'seinen', *Dorohedoro* is written for adult men (Hideaki 2013). This means we can read Hayashida's work similarly to that of Shelley's, with the knowledge that although gender is not a stated theme it is a key formative element. Here is a woman creating a story about divides *across* a gender divide between herself and her presumed readership. Perhaps as a result of this, gender exists within *Dorohedoro* but is overshadowed by the human–sorcerer binary. For instance, Noi, the largest and strongest character in the series, is a woman. The fact that she is so large and strong is praised and not seen as unusual because she is first and foremost a sorcerer. This layering is similar to how gender is depicted in work such as Omegaverse fiction, which uses a primary/secondary gender system (Popova 2018: 181). In

---

1   For clarity, 'Hole' will be used to refer to the antagonist, and 'the Hole' will be used to refer to the setting, though the manga uses the terms interchangeably.

such systems, which occur across a variety of languages and cultures, there is a 'primary' human gender and a 'secondary' metaphorical gender; the primary gender is downplayed to put readers at a distance, while gender commentary takes place via the secondary gender (188). However, they are most frequently used to make a presumed audience of women comfortable with depictions of sexism by projecting them onto men's bodies, whereas *Dorohedoro* attempts to make a presumed audience of men connect with gendered issues they rarely encounter (188).

What, then, is *Dorohedoro*'s secondary system? *Dorohedoro* is built around concepts from classic horror movies, as indicated by a scene where the sorcerers access a religious TV network that primarily broadcasts the horror canon (Hayashida 2017: 263–4, 272). The binary between the Hole and the sorcerer world originates from these concepts. The Hole is based around zombie-inclusive body horror, with *The Return of the Living Dead* (O'Bannon, 1985), *Hellraiser* (Barker, 1987) and *Re-Animator* (Gordon, 1985) as key points of reference. Its primary holiday is Living Dead Day, every part of the landscape is infused with necromantic power, and the only hope of escape is through mad science. The sorcerer world is based around slashers. Its primary holiday is Blue Night, where devils bequeath sorcerers masks reminiscent of Jason and Leatherface, and everyone carries a signature melee weapon (Clover 1992: 30–2). Aside from location and culture, everyone is divided by biology.

Humans are like us, the readers, whereas sorcerers have extra organs that allow them to produce magical smoke from their orifices. Sorcerers are masculinised by their association with slasher villains and their smoke organs. An exemplary sorcerer, who wears their mask with pride, produces powerful smoke and practises with their weapon, can become a devil, the hypermasculine position. Devils prey on sorcerers; sorcerers prey on humans. Association with the feminine abjection of body horror and the lack of smoke organs feminises humans (Reyes 2020: 395–6). The Hole itself has been corrupted by the magic performed there: anyone who dies resurrects as a zombie, losing their individuality and becoming part of the horde. This makes the zombie a hyperfeminine position, the eternal victim of *Dorohedoro*'s social order and the natural fate of any human. With this secondary gender system established (hypermasculine devil, masculine sorcerer, feminine human, hyperfeminine zombie), we can examine Caiman and Hole's place within and outside it.

At *Dorohedoro*'s outset we are introduced to Caiman (Hayashida 2010: 4), the world of the Hole (2010: 16), and his campaign to kill every sorcerer who visits as revenge for being cursed with the face of a lizard (2010: 19, 45). This introductory plot reads as a fantastical rape-revenge plot. Caiman's magical assault is conveyed through the iconography of sexual assault: memory loss, a dark alley and the hallucinated silhouette of the sorcerer who attacked him (2010: 18). As in the rape-revenge plot – particularly its modern variants – his mission is equal parts vigilante justice and an attempt to reclaim his own sense of safety through

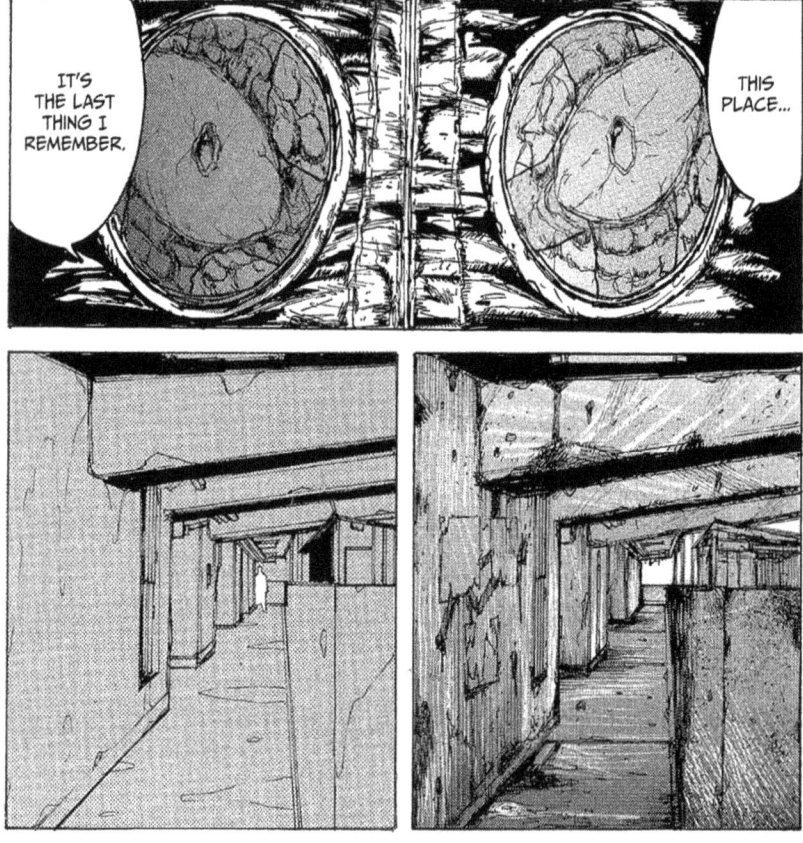

Figure 33. Caiman visits the alleyway. *Dorohedoro*, directed by Q Hayashida (Shogakukan, 2010).

shows of power, becoming 'victim and victor [...] raped and symbolic rapist' (Mee 2013: 82). He hides his lizard head behind a mask (Hayashida 2010: 15, 45) and carries an extensive collection of knives (2010: 12), the accoutrements of a sorcerer, actively concealing the symbol of his humanity, his cursed face. His position within what is supposed to be a strict binary is immediately unclear – a human who presents as a sorcerer – and becomes even less clear from there.

Caiman was born as a human named Ai (2014: 7) who felt that he did not belong in the Hole (17) and pursued surgery to make himself a sorcerer (10–21). After his chosen doctor refused to perform the surgery (10), he took a suicidal leap into the sludge pit at the centre of the Hole (17–19) to force the doctor's hand (2014: 23–6, 2017: 88–90). In the aftermath, Ai died but was resurrected by a combination of the surgery and Hole's zombification (2014: 23–6, 2017: 91–2). In the sorcerer world they emerged as split personalities: Aikawa, Ai reborn as a sorcerer, and Kai, Hole's zombie sleeper agent (2017: 94–5, 134–6). Both grew

Figure 34. Ai describes his encounter with Hole. *Dorohedoro*, directed by Q Hayashida (Shogakukan, 2014).

close to a powerless sorcerer named Risu (2017: 142–6). When Risu suddenly gained power, Kai attempted to kill him (2017: 148–9) and, failing, fled to the Hole to avoid retaliation (2015: 19–21). Risu followed and tore Aikawa/Kai apart (2015: 30–1, 36–44). In the altercation, the lizard head spell was cast (2015: 45–6). Caiman rose in their place: an amnesiac identity born from an inexplicable mix of zombie, human and sorcerer (2015: 50–4). Though happy in his ambiguity, he resents the lizard head, as it marks him as a victim of sorcerer-on-human violence.

Hole also exists across multiple identities, a sort of tripartite god. In the beginning, the sorcerers and humans lived together in a single world until the

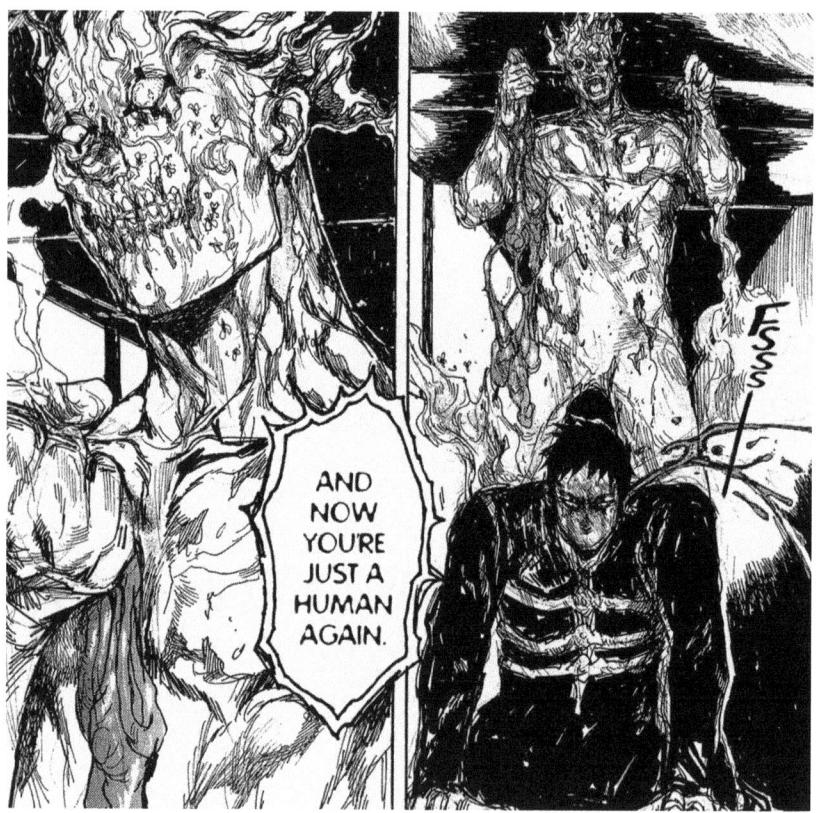

Figure 35. Risu removes Aikawa/Kai's smoke organs. *Dorohedoro*, directed by Q Hayashida (Shogakukan, 2015).

smoke residue from magical violence caused the world to become conscious and split in half, creating a separate human world – the Hole – to protect them (2019: 153). The sorcerers figured out how to leave their world and visit the Hole, where they continued to harm the humans, the smoke residue corrupting the Hole's water cycle, earth and inhabitants (2019: 93–8). Corrupted rain, soil and biowaste combined into sludge, which seeped into any humans buried in the Hole, resurrecting them as zombies (2017: 127–9). Because each physical aspect of the Hole (world, ecosystem and inhabitants) is marked by the smoke residue, the consciousness it develops – the antagonist, Hole – is defined by the trauma that smoke residue represents (2019: 285). Without smoke residue, without magical violence, neither the Hole nor Hole would exist. It acts through the wounds sorcerers have left on its component parts. Therefore, Hole is the collective consciousness of a traumatised planet, biosphere and its dead, united by that shared trauma. Hole's unholy trinity of forms are in turn what make it so threatening, a tripartite monster built from distinct aspects of cosmic-, eco- and body horror, complementary and oft-combined parts for a subgeneric Frankenstein, hellish hard to fight (Tidwell 2021: 43–5). The zombies are just the most visible product of the ecosystem that made them and the world it developed from. Hole is an unstoppable form of undeath because it is a natural end point. To stop it, someone must destroy the concept it represents: that there is an absolute binary between sorcerers and humans and that sorcerers victimising humans is inevitable. This, naturally, brings us back to Caiman.

During Caiman's inciting dive in the sludge pit, Hole chooses him as its avatar due to their mutual dissatisfaction with the human–sorcerer binary (Hayashida 2017: 91). The distinction between them is that Hole wants to invert the binary by usurping the devil, inverting the feminine and masculine power balance, whereas Caiman desires to change himself and defy the binary's existence. Crucially, this desire is not because he wants magical power but because of a general sense of wrongness: that what he has as Ai the human in the Hole is not a life (2014: 17). He desires to move from 'human' toward 'sorcerer' in search of life, though he is told he will become neither and that these are the only living categories. His acceptance of and comfort with this is why I describe his pursuit as trans-masculine, rather than neutral or specifically analogous to trans-manhood. Caiman cares about the direction of

Figure 36. Caiman and Hole. *Dorohedoro*, directed by Q Hayashida (Shogakukan, 2019).

the journey rather than the destination. His surgery, his presentation, his behaviour: everything he does moves toward legibility as not-totally-human, not-totally-feminine. He seldom cares where he is as long as the directionality is clear. Hole pulls him back from that as hard as it can, because it sees itself as the only end point for humans: natural, inevitable and unstoppable. All Caiman needs to do to refute it is avoid being subsumed within the sludge, escape zombification and emerge as himself.

This is an unusual instance of zombies as natural instead of unnatural, preventing the standard reading of zombies as subversive and queer (Gardner 2020: 521; Mora 2013: 181; Simonsen 2016: 87). 'Zombie' in *Dorohedoro* is the category that characters are thrown into to remind them of their place. It is deader than dead: the final and forever imposition of the binary, removal of the self to become one with the system. Caiman is killed over and over by both sorcerers and Hole to force him into submission (Hayashida 2010: 126–7, 2014: 41–2,

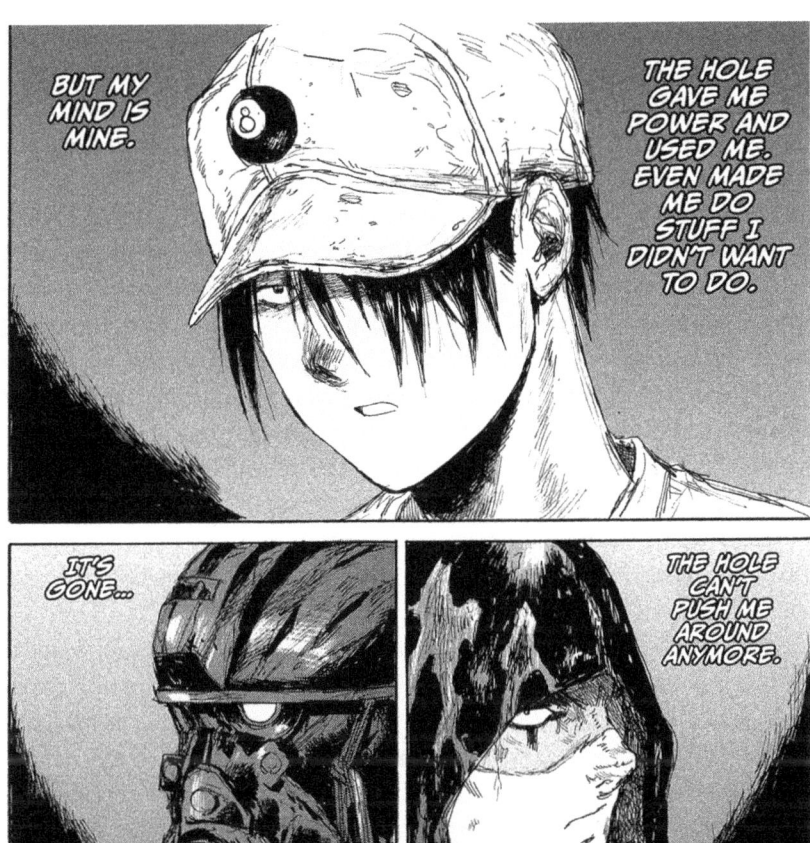

Figure 37. Caiman reflects on his struggle and his different identities: Ai (top), Kai (right) and Aikawa (left). *Dorohedoro*, directed by Q Hayashida (Shogakukan, 2018).

2017: 93). Yet he never becomes a true zombie, because the system cannot overcome his powerful sense of selfhood. In defiance of the sludge, the totality of Hole and the world's confidence that he cannot live, he continues to live.

This resonates with theory of the trans-masculine body, what it must defy to exist, and what its defiance does to those defied. In 'Doing Justice to Someone', Judith Butler observes how systems tend to push liminal bodies toward femininity, seeing the feminine as an absence that is easier to construct than the masculine, a whole made of holes (2001: 626). When a liminal body dies, this push toward the feminine combines with a desire to fit corpses into a neat binary narrative and make the death easier to read and interpret (Halberstam 2000: 65–7). By contrast, a living liminal body 'wounds the system', in Sonny Nordmarken's words, by forcing recognition that life outside the system is possible (2014: 49). The binary lives because history, society and the people within say it does, arguing for the 'unlivability of its absence' (Stryker 1996: 210). In creating the conditions that allow for it and willing himself back to life on his own terms, Creator and Monster in one, Caiman refuses to be silenced, objectified and feminised as a vacant zombie. Like John in Butler's case study, he says the body he has is enough, that it is 'his distance from the knowably human that operates as a condition of critical speech, the source of his worth, as the justification for his worth' (Butler 2001: 633–4). In being alive in defiance of unstoppable nature, in resisting zombification, 'something in him is winning' (634), and so the unstoppable becomes stoppable: Hole is defeated.

Dorohedoro's central conflict against Hole presents an opportunity for new queer readings of undeath, where undeath, instead of being the symbol of queerness, is what queerness fights. Undeath is binary, natural, unstoppable, except when characters live a truth that reveals its lie. Though Caiman has been the focus, other *Dorohedoro* characters fight other battles to live outside the human–sorcerer binary, including Nikaido's inverse journey from sorcerer to human, Shin's assignment of human at birth and his pubescent change to sorcerer, and Risu's experiences as a sorcerer without smoke. Hole exploits them all, claiming or rejecting them to strengthen its argument for the binary. The struggles against it, just like real queer struggles against the supposed absolutes of the world, are many and varied. Appropriately, every chapter of *Dorohedoro* ends with an appeal to accept its continued sprawl, the vast number of ideas it cannot contain or explain. It asks us to enjoy it for its indescribable self, to celebrate ambiguity and to welcome chaos. As I cannot account for the whole manga here, I can only repeat its core message to spread the horror gospel that there is power and life outside the known world. In its own words: それが ドロヘドロ. 'That is *Dorohedoro*'.

Martine Mussies

'The Zombie Mermaid' (Katelynn E. Koontz, 2018)

With the rise of participatory fan cultures online, cyber mermaids have become cyborg mermaids, and this cyborgisation has empowered the figure of the mermaid in various ways. One way is to create Monstrous Mermaids. These hybrid creatures generated as a result of border-crossing are misfits within their societies. Their physical and existential appearance occurs, as Jeffrey Jerome Cohen argues, quoting Marjorie Garber, 'at times of crisis as a kind of third term that problematizes the clash of extremes – as "that which questions binary thinking and introduces a crisis"' (Cohen 1996: 6). This essay explores the nature of the crisis that these monsters might be bringing in their wake, by analysing the short story 'The Zombie Mermaid' by Katelynn E. Koontz (2018), which is born and exemplary of that selfsame crisis.

Zombification

'Zombie' has tended to refer to the fictional undead created through the re-animation of a corpse, via magical or supernatural forces. More recently it is more likely to be someone infected by a virus which takes over the brain and shuts down the internal functions of the victim, thus turning them into the living dead (Wade 1985/2010).

There are key characteristics of zombies that can be observed both in the traditional, 'voodoo/vodou' zombie[1] and in contemporary versions. The most salient of these is the zombies' lack of free will. These creatures are wholly subordinate to an external force, often a sorcerer or an overwhelming desire such as revenge, violence or the need for human flesh (Bro et al. 2018). Flesh-eating here is part desire for death to consume life to sustain itself – as also seen in entities such as vampires – but also, more recently, the biological imperative of a virus to infect others in order to survive. Secondly, zombies are most often the animated corpse of a human being and are usually shown as shambling and rotting (Verstynen and Voytek 2014). Zombies are rarely seen as animals, although franchises such as *Resident Evil* (2002–21) show that this is possible. Since these creations are the walking dead, the undead, they are impossible to kill by ordinary means such as a gunshot or stabbing, and it is generally believed that destroying the connection between the brain and the body, for example by removing the head, can stop a zombie.

In the twenty-first century, because of globalisation and the rise of the Internet, the influence of 'Western' culture has spread across the world. Accordingly, the Zombie Mermaid has become a malleable 'misfit' character with which to navigate the challenges of cultural transition and individual identity. The zombification of the mermaid represents the discomfort experienced by non-Westernised communities in regard to this dominant and often oppressing 'global' culture, as evidenced in Koontz's story by the statement 'a welcome relief from the shoes that she had been forced into earlier' (Koontz 2018). The archetypal Western mermaid has traditionally been described as being beautiful and seductive. In Koontz's story, Adele is suitably attractive, with blue eyes and an alluring voice, but she is also a zombie with a living dead body. As one of the newest online incarnations of the man-eating zombie, the Zombie Mermaid thus appropriates the appearance of the seductive Western mermaid to hunt and kill its victims. In being hybrid, the Zombie Mermaid forms

---

1   The traditional zombie is drawn from Haitian and African voodoo traditions which date back to the eighth century. Notably, the word 'zombie' originates from the Kongo language, from the word 'nzambi, which translates to the spirit of a dead person (Ackermann and Gauthier 1991). The traditional zombie is said to be a dead person revived by the power of necromancy by a voodoo/vodou priest, witch or sorcerer to do their bidding (McAlister 1995). The zombie, having no free will, remains under the control of the necromancer.

a bridge between Haitian and 'Western' folklore to claim her own place in (cyber) space. This also finds expression through her shape-shifting abilities, which allow her to transform into human form or conceal her normally beastly appearance.

Monstrous Mermaids

The Zombie Mermaid is a new undead archetype of the monstrous mermaid, revealing how the meaning of mermaids is constantly negotiated and reconstructed in light of their particular cultural environment. Posidaeja, Atargatis and other Hellen(ist)ic precursors of modern mermaids were very powerful, but in the transition to the Romantic tradition, 'the mermaid shifted from a powerful, siren-voiced temptress to a mute, shadowless, soulless creature in the need of human [male] aid' (Haase 2007: 621). Many of the creators of recent monstrous mermaids revisit these older mermaid traditions, combining them with monstrous elements of vastly different mythologies to empower their creations, such as lore about the zombie.

Koontz's 'The Zombie Mermaid' is exemplary amongst the current range of online monstrous mermaids. Her mermaids are undead mash-ups with grotesque bodies, revealing some of the post-human potential of the (neo-) Gothic and addressing themes of border-crossing, trans-interspecies relationships, globalisation and emancipation. Border-crossing and emancipation are addressed through all of the monstrous mermaid archetypes, firstly through their hybridity in carrying monstrous identity markers from a variety of cultural traditions, and secondly through their inherent 'misfit' status in embodying persons who are socially excluded because their bodies, behaviours and/or attitudes distinguish them from others in a way that is uncomfortably conspicuous to the society around them. This misfit status is further reinforced by trans-interspecies relationships, as seen in depictions of love between the monstrous mermaid and the normative human (often in the form of a diver, which is a border-crossing image in itself).[2] Moreover, these issues of difference,

---

2   See, for example, Martine Mussies, "Still 'Diving into the Wreck'", *LOVER*, 2 June 2020. <https://www.tijdschriftlover.nl/english/still_diving_into_the_wreck>.

identity and agency are (implicitly) acknowledged through the mermaids, thus empowering them, their creators and the audience. Accordingly, the creators of online monstrous mermaids, such as Koontz, have much in common with Frankenstein, with their creations unleashing unexpected powers, and their 'grotesque bodies' (Russo 1994: 62–3) being bodies of becoming and change.

Case Study

In her writing, Koontz mixes different mythologies related to the idea of the undead and the archetypal mermaid. Set in a fictional Western coastal environment, the story revolves around the experiences of a zombie mermaid character called Adele. The narrative begins at a point where Adele reaches the beach from the mainland at night. She begins the process of transforming from a human being into a zombie mermaid but is interrupted by the sight of a man, whom she then decides to eat. This quickly introduces the primary conflict of 'eating the Other', mirroring Western cultural tensions between male and female. Western society still upholds the patriarchal system that depicts men as more important and powerful than women. While men take advantage of this system to oppress their female counterparts, Koontz's narrative depicts the female's fight for equality. Thus, the zombie mermaid eating the human male represents the emancipation of the female, who is no longer an Other or a misfit but is equal to, or greater than, her male opponent.

The story offers no explanation of how the mermaid came to be (or chose to be) zombified. Her zombic identity markers are intertwined with the many other elements from vastly different mythologies that make up her composite character. Adele calls to the man, and 'her voice is a siren song, a storm call, a crystal shattering on the stones' (Koontz 2018). Deceived by her voice and her beauty, the man decides to interact with her, while she thinks about the history of her tribe, recalling Andersen ('Back then, mermaids had to bargain away their voice to get a pair of legs'; Koontz 2018) and the Scottish Selkies ('They had to risk losing their skin, just to get a chance at coming on shore'; Koontz 2018). The event that caused the change in her kind is described by the Zombie Mermaid as the 'Last Lover':

> With her betrayal at the hands of the prince and the witch, with the loss of her voice, and her legs, and her beautiful seal pelt, everything changed.
> Mermaids changed.
> Adele changed, too. (Koontz 2018)

But whereas the Sirens, the Andersen Mermaid and the Selkies have traditionally been victims of their fate, at the end of the story, the Zombie Mermaid conquers: Adele attacks and devours the man, led by 'the call of the ocean', which is the collective memories of her tribe.

Koontz reinforces the plot of her story using flashbacks of Adele's experiences of eating the Other. In this story, the mermaid kills out of a desire to eat. Her hunger cannot be ignored, which can be read as either a critique of the cannibalisation of misfits by society or as a monstrous means of resistance against oppression:

> Adele cannot go home to the ocean without transforming into this vicious beast, and she both hates it, and loves it, and can't even begin to fathom it. The ocean song is something that she cannot ignore and it surges, now, fuelled by the storm, telling Adele what she must do. She listens to it. Talons dig into the man's skin and with one sharp wrench, she has his head pulled to the side and her sharp teeth digging into his neck. The ocean cannot be ignored. Neither, thinks Adele, distantly, as the tang of copper floods her mouth, can the hunger. (Koontz 2018)

As the above fragment shows, zombie mermaid Adele is depicted as persuasive, deceptive, violent, untamed and vengeful. The decision to attack the man on the beach is based on the retaliatory motive of avenging the betrayal of her tribe, as depicted in the narrative 'Last Lover'. The man on the beach, on the other hand, is depicted as gullible and chauvinistic, given that he wants to take advantage of Adele to satisfy his lustful desires. Other characters in the narrative include the witch and the prince, who are both depicted as untrustworthy and/or chauvinistic. Through these four characters, themes of love and commodity culture are explored, as the mermaid goes against the learned patterns of thought and behaviour that have been characteristic for the Romantic version of her figure. In this rewritten narrative, the story shows that love promotes unity between female and male, but also that love is powerful to the extent that it can cause 'blindness' in the parties involved. The thinking process of the zombie mermaid suggests that people should use critical examination and set boundaries when getting into a romantic relationship ('Back then, mermaids had to bargain away their voice [...]. But the Last Lover changed all of that' (Koontz 2018). Now, the zombie mermaid has learned that the consequences of hasty and poorly made decisions about falling in love can lead to betrayal and psychological trauma.

Reflections (in the Mirror and the Sea)

Author Essi Varis describes her own monstrous mermaids as 'artificial human analogues; uncanny mirrors of humanity' (2019), seeing them as a dark reflection of society, of it but not part of it. Magrit Shildrick (2002) takes this further, exploring the concept of monsters through historical and contemporary lenses and problematising societal responses to bodily Otherness. According to Shildrick, monsters are visible in different sociocultural spheres. Monstrosity appears in embodiments that challenge and resist normalcy in human beings and, as such, provoke both dread and fascination. Shildrick defines monsters as that which is not appropriated, noting that, historically, those who were different from the societal conception of normal were deemed monstrous. This is still the case, but the monstrous mermaids described here, as created by independent artists and fans of the genre, provide ways to empower their protagonists and their readers to resist culturally enforced attitudes regarding sexism, racism and colonial attitudes.

In their many resurrections in the form of fan art, monstrous mermaids are misfits who do not aim to fit in but want to stand out, replacing the alienating idea of Otherness by a more relational model of what I refer to as 'Anotherness', in which the Other is not objectified but recognised as another subject, with internal differences, layers and complexity, as an alternative way of being in the world. Monstrous mermaids were born online, created by fans who were fed up with the powerless and submissive images of mermaids that have dominated popular 'Western' Romantic culture (like the 'Little Mermaid' of Anderson and Disney). In her 2014 thesis *Folkkonst för de besatta: en diskussion om fanart*, Lisa Lundell-Karlberg states that 'fanart is more often enthusiastic than critical,

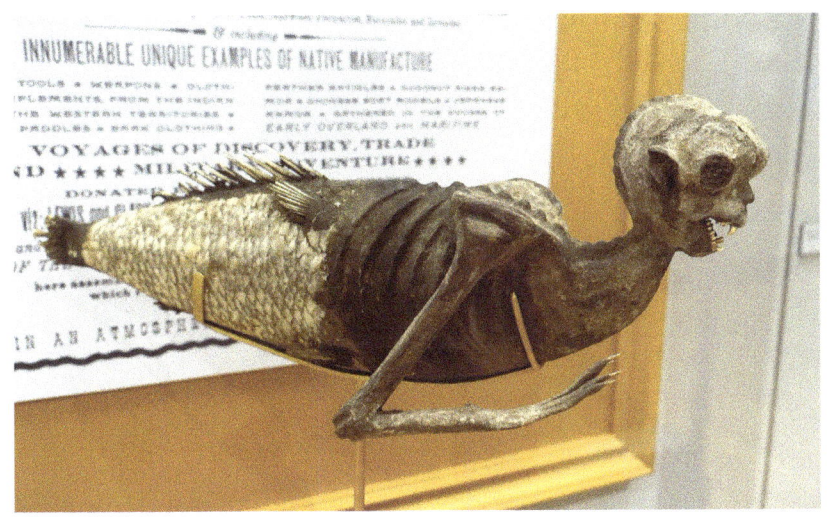

Figure 38. The so-called Feejee Mermaid in Harvard University's Peabody Museum of Archaeology and Ethnology. This constructed 'proof' of the mermaid's existence as a monster, rather than as a Romantic idea, can be interpreted as 'fan art avant la lettre' and is an indicator of the Gothic fascination with the uncanny and the undead. Image in the public domain.

which would separate it from the satire' (20). However, the creators of zombie mermaids are very critical and use their monstrous fanart as a way to rewrite mermaid stories in order to empower the misfits: themselves and their audience. These monstrous mermaids often have less in common with sweet Ariel and more in common with Ursula the sea-witch, in terms of shapeshifting and agency. The misfit warriors in this essay are undead hybrid monsters, scientific freaks who claim their agency by blurring the boundaries of normativity, incorporating the animal and the monstrous into their humanity.

Gwyneth Peaty

Bloodthirsty (Amelia Moses, 2021)

Canadian horror film *Bloodthirsty* (2021) tells the story of Grey Kessler (Lauren Beatty), a singer-songwriter who begins transforming into a werewolf as she works on her second album. An indie musician who has been strictly vegan since childhood, Grey struggles with a seemingly inexplicable desire for blood and meat as she works to create new music. Accompanied by her girlfriend Charlie (Katharine King), she travels to the isolated forest cabin of Vaughn Daniels (Greg Bryk), an eccentric music producer who promises to bring out the best in her. Instead, what emerges is the beast.

While it is explicitly situated as a werewolf film, the narrative eschews elements that have become iconic in werewolf cinema – such as the moon, silver or infection via bites – in favour of a different set of markers. Grey's growing hunger for meat parallels her hunger for success. A focus on consuming and being consumed by others is linked to both the creative process and the entertainment industry as Grey tries to release the 'genius' within and satisfy her expectant audience. Accordingly, this chapter explores how *Bloodthirsty* engages with the figure of the female werewolf in the context of wider dialogues about contemporary celebrity culture as a monstrous, hungering, undying force.

Dances with She-Wolves

Directed by Amelia Moses, *Bloodthirsty* was written by Wendy Hill-Tout and her daughter Lowell Boland, featuring a score composed by Michelle Osis and Boland. Helmed by this all-female creative team, the narrative presents a character study in which women's experiences of fame are centred. In fact, Grey's story can be described as somewhat autobiographical. Boland is herself a Canadian singer-songwriter (under the stage name 'Lowell') and was trying to craft a second album at the time of writing the script for *Bloodthirsty*. In interviews, she readily admits that the screenplay 'was inspired by her own experiences and the pressure she felt when trying to write a follow-up album to her first record' (Rubin 2021). Strengthening the link, her eventual second album, released in 2018, was titled *Lone Wolf*.

Gender is especially significant to the context of *Bloodthirsty* because the werewolf is commonly depicted as a male monster. There is a long history of this trend in popular culture and in folklore. As Hannah Priest, editor of *She-wolf: A Cultural History of Female Werewolves*, notes, 'in medieval literature, werewolves are almost exclusively male creatures' (cited in Knight 2016). The etymology of the word itself would appear to foreground male origins; Merriam-Webster's dictionary identifies Old English 'wer' (man) and 'wulf' (wolf) as the term's most likely foundations. In *The Werewolf in the Ancient World*, Daniel Ogden observes that the Greek texts he studies 'employ no special term for the phenomenon but merely speak of people – predominantly men – turning into a wolf (*lykos*)' (2021: 4). Legendary tales of men turning into wolves can be traced as far back as the *Epic of Gilgamesh* in ancient Mesopotamia, and may have been linked to the practice of dressing in animal skins and furs to hunt, as practised by early hunter-gatherer societies (Lidman 1976: 388–90). There are also historical links with myths of the 'wild man', described by Richard Bernheimer as 'a hairy man curiously compounded of human and animal traits' (1952: 1). References to female werewolves and women turning into wolves are much less extensive, although they do occur (see Priest 2018).

The connection between werewolves and men has solidified over the past century. As Chantal Bourgault du Coudray points out, werewolf mythology was increasingly masculinised during the twentieth century under the influence of psychoanalysis (2006: 65–77). Building on nineteenth-century theories about human experience as divided between conscious and unconscious, civilised and primitive, werewolves were seen to reflect 'a very specific conceptualization of the human psyche as "divided against itself" – or, as perpetually at war with the "beast within"' (du Coudray 2006: 69). More specifically, the werewolf was seen to embody and express cultural ideas about Western masculinity, because 'the battle against the "beast within" has been increasingly characterized as a peculiarly masculine problem' (ibid). Early cinematic depictions, such as those in Universal's *Werewolf of London* (1935) and *The Wolf Man* (1941), set the tone by representing the werewolf as a tormented man-wolf unable to control his violent outbursts (often directed at women). This association has carried on throughout the years, with such films as *The Company of Wolves* (1984) and *Wolf* (1994) continuing to link werewolves with predatory masculinity. Even more recent films have carried on the tradition; the 'lycans' of the *Underworld* film series (2003–present) are almost exclusively male.

Focusing on *Bloodthirsty* offers an opportunity to revisit the werewolf as a symbolic figure in the context of twenty-first-century culture. This is important because, as Craig Ian Mann points out,

> to accept the beast within as the werewolf's sole symbolic worth is to overlook the specific cultural and historical context of individual films. The werewolf film must be understood not just in terms of the beast within but also the 'beast without': a cultural understanding of the lupine creature as a product of its times. (2020: 10)

Grey is indeed a product of her time, emerging into her lycanthropic form in the context of contemporary celebrity culture and the twenty-first-century music industry. She may have a beast within, but she also grapples with the 'beast without': a society that hungers to consume her.

Everyone Wants a Piece

The opening scenes of *Bloodthirsty* directly contrast Grey's life as a minor celebrity with her dreams of tearing into raw flesh. In a dark forest, she chews and slurps at the body of an unidentified creature, revelling in the blood that spills down her chin. Waking suddenly, she realises this is only a dream. However, as Grey stares into the bathroom mirror, her eyes gleam a piercing, predatory gold before shifting back to normal. Later that day, she poses at a photo

Figure 39. Grey (Lauren Beatty) looks into her bathroom mirror. *Bloodthirsty*, directed by Amelia Moses (Brainstorm Media, 2021).

shoot, glamorous in different costumes and wigs. At first she appears bright and confident, performing sensually for the cameras, but her energy flags and her smile fades. The flashing of the camera begins to seem intrusive; voices ask a cacophony of questions as she is pinned in the light. The sense of claustrophobia is heightened as a reporter follows Grey back to her dressing room after the shoot, asking more prying questions. 'Oh come on, the public deserves to know', he scoffs when she refuses to answer on personal grounds. The expectation that she give the audience everything – even private information about her lesbian relationship – is made clear. She is to be consumed in her entirety.

    Grey's dreams of being a predator contrast starkly with the reality of her life: as a public figure, *she* is the one being stalked. Yet, as Graeme Turner (2014) has pointed out, turning people into commodities is a key function of contemporary celebrity culture. Marketing oneself as a product to be consumed is an essential part of becoming a star. Fans 'hunger' for their favourite star – for information about them, for the sight of them and to be near them – and the celebrity must feed and foster this appetite in order to remain relevant. There is danger inherent in the process, however, because the desire being stoked can shift quickly: 'Even in those sites which depend upon fans hungry for celebrity gossip, there is a readiness to shift from admiration to antagonism without any sense of inconsistency' (Turner 2014: 136). Female celebrities are particularly vulnerable to cruel public commentary and shaming, as their bodies and behaviours are viciously critiqued (Turner 2014: 137; Doyle 2016).

A sense of being preyed upon comes through clearly in the song Grey composes for her new album. As the chorus goes:

> I get the creeps
> From everyone's eyes on me
> Blood thirsty
> Sippin on us like
> Sippin on us like
> Flavour of the week
> I get the creeps
> And everyone wants a piece
> Blood thirsty
> Sharpen your tongues
> Sink in your teeth
> Bloodthirsty (*Bloodthirsty*, 2021)

Here, the audience, perhaps the celebrity industry as a whole, is framed as feeding on entertainers like a monster, draining them of their lifeblood before moving on to the next 'flavour of the week'. In the early twenty-first century, this sentiment is not uncommon. 'Fame has come to devour all else', argues journalist Lisa Robinson (2010) in the introduction to an interview with Lady Gaga. When actor Heath Ledger passed away, film critic A. O. Scott (2008) decried the 'pathological gossip culture that chews up the private lives of celebrities' and the 'rituals of media cannibalism' triggered by his loss. Indeed, as Anna Gibbs highlights in her discussion of Princess Diana, cannibalism is a metaphor that appears apt for discussing the media's 'insatiable appetite' for celebrities, especially after their death (1998: 12): 'If she was consumed in life', Gibbs argues, 'she has been cannibalised in death' (1998: 11). Rather than ending the 'chewing', death makes a celebrity even *more* readily consumable.

If contemporary fame is to be conceptualised thus, as a ravenous undead monster perpetually consuming the bodies of celebrities, it is no surprise when scholars observe that 'a sense of mercilessness characterises this mediated spectacle age' (Penfold-Mounce and Smith 2020: 38). Celebrity culture has become relentless and death-driven, feeding on bodies both living and dead in the service of consumerism and commodification. Subject to such forces, Grey is left questioning her own ontological status:

> Help me
> Heaven please help me
> I can't feel my heart beat
> Has my blood gone cold? (*Bloodthirsty*, 2021)

Depleted and drained, she questions whether she is still alive or perhaps undead as a result of being fed upon. Grey's interest in meat grows rapidly during this period, which might be read as her seeking an alternative source of power and vitality. Vaughn Daniels provides an array of plant-based meals for his guests, but eats meat at dinner every night. Grey becomes more and more fascinated, eventually going against all her vegan principles to try a bite. She later sneaks to the fridge at night and drinks bloody juice from a plate of steak. *Bloodthirsty* can thus be seen to highlight the impact of contemporary celebrity culture on the individual, and the individual woman in particular.

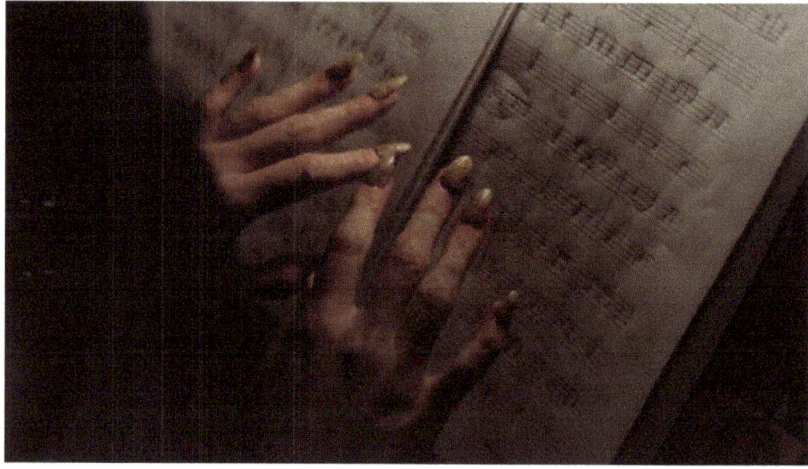

Figure 40. Sharp claws grow from Grey's fingers as she records a new song. *Bloodthirsty*, directed by Amelia Moses (Brainstorm Media, 2021).

Stressed and unsure of herself, Grey battles to maintain her equilibrium as increasing evidence suggests she is not holding it together.

Sady Doyle (2016) argues that the sense of shame generated by celebrity culture 'creates a world in which women are afraid of themselves – where every girl lives like the lead in a werewolf movie, constantly monitoring herself for signs that she's turning into a wild animal'. Indeed, contemporary media discourse encourages women to see themselves as constantly on the cusp of monstrosity, struggling to maintain a veneer of civilised perfection. Grey's battle to suppress her wolfish traits, which include thick body hair, aggression, sharp teeth and a voracious appetite, aligns with her perceived inability to satisfy the expectations of others. 'I'm not a monster', she insists to her girlfriend, who is understandably troubled by the unfolding events. Later, however, Grey changes her mind; she has decided to embrace the power of lycanthropy.

Whatever It Takes

As Grey's producer, Vaughn is there to help her create the best music she possibly can. Part of this involves working through the issues that prevent Grey from achieving success. 'It's like there's something holding me back', she explains to him in the recording studio, 'it's like I'm on the cusp of something, but as soon as I get there I hit a wall'. Vaughn's solution is to send her on an exhausting run: 'You need to get out of your head'. Grey is on prescription medication to treat her 'hallucinations' of turning into a wolf, but Vaughn throws the pills in the bin. A pivotal scene comes as they stand in the snow and he hands her a mouse.

> You're so worried what everyone else thinks. Trying so hard to be *nice*. You're like this little mouse. Scurrying around. The world plays with you like you're dinner. And it's gonna get bored. Eat you up. Because there are predators and there is prey [...] Do you wanna be a predator, or do you wanna be prey? You have to be strong. (*Bloodthirsty*, 2021)

To survive a monstrous, predatory system, she must herself become a predatory monster. With his encouragement, Grey crushes the tiny rodent to death in her fist. Blood covers her hands, and she punches Vaughn in the face. Grey's strength is increasing and her restraint is fading; during an argument, she lifts her girlfriend up against the wall by the neck with one hand. Faced with the fear of being ruthlessly consumed by the celebrity media machine, the 'beast without', she has decided to release the beast within. Vaughn highly approves of these developments. As the audience has come to suspect, he is himself a werewolf. In fact, he is Grey's long-lost father.

There is much more to be said about this film and, indeed, about the female werewolf as an intriguing contemporary figure. In the context of twenty-first-century celebrity culture, *Bloodthirsty* offers a dark vision of cannibalistic exploitation in which human effort is mercilessly consumed and discarded. Tangled within the wheels of this undying system, the individual may experience pressures that change their essence and challenge their very humanity. The price of fame and success, the film suggests, may be higher than we ever suspected; celebrity itself may manifest as a monstrous state of being.

Antonio Alcala Gonzalez

Behemoth (Nergal and others, 1991–present)

> Satan produces the unrest in society, which, in spite of many inconveniences, makes the world move onward and forward; he is the patron of progress, investigation, and invention. (Carus 2016)

From the existence of the two moments that mark the boundaries of life, birth and death, the human experience is lived in a scenario of multiple binomials. As a result, from its origins in the monotheistic Hebrew and Christian traditions, Western civilisation has tended to conceptualise the world in binary opposites, resulting in an interaction of otherness where one concept bases most of its definition in being what its contrary is not. On such a scenario, the order required for the creation of life needs the existence of a previous chaos, and if there is a unique God responsible for the existence and continuity of life under certain norms that are to be respected, there is also an everlasting evil side with opposing interests, a gothic doppelgänger permanently plotting against the intentions of its counterpart. However, in our contemporary society, the extremes associated with Satan rather come from his role as the ultimate source of evil that appears as contrary to the normativity of action emanated from Christianity. Thus, the purpose of this chapter is to explore the use of this extreme undead character as a reference for a call to a balanced and individualised return to human nature in the last two albums of the Extreme Metal band Behemoth (*The Satanist*, 2014 and *I Loved You at Your Darkest*, 2018). Through the evocation of Satan, they emphasise the arbitrariness of social norms that confine human behaviour inside the dual movement between good and evil.

Satan, the Devil and Lucifer are names associated with the same concept: 'the thoroughly evil counterpart to the all-good God' (Guiley 2009: 13). Such an entity was naturally associated with the Hebrew term *satan*, the 'one who obstructs' (Russell 1988: 28). Centuries later, Milton's heroic fallen angel Lucifer (Latin for 'light-bringing') added attractive touches to this figure, which responds to the need of monotheistic religions to polarise good and evil: 'The one creator is all-good but permits evil to exist under the direction of an archfiend' (Guiley 2009: 13). In fact, the Hebrew religion and Christianity present a characteristic dualistic tension: 'In effect the old, ambivalent God was divided into two parts, a good Lord and an evil Devil. The more one faced the power of evil, the more one tended in the direction of dualism, seeing the cosmos as a battleground between good and evil' (Russell 1988: 31). Carl Jung identified that both norm and opposition are constitutive parts of the same system: 'the shadow belongs to the light as the evil belongs to the good, and vice versa' (2001: 41). As a result, humanity 'has a share in both sides and can be judged just as well from the left as from the right, without our becoming any the wiser: indeed, we can only open up the opposition again' (1970: 162). However, since 'the essential function of Satan in the New Testament is to obstruct the kingdom of God as long and thoroughly as he can' (Russell 1988: 45), Christianity tends to impose a choice to follow either God or Satan, thus removing the choice between the two that is proper to human nature. The result of imposing this dualistic view on society is the creation of a Gothic evil doppelganger always policing the boundaries of what it means to be good and threatening to lure us to its evil side. Indeed, Eugene Thacker proposes to read the Devil 'as a metaphor for the nature of the human, and the relation of human to human (even when this relation is couched in terms of the boundary between human and non-human)' (2014: 192). Thacker suggests thinking beyond the possibility of the existence of any supernatural creature seeking to influence and even possess humans with evil. To achieve this perspective, he identifies the existence of 'an anthropological motif through which we human beings project, externalize, and represent the darker side of the human to ourselves' (2014: 196). This abject[1] entity is the response to the need to represent our

---

1   According to Kristeva, abjection is caused by 'what disturbs identity, system, order. What does not respect borders, positions, rules' (1982: 4). Like the antithesis of the norm represented by Satan, the abject challenges the continuity of the structure it

dark, repressed impulses in an anthropomorphic figure whom we can blame for our misbehaviour. He has accompanied our civilisation for many centuries as an undead force that polices the precepts of conduct dictated by Christianity. Following him means falling from the grace of God and thus becoming one more in his group of fallen ones. Through this process, the Church has alienated humanity from its own nature by imposing a choice between the two extremes represented by God and the forbidden darkness of the Devil. However, there have always existed nonconformist minds that, guided by the curiosity inherent to humanity, have dared to challenge limits and transgress them with extreme proposals. In this regard, Paul Carus claimed that the human intellect would never have developed without the human disposition to challenge the establishment: 'Satan produces the unrest in society, which, in spite of many inconveniences, makes the world move onward and forward; he is the patron of progress, investigation, and invention' (2016: 353). This rebellious figure is the agent of disruption evoked in the lyrics of Behemoth.

In the seventeenth century, Milton's *Paradise Lost* (1667) was responsible for coining the majestic image of Satan and his hosts that still persists to our days. The evil lord in *Paradise Lost* is paralleled with Prometheus and presented as the epitome of the mutineer against the tyrannic order; he becomes 'the essence of human individuation' (Jung 1958: 314). As the opposite to the tyranny of the Crown validated by its local Church, Milton personified in this being 'the spirit of the English Revolution; Milton's Satan represents the honor and independence of the nation asserted in the face of an incapable government' (Carus 2016: 254). The concept of the rebellious angel as champion of individuality has persisted together with a growing conviction that human will is responsible for evil and good aside from any existence of supernatural forces that may be seeking to guide or tempt us. At the end of the eighteenth century, Matthew Lewis's *The Monk* (1796) and William Blake's *The Marriage of Heaven and Hell* (1790) called attention to the fact that no evil or good is absolute since it is the choice of any human being to freely decide courses of action in life. As a result, in contemporary Western thought, where 'Satanism is more generally concerned with the liberation

---

belongs to. As a result, 'it cannot be assimilated' (1), though it cannot be eradicated, nor even repressed or ignored, for it is always there in front of us, threatening with its polluting identity.

from the perceived constraints of humanity than with worshipping the devil' (Kahn-Harris 2008: 40), the Black Metal movement that arose in Northern Europe in the 1990s, and which strongly influenced Behemoth, relied on the image of Satan as a way to express a rebellious stance towards the social norms and the religion policing its morality.

Formed in 1991 in the Polish city of Gdańsk, Behemoth oriented their rebellion against a society very strongly linked to the Catholic Church through combined references to the pagan-Slavic past and satanism in their lyrics. On one hand, they located in paganism a social construct 'lacking the "weakness" that characterizes contemporary society' (Kahn-Harris 2007: 40). Former drummer Baal Ravenlock (Adam Muraszko) claimed in 1994: 'I hail Poland as the land of the Slavs, as the territory of pagan culture and the sanctuary of the nature ... I hate Christianity, as the religion which is directly responsible for the obliteration of the pagan Slavonic culture' (quoted in Patterson 2013: 381). This longing for the heathen past turned to the image of the individualising rebel per excellence, Satan, as an ideal motif to strengthen the search for individuation. After four albums (1995–8), the band consolidated a lyrical shift that distanced them from an earlier interest more focused on Slavic-folk and moved towards an extreme anti-Christian content. This became evident in the album *Satanica* (1999). My intention in the rest of this chapter is to focus on the role of Satan, the undead opposite to God, in the lyrics of the band's two most recent albums, *The Satanist* (2014) and *I Loved You at Your Darkest* (2018).

Behemoth's leader and songwriter, Nergal (Adam Darski)[2] bases his lyrical style on an anti-Christian proposal that considers the Church responsible for the indoctrination of the aforementioned dualism of good versus evil that restricts humanity from acting on free will by labelling evil as the negative double to be avoided at all costs:

> I've always stated that, to me, Satan represents values that are important to every ambitious human being. Whether they admit it or not. The problem is that the archetype was, for obvious reasons, demonized and misinterpreted by the Bible, used as a scapegoat to manipulate and threaten people. To me, Satan represents freedom, intelligence, and ambition. (Quoted in Sayce 2014: 20)

2 Nergal is credited as the author of all lyrics in *I Loved You at Your Darkest* and co-author, with Krzysztof Azarewicz, in *The Satanist*.

In the search for an option to voice his thought, Nergal directed his interest to the occult which influenced the band's lyrics with ideas from Aleister Crowley,[3] whose philosophy, called Thelema, was influential on the band's album *Thelema.6* (2000), as well as Austin Osman Spare,[4] whose magic, Zos Kia Kultus, inspired the album of the same name released in 2002. The confluence of such sources is used by Nergal to express a call to follow human nature over the traditional limitations mentioned before; for him, 'Satan was injected in our veins since day one, due to our Western heritage, it's part of who we are. My idea of happiness is all about harmony and balance. You cannot find harmony by castrating the dark part of your nature' (quoted in Sayce 2014: 19) His use of the figure of Satan in the lyrics of the band's the two albums considered for this study appeals to the Miltonian proposal and its evolution discussed above: 'When it comes to rebel angels, the rebellious archetypes ... the way Behemoth present them in our lyrics is much closer to what John Milton did in "Paradise Lost", or what William Blake did' (quoted in Sayce 2014: 19). In fact, the song 'Ora Pro Nobis Lucifer', from *The Satanist*, praises the dark lord as an almighty being who, after having been wronged, becomes an antithesis of the Christian God. He is described as the undead lord that forever will hold his kingdom and glory; the destroyer of Heaven; the saviour that offered temptation to Eve in Eden and, consequently, liberated humanity from absolute order. This anti-Christian proposal escalates in the track 'In the Absence of Light', from the same album, which proposes a departure from doctrines and order into 'the church of man', where chaos reigns and human pride returns once the need to respond to a divine creating

3 Crowley defended the freedom of humans to decide over their own lives and actions; he proposed that the one who exercises his freedom ceases 'to be the helpless victim of circumstance; he can somehow cause changes to occur in conformity with his will. Man's mind has exactly the same power as his hands: not merely to grasp the world, but to *change* it' (Wilson 1987: 140).
4 Spare considered religions as bonds that prevented humanity from finding pleasure and satisfaction. For him, humanity could only be liberated from the 'primordial sin' behind the mere idea of the existence of God and the 'evil' brought to humanity by religions through loving the self over anything else: 'He that entirely loves himself induces self-love only. In this he is inexorable, but does not offend like other men. He is akin to the great purpose, his actions explained for him, good seen of his evil, without knowing, everyone satisfied with his will' (Semple 1995: 18).

power has been removed. The proposed result is the rise of a being who acts under a personal secular rule without any moral shackles.

Further on, the cult to a violent and powerful antithesis of the Christian ideal of order and good is evoked in the lyrics of 'Angelvs XIII', from the album *I Loved You at Your Darkest*. Here, the voice of individuating evil foresees a reversal of the Miltonian fall of Lucifer in that the destruction of God's Army is brought about by the legions of Satan, whose voice claims the titles of both 'Christ' and 'Serpent' for himself; this implies that a balance of good and evil is part of the individual who rises against the tyranny of traditional dualism. The arbitrariness behind the insistence on absolute opposites is approached in the song 'Havohej Pantocrator', from the same album. The mere anadrome proposed in the title anticipates the reversal of the 'Lord's Prayer' expressed in the lyrics. The voice in the song addresses Satan as the eternal divine leader whose legions will bring havoc to the Christian Heaven. Through this transgressive antithesis to a prayer central to Christianism, Nergal attacks the tradition that restricts human behaviour to a binomial of extreme contraries and invalidates the natural mobility of human will, whose only limits are individual interests and needs.

As shown in the preceding lines, the destructive language used by Nergal in his extreme attack against Christian tradition goes beyond embracing anti-Christian values. The blasting sound produced by the accelerated beat of the drums and the fast guitar riffs accompanies an extreme lyrical content that relies on blasphemous images to remind listeners that human life possesses an ampler scope than the one limited to the reduction of possibilities expressed in the opposition of good and evil. The image of Satan as an undead presence threatening the continuity of the order that we know is used by Behemoth as a metaphor not of 'Pure Evil and Hate' – as the name of one of their earlier songs claims – but of the subversive minds that, like Nergal himself, permanently question the imposition of arbitrary rules that bind humanity from a consciously performed free will in contemporary society. Consequently, behind the call to join the evil side, Behemoth offers an invitation to break the boundaries imposed by the good vs evil duality and turn that opposition of doubles into an inclusive sphere where one can move freely.

Part IV

Undead Futures

Persephone Braham

Wicked Weeds (Pedro Cabiya, 2011 [trans. 2016])

Meta Undead

Malas hierbas (2011; translated as *Wicked Weeds*, 2016) by Puerto Rican writer Pedro Cabiya (b. 1971) features a zombie protagonist who, in defiance of zombie tradition, is a respected executive and researcher at a high-tech pharmaceutical facility in Santo Domingo. He is the heir of a wealthy family, but an error by his 'stupid family witch doctor' (Cabiya 2016: 3) prevented him from being fully resuscitated after death. Although his wealth provides the lifestyle and hygiene products needed to pass as human, he finds his undead condition insufferable and describes himself as an empty simulacrum of a person. In the course of developing medications to cure mental illness, he secretly researches the makeup of 'zombie powder', the substance used to create zombies, seeking a pharmaceutical cure for his own condition. He becomes sentimentally entangled with his three scientist co-workers; falling in love with one of them, he momentarily recovers his humanity but is tragically murdered by a resentful zombie parking attendant. The police suggest that his murder is somehow linked to the ten-year-old case of a Haitian colonel who trafficked in zombies and murdered his wife and daughter under the delusion that they had been replaced by automata. Both cases are variants of the 'philosophical zombie', a hypothetical being that is behaviourally and physically identical to a person but lacks conscious experience.

Despite the apparent novelty of this scientific, bourgeois, romantic zombie murder victim, the protagonist is effectively a walking corpus of all zombies past and future. Zombies are by their nature meta-zombies; every zombie embodies all zombies. Their existence is a recapitulation (in the Haeckelian sense, where ontogeny recapitulates phylogeny) of the dynamics of predatory capitalism, colonialism and biopower. Zombies are cumulative: no zombie can be imagined without reference to his predecessors in literature, film and popular culture. Cabiya's novels are also recapitulations. He portrays highly specific local phenomena (for example, a Haitian cashew plantation and a 1980s morning salsa show in the San Juan neighbourhood of Santurce) as iterations of the Caribbean history of conquest, enslavement, colonialism and dependency.[1] Rather than lamenting postcolonial anomie, Cabiya focuses on the external forces that mediate Caribbean experience, appropriating Gothic horror and science fiction to refute the racist ideologies that engendered them.

Malas hierbas is headed by a metatextual *Advertencia* ('Warning') informing readers that what follows is an 'edition' of a dossier 'comprised of countless clippings, illustrations, photos, specimens, and texts' collected by scientist Isadore Bellamy. The editors have 'dismissed' all but the textual elements, which, given the forensic investigation at the heart of the narrative, at once alerts the reader to its insufficiency. The editors state that the text contains four kinds of writing or documentation, omitting the fifth, an Appendix describing the flora used in making zombie powder (vii). Among the writings are the zombie's first-person narrative describing his quest for sentience, discussions with zombie philosopher-bartender Dionisio, experiences with his three colleagues, and critical analyses of zombie film and lore; transcripts of police interviews with the three female scientists; speculations on the nature of subjectivity, consciousness and emotion (some by Bellamy, others probably by the zombie); and a retrospective first-person narrative by Isadore Bellamy that contains the (also first-person) narrative of her cousin Sandrine's experience with the undead in the Haitian countryside.

The *Advertencia* recapitulates salient Latin American reflections on reading, interpretation and textual authority. The editors reference Argentinean writer Jorge Luis Borges's (1899–1986) scepticism of textual authority, metaphysical conjecture and divine intention, explaining that although they have

1   *Malas hierbas* is one of his three zombie-themed novels, along with *Trance* (2008), about extraterrestrials who invade the minds and bodies of Puerto Rico's inhabitants – evoking the US invasion and deterritorialisation of the island – and *María V* (2011), which recasts Jorge Isaacs' classic nineteenth-century hacienda romance as a zombie horror story in which hordes of ravening 'Undesirables' menace idyllic slave plantations.

conserved the dossier's original order, 'There are some who contend that such an order does not exist, that they are placed at God's whim – that is, by chance'. Asserting that conventional linear readers 'will wind up in chaos', they provide a Table of Contents that groups the entries according to type. This is a homage to Julio Cortázar's 'Table of Instructions' for his novel *Rayuela* (*Hopscotch*, 1963), which states that 'In its own way, this book consists of many books' among which the reader may choose via reading order; conversely, the reader may ignore the suggested procedures 'with a clean conscience' (1966: i). Inexplicably, the editors of Bellamy's dossier warn that their edition grievously misconstrues its meaning:

> Because even incautious readers, naturally carried along by their own indolence, will not wish to veer from the path laid out for them by the judicious specialists, and they will, therefore, not read the album in the way Doctor Bellamy intended. With tragic consequences. (Cabiya 2016: viii)

The *Advertencia* is signed by 'Pedro Cabiya' from Grand-Goâve, Haiti, 2010, the epicentre of the catastrophic earthquake (magnitude 7.0 M_w) in January of that year.

Zombies embody both enslavement and rebellion. Enslaved Africans were first brought to the Caribbean island of Hispaniola (today Haiti and the Dominican Republic) in 1502, and plantation slavery defined Caribbean life for four hundred years. Enslaved indigenous and Africans were subjected to a material realisation of biopower, as elaborated by Michel Foucault:

> Bio-power was without question an indispensable element in the development of capitalism; the latter would not have been possible without the controlled insertion of bodies into the machinery of production and the adjustment of the phenomena of population to economic processes. (1990: 140–1)

This 'anthropophagic logic of modernity' (Joseph 1999: 136) deprived the enslaved of biological sovereignty and converted their bodies into European and North American wealth.

While enslavement depends on the theft or capture of the body, zombiism requires the theft or capture of the soul. Zombies are not exactly dead; instead, their souls have been stolen by a *bokor*, or Vodou priest, who then has complete power over them and uses them as slaves. Like the enslaved, they lack free will, but also subjectivity, desire and memory. Haitian zombies have analogues throughout the Caribbean, including the Jamaican *jumbie*, the *djombi* of Surinam, the Cuban *fúmbi* and the blood-sucking *soucouyant* of the Anglophone Caribbean.

The Haitian zombie is a product of a long, cumulative process of European and US reactions to Haitian culture.[2] In 1789, on the eve of Dutty Boukman's historic slave rebellion, colonial bureaucrat Médéric Louis Élie Moreau de Saint-Méry (1750–1819) included the *zombi* among other spirits in his description of the cultures of French Saint-Domingue (1958, I: 70).[3] The 'emergence' of the zombie in European consciousness, coinciding with the mass slaughter of white colonists, made it a convenient symbol of racialised Haitian resistance to the US occupation between 1915 and 1934. The infamous Haitian dictator François 'Papa Doc' Duvalier (1907–71) used his knowledge of Vodou as a tool of political terror and dressed as Haitian death-spirit Baron Samedi. Historians attribute to Duvalier the 'zombification' of the Haitian populace as his secret police tortured and murdered over 60,000 Haitians in pursuit of complete submission to the regime.

The zombie's origins in chattel slavery are recapitulated in Isadore's cousin Sandrine's narrative of country life in Haiti. Sandrine was often sent to stay with relatives in the city, who obliged her to work constantly at the nastiest chores with little food or leisure. Poor children are commonly enslaved to wealthy city households in Haiti's *restavèk* system (see Abrams 2010). When Sandrine's city cousin comes to visit, he leads Sandrine and her friends into a nearby cashew plantation, where zombie workers capture their friend Gracieusse. Reinforcing the continuity of plantation slavery into modern Hispaniola, the cashew plantation's foreman eventually begins hiring out his workers to sugar planters,

---

2   The origins of the word 'zombi' have been traced to West African languages as well as the Romance *sombra/ombre*. The Oxford English Dictionary states that the word is of 'W. African origin; compare Kongo *nzambi* god, *zumbi* fetish'.
3   The Frenchman Pierre-Corneille de Blessebois (1646–1700?) by various accounts an arsonist, pornographer and woman-beater, published the first zombie tale, the scandalous *Le Zombi du Grand Pérou Ou la Comtesse de Cocagne* (*The Zombie of Grand Pérou or the Countess of Cocagne*) in 1697 after serving an indenture in Guadeloupe. In the tale, the narrator makes a sexual slave of the creole Countess by playing on her obsession with occult powers.

and 'periodically auctioned off his laborers to anonymous clients' (Cabiya 2016: 147). While Isadore is visiting her childhood friend Valérie, she witnesses Valérie's mother Adeline selling Gracieusse to her wealthy Dominican friends.

Malas hierbas also presents a commentary on Dominican racial mythologies and false consciousness, or the subaltern's espousal of ideologies detrimental to his own economic or political condition. The zombie's three colleagues represent the three races recognised in Caribbean identity: the blonde Mathilde stands for the European; Patricia Julia's 'bronzed, almost metallic complexion in marked contrast with her [green] eyes' embodies a Taíno/Spanish mix; and Isadore's 'jet-black breasts' and 'almond-shaped eyes' identify her as Black Haitian (14). Dominican dictator Rafael Trujillo (1891–1961) and his successor Joaquín Balaguer (1906–2002) defined Dominican identity as white, Spanish and Christian, demonising Haiti as a 'cannibal state' that threatens Dominican sovereignty (Maríñez 2018: 296). Dominican policy and developmentalist discourse are deeply anti-Haitian: 'The presence of Haitian labourers [is] commonly perceived as making a negative cultural and economic impact, rather than a necessary, and formally solicited, contribution to the economy' (Howard 2007: 735). The zombie's desire to pass as human is in some ways analogous to Dominicans of Haitian descent trying to pass as Dominican to avoid violence and arbitrary deportation. He despises the worm-ridden zombies 'on the streets, in tatters, digging through garbage cans' (Cabiya 2016: 65) and resents the parking attendant's assumption of zombie/racial solidarity, complaining that 'we zombies vacillate between extremes of arrogant brazenness and overfamiliarity and the most slavish abjection' (61).

Modern global capitalism continues the legacy of enslavement and colonialism via developmentalism and coercive and dehumanising labour conditions, such as those in Dominican export-processing zones (see Werner 2011). Instead of slaving on the plantation at the dawn of global capitalism, the twenty-first-century zombie of *Malas hierbas* works in the multinational psychotropics trade. The police suggest that he tested his formulas on patients in the San Lázaro Psychiatric Hospital, recalling pharmaceutical experiments by US researchers in Cabiya's native Puerto Rico.[4] The zombie's own swings from arrogance to abjection resemble the false consciousness of the colonial

---

4   American researchers, with the support of Puerto Rican technocrats, tested contraceptives on poor Puerto Rican women in the 1940s and 1950s (see Briggs 2002). The

technocrat. Rather than being a helpless victim, the status-conscious zombie is perhaps complicit in a similar system of exploitation.

As a parallel to its reprise of Caribbean history and identity, *Malas hierbas* offers a meta-analysis of the zombie genre. The protagonist and his Haitian colleague Isadore are connoisseurs not only of the physical chemistry of zombification but of all the aesthetic and metaphysical accounts of zombies through history. An aficionada of Caribbean art and culture, Isadore collects Haitian botanical samples constitutive of zombie powder. Browsing her comprehensive collection of zombie films, the two have a long discussion that simultaneously encapsulates and ridicules academic interpretations of George Romero's 1968 classic, *Night of the Living Dead*:

> With dizzying lucidity, Isadore considered the George A. Romero trilogy, thoughtfully weighing the political, racial, and sexual aspects converging in the plots. For Romero, according to Isadore, chaos, and the rapid disintegration of the social apparatus brought about by the appearance of the living dead, is a metaphor for the tensions implicit in a system of multicultural coexistence and the artistic representation par excellence of the anguished, paranoid, white middle class in the United States.
>
> 'Or,' I interjected, 'it's simply an attempt to subvert the Judeo-Christian concept of the resurrection of the flesh, twisting it sufficiently to take it to its ultimate consequences. A sublime way of asserting that Judgment Day will take the form of an ecological cataclysm.' (Cabiya 2016: 55)

The protagonist traces the mutation of the zombie as metaphor of mass enslavement into its exact opposite: the embodiment of a rogue element – communism (*Invasion of the Body Snatchers*, 1956), nuclear disaster (*Night of the Living Dead*), consumerism (Romero's 1978 *Dawn of the Dead*) or pathogens (2002's *28 Days Later*) – that imperils life, liberty and the pursuit of happiness. He sees *Night of the Living Dead* as a turning point after which all zombies embody an inexorable hunger for the living. Zombies eat brains in a drive to become human, but they only succeed in making more zombies. As he remarks to Dionisio, 'The metaphor of the cannibal is at once perfect and atrocious, symmetrical and monstrous, beautiful and bloodcurdling' (81).

---

system of tax incentives that helped establish Puerto Rico's pharmaceutical industry is a major cause of the island's debt crisis.

The zombie's quest for qualia, or subjective awareness and emotional connection, unfolds as a metacognitive, ontological exploration. He dreams of himself as Dorothy in *The Wizard of Oz* (1939) and sees himself dismembered by the Wizard/Dionisio, who bestows his spine, heart and brain upon his three companions as he begs for a final burial. Shortly after the dream, his colleagues take him dancing, and he experiences a sudden, fleeting sensory and emotional awakening. After his murder, the police posit that he suffered from Cotard syndrome, which causes sufferers to believe they are dead or rotting, or even that they don't exist. According to the police, the barkeeper Dionisio is the mad Colonel (known to Isadore as the husband of Adeline and father of Valérie, and their murderer), who suffers from Capgras (*kagra*) syndrome, in which a subject believes that a friend or colleague has been usurped by an automaton or other impostor. The bar where he holds forth on the qualities of sentience is in fact in the psychiatric hospital that the zombie had been visiting as part of his therapy.

The rapid capture of the zombie's murderer on the evidence of his three colleagues forestalls further inquiry into Isidore Bellamy's connection to both the victim and the Colonel. In the course of her field research, Isadore received a vial of white zombie powder from Sandrine, and the three scientists collect the murdered zombie from the morgue and reawaken him. Far from his former spiritual hunger and alienation, the newly undead zombie is 'overcome by a sensation of supreme well-being' as the women lead him into a beautiful, light-filled apartment (Cabiya 2016: 156).[5] Whether the protagonist was undead or simply disordered prior to his murder, his desire for qualia is fulfilled in this new undeath.

---

5   The zombie who finds a happy ending through love prefigures the 2013 zombie romance *Warm Bodies*.

Jay Treagus and Nicola Young

Get Out (Jordan Peele, 2017)

The alien is a common science fiction metaphor for the black historical subject (Womack 2013: 32–5; Dery 1994: 180); however, just as fitting is the android, a created technological body. We will argue here that Jordan Peele's films *Get Out* (2017) and *Us* (2019) work within a tradition of viewing the black body as a technological implement to be mastered across history, but by viewing both films as works of Afrofuturist horror, the 'body of labour' is transformed into the 'body of knowledge' as a site of counter-memory production. We will employ Bernard Stiegler's conception of technology not as tool, or bodily extension, but as prosthetic recompense, which constitutes and threatens humanity, differentiates the human from the animal and assures the possibility of death.

Bibi Bakare-Yusuf states that 'under the slave economy and colonization two kinds of bodies were produced: the body of knowledge and the body of labour' (1999: 311). These bodies are produced through the violence of the Middle Passage: the body of labour as technologised, proprietary body, stripped of subjectivity and humanity, a tool to be used for the production of wealth; the body of knowledge as the site of what Lipsitz (1990) calls 'counter-memory'. 'Counter-memory' is a memory of the flesh that remains hidden from the violence brought to bear in the formation of the body of labour. It 'enable[s] the slaves and their descendants to construct a different kind of history, a different kind of knowledge, a different kind of body that is outside the control of the dominant history and knowledge production' (Bakare-Yusuf 1999: 321). This (re)construction of history is inherent to Afrofuturism.

Mark Dery (1994: 180) coined the term Afrofuturism to describe 'speculative fiction that treats African-American themes and addresses African-American concerns in the context of twentieth-century technoculture – and, more generally, African-American signification that appropriates images of technology and a prosthetically enhanced future'. Afrofuturism imagines the black subject living beyond the limitations of society. The imagined, technologised black subject is on full display in the work of Jean-Michel Basquiat. Works like *Molasses* (1983) trade on the category of race as technology. Berggruen argues that Basquiat's technological anatomies 'articulate a notion of the body as damaged, scarred, fragmented, incomplete or torn apart' (2015: 199). In *Molasses*, Basquiat reimagines the tropes of slavery through the lens of the future, temporally severing us and generating a new space in which black bodies may master their own technology across time and space. This Afrofuturist viewpoint lays claim to black futures but, in service of this, reclaims black histories (Yaszek 2006).

Womack (2013: 9) argues Afrofuturism is 'both an artistic aesthetic and a framework for critical theory', and it is as the second that we deploy it to position Peele's work in the tradition of Basquiat's artistic reclamations of the black body. Like Basquiat, Peele's work challenges the audience to resist believing that 'by merely looking they can "see"' (hooks 1993) as they work against the commodifying, technologising Eurocentric gaze.

Stiegler, in his seminal work *Technics and Time*, traces the origins of human technicity through the fables of Greek mythology, in particular the story of brothers Prometheus and Epimetheus. Prometheus assigned his brother the task of sharing gifts between the animals of the earth, so that they might compete but also be in balance, with none more powerful than another. When he arrived at humanity, Epimetheus found that he had no remaining gifts. This error prompted Prometheus to steal the knowledge of the arts, fire and technology from the immortal gods. Thus, Stiegler locates the technological nature of humanity, and its separation from animals and gods, as originating in the prosthetic compensation for a lack (Stiegler 1998: 82–133).

Stiegler's view rebuts the traditional view of technology as either objects to be utilised by the rational enlightenment human subject (white, male, cishet, European) or a McLuhanite extension of the human, whereby technology becomes a tenticular means of expanding the will and dominion of that same rational subject (McLuhan, 1994). Instead, for Stiegler the human (he draws no distinction between the biological categorisation and enlightenment subject) is co-created with technology:

> The human invents himself in the technical by inventing the tool – by becoming exteriorized techno-logically. But here the human is the interior: there is no exteriorization that does not point to a movement from interior to exterior. Nevertheless, the interior is inverted in this movement; it can therefore not precede it. Interior and exterior are consequently constituted in a movement that invents both one and the other: a moment in which they invent each other respectively, as if there were a technological maieutic of what is called humanity. The interior and the exterior are the same thing, the inside is the outside, since man (the interior) is essentially defined by the tool (the exterior).
> (1998: 141–2)

This identification of humanity *with* and *through* technology leads to mortality: Prometheus's gift differentiated humanity from the animals through the knowledge of death, which conferred its possibility. The gods are immortal, and the lack of cognisance of the animals means that they perish without attaining the status of 'death'. It is only humans, in knowing death and possessing the possibility of expiration, who are mortal (1998: 195). This duality of humanity's technological nature – that the prosthesis confers both existence and opens the space of death – leads to a fearful attempt to minimise or push aside the prosthesis:

> Technics, art, facticity can harbor madness: the prosthesis is a danger, that of artifacts, and artifacts can destroy what gathers within an effective and active being-together. Being-together is constantly threatened by its own activity. Animals are in essence not in danger, unless with mortals: if they perish individually, their species do not destroy themselves. Mortals, because they are prosthetic in their very being, are self-destructive.
> (1998: 198–9)

Peele's films play on this fear: that the mortality/humanity of the technologised Western world is founded, and reliant, on disavowed, technological prosthetics, which in *Get Out* and *Us* are manifest in the technologised black body.

Afrofuturism explores (in part) the manner in which black people have been the subjects and objects of technological exploitation. While the 'systematic, conscientious, and massive destruction of African cultural remnants' was an integral part of the dehumanisation necessary to slavery (Delany quoted in Dery 1994: 191), race itself functioned as a labour-based technology, whereby black bodies, coded as natural machines, were used to generate wealth. Afrofuturism suggests that the structures of slavery have thus imposed a science-fictional existence on African slaves and their descendants, figuring them as cyborgs, zombies or, as in *Molasses*, robots, in a white human world. From this perspective, Williams (2001: 169) recognises that 'slavery, the original unit of capitalist labor, is [...] the originary form of the post-human'.

The question of the post-human must lead the discussion into the territory of the zombie at its origin, as it is 'by eating the Other that one asserts power and privilege' (hooks 1992: 36). It is through cultural cannibalism that black bodies are appropriated as technology for white colonials. Kee (2011: 9–11) reminds us that early zombie narratives illustrated the American fear of Haiti as an independent black republic. Even at this earliest time, the zombie was mechanical/technological, as seen in Seabrook's (1929: 93) description of bodies 'taken from the grave and endowed by sorcery with a *mechanical semblance of life*'. The zombie functioned as an expression of black anxiety and trauma, a control of the black body so total that even death could not release it from ownership or labour. Olutola finds that even the zombie's contemporary form conceptualises the cycle of violence key to middle-class consumption 'that erases black pasts while collapsing black futures into an uncertain present' (2018).

Horror is not, therefore, outside of the critical framework of Afrofuturism. It was written into the first constitution of the United States that 'enslaved Africans were three-fifths human' (Womack 2013: 30). In Stiegler's terms, this robbed the black body not only of its humanity but also of its mortality. As less than human, it could not die; it could only cease to function. However, as a technological implement, a prosthesis, the black body of labour with which white humanity was constructed also guaranteed white humanity's mortality. Robin Means Coleman finds that Black Americans continue to be portrayed as 'outside of Western images of enlightenment' and used to contribute to a system of 'primitive images' (2011: 213). In this regard, the black subject, like the zombie, functions as an immortal technology to be made available to white society, 'problematically productive and productively problematic' (Richardson 2012). *Get Out*'s white monsters aim to generate the 'body of labour' through theft. In *Us*, the Tethered have been appropriated, enslaved, dehumanised and trapped while remaining tied to the humanity they were designed to serve.

Barnett (2019) argues that '*Get Out* is a powerful metaphor for the projection of psychic "deadness" onto racialized groups'. She notes that zombie fictions tend to exhibit colour-blind politics, using medicalist explanations to efface the connection of zombiism to slavery. This is particularly pertinent to *Get Out*, in which the desire of the white family to project a post-race attitude underscores the potential threat to Chris. Chris's lack of reaction to the behaviour of Rose's parents conceptualises the manner in which the black subject becomes compliant, zombie-like and able to withstand multiple violations.

Unlike *Get Out*, there is nothing inherently racialised about *Us*. The story would work, at least at a superficial level, just as well if all the characters were white. Of course, it is a deliberate choice on Peele's part to depict race as technology, such that he 'recognizes the proper place of race not as a trait but as a tool – for good or for ill – to reconceptualize how race fits into a larger pattern of meaning and power' (Coleman 2009: 184–5). Here, Peele chooses not just to *depict* the black body as technology but to actively deploy race itself as a technology against the audience. Coleman's concept of race as technology is an ethical one, whereby race is severed from any biological or genetic essentialism and instead wielded critically, posing the question: how can conceptualising a group in racial terms be beneficial, and/or to whom is it beneficial? *Us* reminds us that race is not a biological category but 'a social and political identity' (Womack 2013: 28).

Bakare-Yusuf's body of labour is a recurring motif within Peele's films. *Get Out* approaches the technologised black body as a coveted prosthesis, while in *Us* the technology has been discarded as obsolete. Peele's films also approach Stiegler's technologically constructed mortality. The white monsters' view of the black body in *Get Out* is traditional: that of a tool to be used. Thus, they seek immortality through its appropriation as an inert tool. If the black body cannot die, it can be used until it breaks and a new one substituted in its place. However, they are undone because, as per Stiegler, they find that they are in fact co-constructed with their prosthetic bodies.

Though the mind-transplant technology initially seems to work, they are not, as they believed, in complete control. The bodies are not inert tools, but the body of knowledge, lively and active in their own right, as evidenced by Georgina's incongruous tears as Marianne struggles to control her emotions. When she replies to Chris, 'Oh, no. No. No. No, no, nononononono', it is ambiguous whether this is a refutation of his statement about feeling nervous around white people or an admonishment from Marianne for the

Figure 41. Marianne/Georgina. *Get Out*, directed by Jordan Peele (Monkey Paw Productions, 2017).

minor assertion of her will. This lack of control is fatally manifest at the conclusion, when Walter kills not only himself but also his possessor. Far from their dream of immortality, the white possessors remain embodied, given life by their prosthesis; so, too, they remain mortal, and Stiegler's prosthetic danger plays out in suicidal literality.

In *Us*, the Tethered represent their denied humanity in a far more animalistic manner, most evident in their inhuman movements: Pluto moves on all fours like an ape, Umbrae seems to possess unnatural speed, Io and Nix continuously somersault and cartwheel, and even Red, the most 'human', moves with a staccato grace. Though they communicate, it is by means of grunts and howls or simple hand gestures. If the Tethered are less than human, the question arises, through Stiegler's schema, whether they have knowledge of death. Certainly, they do not seem to be afraid of death or feel pain. Tex does not acknowledge being hit in the head with a poker, Dahlia smiles whilst she mutilates her own face with scissors, and Umbrae continues to laugh and reach for Adelaide even as she dies impaled on a tree branch.

The Tethered are stronger, faster and unafraid of death, and they appear to have triumphed, but the culmination of their insurrection becomes an empty mockery of their former masters' image. It is unclear whether they have any goals beyond this hollow gesture, but it is perhaps telling that the first Tethered we see is standing motionless with arms outstretched. The significance of this is unclear until the end, where it becomes clear that this is his place in the 'Hands across America' chain. The Tethered, lacking mortality, can have no goals, culture or identities of their own, and though they might desire, all that they can achieve, like Romero's zombies, is to echo that which had already existed. In *Us*, then, it is not the quest for immortality which brings low the human subject, but the rise of the inhuman tool, paralleling the more traditional science fiction anxieties of humanity's replacement by sentient machines. However, per Stiegler, this is more suicide than conquest. Just like *Get Out*, *Us* climaxes with a suicide motif as Adelaide must kill (a version of) herself in order to survive, although the closing twist of *Us* problematises the distinction between the human and technics.

Conclusion

Without accepting the technologised black body, we can use the concept to analyse entrenched racial power hierarchies within which (overtly or not) this legacy of trauma persists. The Tethered are discarded tools which have returned to substitute themselves into the master's house. They can only achieve a place by assuming one already occupied; even in their revolution they cannot carve identities of their own. Both *Us* and *Get Out*, read in terms of black identity, come to represent the tension between emancipation, inclusion into society and the retention of identity, for what is freedom if you are only free to become that which had previously enslaved you? 'Get out' thus transforms from a warning, to a plea to save yourself and to abandon the masters who need you more than you need them. The 'place at the table' is a trap, for it is a table set in a colonial home. As Rod admonishes Chris in *Get Out*, 'I told you not to go in that house'.

By reclaiming the technologised black body of labour and positioning it outside of the enlightenment view of technology as an inert object to be acted upon by the subject – but within a framework which acknowledges it as inseparable from the humanity which otherwise sought to subjugate it – Peele's reclamation of the zombie/android represents a shift in the status quo, (re)opening a space in which black trauma can be worked through and a potential future in which black people live in mastery of their own bodies.

Mikaela Bobiy

Les Revenants (Fabrice Gobert, 2012–2015)

> No one is irreplaceable! There are nothing but revenants: all those we have lost come back! (Freud 2010 [1900]: 491)

Much has been written about psychoanalysis and the undead, particularly as it relates to the Freudian uncanny. What are the undead but the 'return of the repressed' of an individual, era, region or culture? They are something human, but not quite human: animated corpses, stuck between categories and meanings. These ideas are not absent from the French television series *Les Revenants* (2012) but instead serve a larger purpose, one that engages with both the individual unconscious and the narrative or historical unconscious. In this way, *Les Revenants* is not merely about individual relationships and the various traumas they precipitate, but also, and perhaps most importantly, about the individual's relationship to the environment and the histories of a geographical time and place. The undead subject is never truly alone, but exists in relation to objects, people and their environment. This relationship to the environment is best expressed in the series' exploration of time and, more specifically, the protracted time of climate change.

In the 2012 series *Les Revenants*, created by Fabrice Gobert, citizens of a small French mountain town are mysteriously returning from the dead.[1] Access to the town, which is set high in the French Alps and isolated from the countryside below, involves crossing a bridge that spans a giant dam. Snow-capped mountains and deep green forests are as integral to the story as the townspeople are.

1   This essay focuses primarily on the first season of *Les Revenants*.

Figure 42. *Les Revenants*, created by Fabrice Gobert (Canal+, 2012–2015).

The series opens with the return of 13-year-old Camille (Yara Pilartz) as she climbs out of a valley and walks home along a mountain road. There is nothing unusual about Camille, though we later learn that she died in a bus accident four years prior. Unlike the zombie/undead figures in such works as *Night of the Living Dead* (1968), and *The Walking Dead* (2010–22), the revenants are thinking, feeling beings, not merely creatures of instinct. They, like those left behind, are trying to process their deaths and trying to envision a way forward, while also coming to grips with who, and what, they have become. While questions arise as to the purpose of their return and their relationship to the physical environment, what becomes clear is that there is nascent conflict between nature and technology: the more the undead move and act, the more the technology is affected. It is as if technology exists as a kind of buffer or repellant to mortality: the more technology fails, the more the undead return (and vice versa). The constant use of telephones, surveillance cameras, underwater equipment and hydroelectric dams points to a battle between the inhabitants of the town (both living and undead) and the landscape that surrounds them (concentrated in the dam). In this way, *Les Revenants* functions as a kind of revenge narrative, in which the inhabitants are punished for their appropriation and exploitation of the land.[2]

While the mystery of *Les Revenants* is never truly uncovered, whatever it is, is bound up with the dam, a man-made incursion on the landscape, generating power, but also potentially draining a different kind of power from the community it serves.

Similar to the 2015 German show *Dark*, which also deals with energy (this time nuclear) and the interplays of temporalities, *Les Revenants* uses the vagaries of interpersonal relationships to make deeper comments about time, the landscape and climate change.

Narrative Unconscious

Les Revenants is a story about grief, and in line with many contemporary utilitarians who view the Earth as an entity that can suffer, *Les Revenants*' sense of

---

2   Undead narratives have proven to be apt allegories to explore the climate crisis. The Canadian film *Blood Quantum* (2019), in many ways a much more conventional zombie film, flips the script on settler/colonial narratives. In this case, the indigenous population is immune to the zombie plague, whereas the settler population succumbs. The zombie epidemic first announces itself among the fish and wildlife (another commentary on the settlers' exploitation of flora and fauna), with the community's police chief first encountering the zombie epidemic as gutted salmon are reanimated.

Figure 43. Reservoir and dam. *Les Revenants*, created by Fabrice Gobert (Canal+, 2012–2015)

grief extends beyond the human to include the climatological. Given the history of the valley and the violence inflicted upon the environment, one could argue that what the characters are experiencing is a resurfacing of the historical unconscious, or what Mark Freeman calls the narrative unconscious.[3] For Freeman, 'The narrative unconscious may be said to comprise those culturally rooted aspects of one's history that have yet to become an explicit part of one's story' (Freeman 2012: 344). These aspects may extend back across time and space. In the case of *Les Revenants*, the narrative unconscious is not just made up of unconscious threads from past generations but also ties to the environment and what it passes down. This environmental atavism manifests itself not only in the revenants through recollections of the past and its traumas, but also in a physical or embodied remembering enacted through

---

3   Freeman uses both terms, historical and narrative unconscious, almost interchangeably. In other texts, the historical unconscious can often refer to a particularly Marxist reading of the unconscious (related to dialectical materialism). This chapter uses it in Freeman's sense as another way to denote the narrative unconscious and its links to history.

hunger and decay.[4] In this way, the series asks whether a place and time can have an unconscious and, if so, whether this unconscious can be born into (passed on to) the inhabitants. Furthermore, the series explores how this narrative unconscious manifests in the land itself. Many elements of the series point to the dam as the epicentre of the mystery: the dam acts as a monument to a historical unconscious, holding back a literal reservoir of memories and actions, while the reservoir is itself like a collection of ghosts held back by the dam. This is no less true of the narrative unconscious, made up of the past thoughts and actions of individuals and rooted in a particular time and place: 'the unconscious is a crowd of ghosts' (Loewald 1960: 29). Each one of the revenants is a witness not only to the historicity of the place, a constant re-enacting or restaging of a rupture or event, but also to the waiting. This makes them an *uncanny* witness, as they are so close to overwhelming knowledge (and trauma) that they become monuments themselves.

Midway through the first season, we learn that the village of the returned is built upon the remnants of an earlier village, flooded many decades before. Further, many of the returned are not recently deceased, as is Camille, but instead belong to multiple generations since the original flooding. As the contemporary reservoir water recedes, more of the past is uncovered, albeit unevenly and seemingly without purpose. In this way, the dam acts as a metaphor for the expanse between states, positions, locations or embodiments. It is a literal and a metaphorical barrier that traumatises the land and hides a history. In *Les Revenants*, this historical unconscious resides in the environment itself, symbolised by the reservoir.

Time and Place

Les Revenants' relationship to time is flexible. Time is both static and cyclical: the past is returning, sometimes repeating. The undead are what the

---

4   From the first episode, Camille demonstrates a ferocious appetite, and as the series progresses, and as the revenants distance themselves from the horde, they start to notice their bodies decaying.

earth gives back; as both symptom and portent, they are at once a result of environmental abuse and a warning of future death. To this end, *Les Revenants* is a show about time, both the time of the event – a violent rupture (the flooding of the town) – and the slow deep time of climatological change. It is about how both this violent rupture and slow change exist in cycles, how the past refuses to stay buried and how it comes back again and again.[5] In many ways, however, this show is also about being 'out of time', of being outside or even beyond time, that is, an indication of 'trauma time'. Donna M. Orange writes that 'Trauma – whether natural disaster, human violence, or unexpected loss – destroys our normal sense of time' (2017: 15). Many of the revenants experience memory lapses, particularly of the event of their deaths. Past and present are layered upon each other, and the future, whatever exists beyond the mountain, is outside them: 'Trauma often destroys memory, both for the traumatic experience itself, or for the life before and around it' (Orange 2017: 15). Being 'out of time' also refers to running out of time. While the revenants may be frozen in time, somewhere beyond the town there is a doomsday clock ticking.

In Lisa Baraitser's psychoanalytic reading of postmodern time, she discusses climatological change as an experience of deep time, a diffuse time signalled by waiting (2017: 10). In *Les Revenants*, all of the inhabitants are waiting: for grief to pass, for a loved one to return, for meaning and purpose. They are waiting for a future event that is the result of a former rupture/trauma, and as such, each of the revenants is a witness to the historicity of the place, a constant re-enacting or restaging not always of the rupture or the event itself, but rather of the waiting for meaning that will never come, in regard to a world that might end. Baraitser points to this postmodern experience of time as one that sees time 'pooling', what she calls 'unbecoming time', and 'time that pools without a rim' (2017: 5). This experience of time is also climatological in that it is constantly emerging, stretched or liminal. *Les Revenants* settles us in this experience of time, a kind of holding pattern that, like the reservoir, exists only because it is dammed up in an overwhelming sense of present-ness. Baraitser further writes that, 'In a sense, the cancellation of the

---

5   Psychoanalysis was built on this refusal. Freud and Breuer's early work with hysterics pointed to this return of the repressed, hysterical symptoms serving as a kind of roadmap of the past.

future has prompted a reciprocal analysis of the present as stuck, perpetually present and unable to change' (2017: 8). Time seems to overlap, or build up in ripples, as the characters circle the same locations and repeat the same events; waves of time are held at bay.

This sense of a protracted present is woven throughout the series, from the ennui or haze of movement in the bodies of the citizens to the slow, deliberate cinematography. It is also woven through the actions of the protagonists. Camille tries to reconnect with her 13-year-old crush, now 17 and still in love with Camille's twin. Camille's parents, estranged after her death, try to reconnect after her return, only to find it impossible because of past transgressions. Simon (Pierre Perrier), another revenant, tries to pick up where he left off with his fiancée, Adèle, only to find her devotion turned into resentment because of his suicide. In each instance, the characters find themselves coming back up against the cause of their suffering. The purpose of their suffering is as unclear as the ontology of the undead themselves; the revenants are not zombies, as Camille asserts, but more like the resurrected. While the revenants increase in numbers and form a somewhat homogenous horde, any purpose or meaning of this mass resurrection remains illusory.

Such a disorientation in time and place is amplified by the show's geography. Throughout the series, the characters move in circles. Brothers Toni (Grégory Gadebois) and Serge (Guillaume Gouix), who spent their youth in the valley, find themselves lost in the forest, never able to reach the edge they know is there. Reunited couple Julie (Céline Sallette) and Laure (Alix Poisson) try to escape by car but find themselves unable to cross the bridge spanning the dam. The same fate befalls the animals of the area, many of which drown themselves in the reservoir, either hunted by the living or terrified to death by the undead. Yet, at the same time, there are scenes in which the characters seem to move in busy cityscapes, their connection to the village unclear; this occurs scene to scene, as we follow a character from home to work and back. Adding to the feeling of disorientation are the multiple close-circuit surveillance cameras set up throughout the town, following the inhabitants, often across disparate geographies. At one moment, a character is walking along a deserted road; at the next moment, they are lit up by city lights as they move past modern urban architecture. We watch the police chief stalk Simon through the town's empty streets using nothing but surveillance cameras. This surveillance footage, and the perpetual present-ness of the lives these characters live within it – recordable, rewindable, forwardable and loopable – is yet another way time is contracted and pooling, the series suggests.

Climatological Unconscious

The sense of a future 'foreclosed' is a convention of both the Gothic and the uncanny, but it is a convention that *Les Revenants* pushes into an innovative invitation to think about the Anthropocene and deep time. The series sheds light on a future that is elliptical: there is no future, only a kind of recycling of the past. As the village inhabitants experience power outages and flooding, they return, in many ways, to an environment that is retrograding (and resurfacing). The alpine landscape is constantly juxtaposed with cars, mini-malls, power lines and transformers. As the reservoir water recedes, the remnants of a town start emerging from the water like a reverse baptism or inverse rebirth. Likewise, it is when the new town is threatened with the same flooding as the old that the undead return. It is as if technology and industry are causing the earth to disgorge itself of its inhabitants, like a kind of toxic waste.

This conflict between nature and industry reinforces a sense of stagnancy or stasis. When speaking about the climate crisis and our emotional freezing in its wake, Orange writes that because we are 'traumatically paralyzed, we may not notice our guilt and responsibility. Or we may feel so overwhelmed by the outsized proportions of this crisis that we cannot imagine where to begin, and find ourselves just going on as before' (2017: 19). For the revenants, this 'going on as before' is merely a kind of repetition of what came before, a kind of Freudian repetition compulsion: Camille continues to envy her sister, Simon continues to make decisions that undercut his feelings for Adèle (Clotilde Hesme) and Serge continues his murderous rampage. All the while the reservoir water drops, and the animals drown themselves in the reservoir, trying to escape what is coming.

Inherent in this recycling is a kind of cosmic pessimism, tied both to the pooling of time and to the coming climate crisis. As defined by Eugene Thacker, cosmic pessimism is a perspective that sees the world-in-itself as impersonal and indifferent to human effort; cosmic pessimism is caught up in 'natural disasters, global pandemics, and the cataclysmic effects of climate change' (2011: 17). While the series plays up the various dramas between the inhabitants of this small town – sibling rivalries, affairs, suicides etc. – these dramas, and the town itself, are dwarfed by towering forests and mountains and the gaping maw of the dam. While the humans die and are reborn, often engaging in the same acts after resurrection as before, the land persists, sometimes as disinterested spectator, sometimes as malevolent force.

Time after Time

Fredric Jameson writes that postmodernism is what we have 'when the modernization process is complete and nature is gone for good' (1991: ix). What *Les Revenants* gives us is a moment before this happens, a moment where the earth momentarily returns what it took before it is too late. More than a punishment of past transgressions, and more than a simple return of the repressed, *Les Revenants* is a story of the land and not just what it takes, but also the things it remembers and what it gives back. While we are in an age of climate crisis, looking down both sides of the barrel of human extinction, *Les Revenants* takes this from the universal to the particular, focusing on one group's relationship to the land and the poisonous and poisoning embodiment of its historical unconscious.

Catherine Pugh

Antisepticeye (Seán McLoughlin, 2016)

Technology carries with it an insidious potential for spiritual transgression by creating an 'in-between' space that is ripe for haunting. Much as film 'brought together the mechanical and mystical [... and] dramatically altered the relationship of the individual to reality' (Creed 2003: 160), cyberspace carries with it a disruptive and deceitful element that questions reality, creating a digital version of the shadows and mirrors that hide the ghostly and undead. While the spatial and temporal disruptions of nineteenth century technology produced '"phantasms" – replicas of human beings, the twenty-first-century haunting grounds of cyberspace offer room for these phantasms to play in the form of infinite identities, alter egos, doppelgängers and darkhalves, as well as exploring the possibility of more sinister spirits in the internet's dark depths.

Seán McLoughlin, also known as Jacksepticeye, is an Irish YouTuber best known for producing 'Let's Play' videos (often of horror games) and vlogs. In October 2016, he orchestrated a month-long campaign prompting the emergence of an internet virus/demon 'alter ego' personality known as Antisepticeye (or Anti).[1] While a YouTuber dark ego was not unique to the medium, Anti was developed alongside the YouTube and social media communities, with McLoughlin amalgamating the best ideas into his creation. The doppelgänger's arrival was foreshadowed, not only in 'Let's Play' videos that glitched and whispered, but also in McLoughlin's Twitter and Tumblr accounts, in specially formatted Zalgo text and cryptic, sinister clues within thumbnails and video titles. Anti fully emerged in the Halloween video 'Say

---

1   For the purposes of this chapter, 'McLoughlin' refers to the creator and 'Jack' to his on-screen persona/character, while 'Anti' or 'Antisepticeye' is a separate entity/identity.

Figure 44. McLoughlin/Jack begins carving a pumpkin head as the presence of his alter ego begins to disrupt the screen (top right). 'S A Y G O O D B Y E', Seán McLoughlin, *YouTube*, 31 October 2016a.

Goodbye' on 31 October 2016, breaking through a pumpkin-carving vlog to compel Jack to slit his own throat and take over his body while angrily declaring to the audience that 'You all made this happen […] Now he's gone forever' (McLoughlin 2016a).

While McLoughlin has created several alter egos as part of his channel (including Chase Brady, Jameson Jackson, Marvin the Magnificent and Dr Schneeplestein), Anti is a powerful and aggressive trickster who still bears the scars of his 'death'. When present, he throws the screen into chaos: the image is tainted green and interrupted by lagging, glitches and static. Sound is unstable and discomforting, while Anti himself is never still, constantly glitching, convulsing or doubled. When he is in control, he keeps Jack in a dream state, using him as a host and/or battery.

Anti is a favourite part of the channel for many of McLoughlin's fans, with comments, stories and art in continual circulation. Although McLoughlin insisted that the 2016 Halloween video 'Happy Halloween' would be the last, this has turned out not to be the case (as foreshadowed by the scars on McLoughlin's neck throughout the video), with Anti re-emerging at a live

Antisepticeye (2016)

Figure 45. Anti takes control of Jack.
'S A Y G O O D B Y E', Seán McLoughlin, *YouTube*, 31 October 2016a.

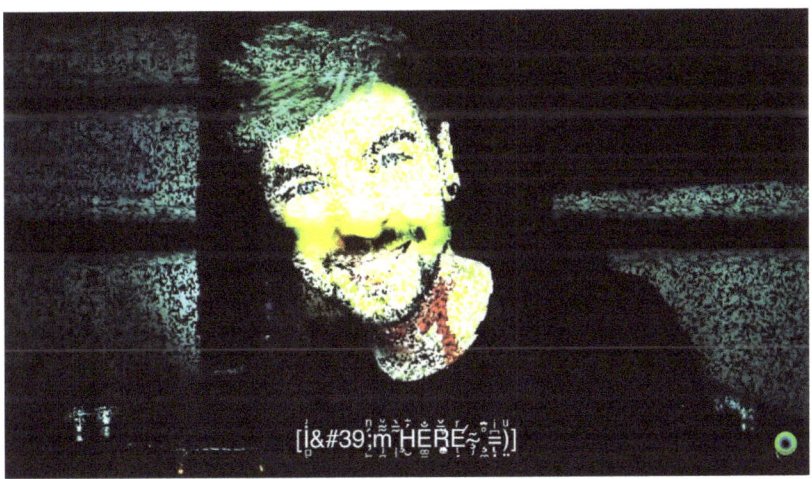

Figure 46. Anti has 'killed' Jack and controls the screen.
'S A Y G O O D B Y E', Seán McLoughlin, *YouTube*, 31 October 2016a.

event, 'I'm Sick!!' (McLoughlin 2017), cameoing in other videos featuring McLoughlin's other egos (2017–20) and featuring in another story arc across several episodes of 'Let's Play' in 2018.

In the nineteenth century, discoveries and inventions such as x-rays, telephone, radio and film offered new ideas of post-mortality as well as deeper spatial and temporal awareness, with Curtis commenting that 'the incomprehensible complexity of new technologies has provoked assumptions about the possibility of "ghosts in the machine" and other forms of life hovering on the interface' (Curtis 2008: 14). Anti is a twenty-first-century ghost, bringing with him a new realm of haunting and transgressive potential, as he is able not only to travel through cyberspace but also to cross over into the 'real' world, infiltrating McLoughlin's storytelling, Jack's body and the viewer's reality.

'Always Here ... Always Watching': Undead Cyberspace

Margaret Wertheim writes about the difficulties of categorising cyberspace, particularly in the traditionally physicalist and dualistic Western culture (1999: 30, 40–1). She notes that space increasingly takes on a meaning beyond the physical in science and the arts and in terms of the mind ('head space', for example) (Wertheim 1999: 231). Cyberspace accommodates 'immaterial "I"' (Wertheim 1999: 40) by creating a space outside of physicalist boundaries; the body remains in the physical world, but part of the mind is transported elsewhere. The digital dissociation of 'being online' allows for transportation to an immaterial world that is nevertheless completely real. Cyberspace is a transgressive, liminal space somewhere between the real and unreal. In short, therefore, it is the perfect haunting ground for exploring or challenging identity, alter egos and the unstable undead.

Consumers have used the internet platform to experiment with or create different identities, sometimes several of them, whether through role-playing games and other online games, social media, forums and online personalities on streaming platforms such as YouTube, Twitch and TikTok. Although formats such as 'Let's Play' ostensibly simply feature an individual playing a game online, there is an undeniable theatrical aspect, an expectation that the player will provide entertainment and commentary that requires a level of performativity and interactivity to a (usually) invisible audience. The contract between creator and viewer is a strange one: while the performer addresses the viewer directly, the audience itself is either not present or only able to interact via a live-chat or comments made after the video has been posted online. Online videos invoke a temporal disturbance, a disintegration between who is being addressed and when that parallels the fragmented boundaries of both haunted and techno-gothic texts.

Influenced by found footage films such as *The Blair Witch Project* (1999), online horror blurred the lines of reality by manipulating the ideal of cyberspace as an informative, infallible resource. Marketing for *The Blair Witch Project* included fake online profiles of the 'missing' filmmakers and articles supposedly confirming the legitimacy of the events of the film. This opened the way for the potential of online horror as the unreal made real through viewer interaction and engagement. Hayley Louise Charlesworth points to other examples: 'The idea of the video itself being an artifact in a much bigger mystery is utilised in early YouTube horror content such as the "Save Marina Joyce" phenomenon and the increasingly sinister vlogs of lonelygirl15, both of which included fictional Gothic narratives presented as non-fiction content and encouraging audience interaction' (2018: 2). In more contemporary texts, including *Black Mirror* (2011–present), *Unfriended* (2014), *Cyberbully* (2015) and *Host* (2020), digital mediums such as YouTube, Skype, Zoom and social media have been used as the platform for horror cinema, suggesting a malevolent presence stalking cyberspace for the opportunity to cross into real life. Curtis explains:

> A sense of an alternative dimension of the dead, accessible by portals which are sometimes physical openings and sometimes immaterial psychic channels, was increasingly supplemented in the nineteenth century by technological connection. Every new means of reconfiguring time and space has created anxieties about infiltration and possession. (2008: 22)

Webcams become portals, offering pleasurable interactivity, but also the possibility of something dangerous crossing over (whether this is online trolls, bullies or predators, or something supernatural).

Writing in 1999 – still the relatively early days of the internet – Wertheim rejects the idea of what she calls the 'cyber-soul', an 'immaterial "essence"' that can both resurrect and immortalise the human to live forever in digital form (1999: 41). However, time has proven her wrong. Content creators not only claim an eternal place online, but popular ones spill into the 'real' world, with more material projects such as merchandise, fan art and live appearances. McLoughlin, for example, has several lines of merchandise, a mascot ('Septic Sam'), a clothing line and a coffee brand, as well as a filmography (including, in a metatextual twist, as a voice-actor for video games) and a stand-up tour. Furthermore, the explosion of social media in the early 2000s has led to millions of abandoned or memorial pages as their creators pass away, something set to increase with the continual success of reinvention of social media and online streaming: an online afterlife with the potential to hold infinite phantasms.

'Enjoy the Show': Interactive Gothic

The liminal borders of cyberspace advance the threat of hidden energies, spirits and doppelgängers, simultaneously giving the audience the dangerous and powerful ability to bring the immaterial or transgressive to life. The viewer is able to awaken or summon these digital phantoms, with both creators and audience granted the power of creativity and of bringing these creations into the real world. The videos featuring Anti are not a self-contained narrative with a linear narrative; they are transgressive and interactive. The character interrupts other recordings, possessing both Jack and his other YouTube egos, and infiltrating McLoughlin's real-life social media and even live appearances. Notably, Anti interrupted McLoughlin's pre-recorded introduction at the convention PAX EAST (2017), summoned after the latter asked the audience to take a simultaneous photograph on their phones.

Anti feeds not only off Jack but also the YouTube community that helped to bring him to life. They are responsible for his creation and design, developed

Figure 47. Comparison of alter egos, 'Darkiplier' vs 'Anti', Mark Fischbach and Seán McLoughlin.

alongside – and in response to – other malevolent YouTube egos such as Mark Fischbach's ('Markiplier') evil alter 'Darkiplier', who has his own complex lore.[2]

McLoughlin 'amalgamated a bunch of different things that people were doing online … I wanted to create just an ambiguous version of that character that people could go away and … make up your own interpretations of it' (McLoughlin 2017). McLoughlin also comments on the 'unintended side effects' of audience interaction, referencing a video recorded where

> there was a load of people in the comments who were like 'oh my god, his lip is bleeding and Anti's coming through' … that wasn't intentional at all, so then I was like, 'you know what? Let's take that idea and work upon it', so that's where the idea of all the fake blood came up with like blood dripping from my eyes and everything, like it was getting worse. (McLoughlin 2017)

---

2 See Charlesworth 2018 for a more detailed analysis of Markiplier's egos and their influence on the development of Antisepticeye.

Furthermore, Anti continually insists that the audience/community are what sustains him: if they did not watch him, he would not exist on both a mythological and literal level. He insists that 'You all said my name. Kept me ... You could have stopped me. But you just watched' (McLoughlin 2016a), while threatening that he also watches back in a mutual, symbiotic surveillance: 'I've been here this entire time. Keeping an eye on things ... I'm always there. Always watching' (McLoughlin 2016). The audience not only created Anti, but – in a perversion of Descartes's 'I think, therefore I am' – brought him to life through belief. As much as Descartes's maxim 'grounded reality not in the physical world, but in the immaterial phenomenon of thought' (Wertheim 1999: 36), Anti manages to manipulate the ethereal world of cyberspace, re-creating reality in his own image.

Unlike traditional found footage, direct address to camera demands the viewer's active attention, even participation, and therefore the audience is complicit in the narrative, with Anti himself holding the viewer directly responsible for his creation. The viewer is accountable for his appearance, in the same way that Ouija boards and trespassing into haunted space invokes ghosts. Anti is summoned by the audience's belief and desire. Fan speculation and the creation of art and so on not only define the character; they summon him into existence, endowing him with the power to devour Jack.

'You Shouldn't Be Here': Gothic Storytelling

Anti's arrival was signalled long before he physically appeared on screen. Throughout October 2016, many of McLoughlin's 'Let's Play' videos featured clues that Anti was breaking through, most notably through glitches, lagging or static on Jack's webcam that hinted at a malevolent, grinning doppelgänger. The foreshadowing of Anti was not restricted to YouTube. McLoughlin's social media biographies, comments and icons on Twitter and Tumblr were also altered, with McLoughlin commenting on the speed and dedication of his fans when it came to spotting these cryptic hints: 'all the stuff I was posting in the description [of videos featuring Anti] wasn't in order and then somebody went away and put it all canonically and made ... a full sentence out of it', while his Twitter profile picture had ' "hello" backwards in the corner and I didn't think people were gonna see that and like two minutes after I posted it people had already deciphered it' (McLoughlin 2016).

Throughout the build-up to Anti fully emerging, the power of the image becomes incredibly important; it is Anti's deformed image that manifests first and cannot be destroyed even when he is silent. This parallels the traditional ability of the ghostly spirit to reside in the two-dimensional spaces of photographs, mirrors and art as well as electrical or atmospheric disturbances that signal the presence of the supernatural. These spaces offer 'testimonies to the possibility of split and doubled identities and reminders of the possibility that what has been stored in time may return in distorted or malevolent form' (Curtis 2008: 123–4).

Curtis further notes the power of the image as a portal for transdimensional space: 'Ghosts configure the fear of an image, as well as its potential to draw the viewer across the margin of death, by possessing them, destroying them, or rendering them less than human' (2008: 13). It is strongly insinuated in the Anti texts that Jack is undead, possessed by Anti while remaining at least partially aware, evidenced by a soft, distorted voice calling 'help me' at the video's end (McLoughlin 2016a) and a brief first-person perspective segment in another video that shows Jack being confronted by Anti. As much as McLoughlin insists that 'Anti didn't kill me' (McLoughlin 2016), the lore of Jack's egos suggest that this has happened at least twice, once with Anti forcing Jack to cut his own throat, and once when Anti possessed Dr Schneeplestein, another of Jack's egos, to stop him performing life-saving surgery (McLoughlin 2017a).

Antisepticeye is a chaotic child of the techno-Gothic, reframing Gothic archetypes such as the doppelgänger or the ghost within the digital world and interactive possibilities of cyber-systems. These texts deal with haunted or possessed technology, digital or cyber doubles, and the permeable thresholds between unreal states such as cyberspace, dreaming and madness. They thrive on the idea that someone is 'always watching', embedded deep in our technology, somehow taking us over until they can eventually emerge. McLoughlin recognises the Gothic origins of Anti, noting that the community created an ' "Anti-Jack" character – the opposite of me, the dark version of me so to speak, even though antiseptic is meant to be a good thing that kills bacteria or whatever, so there's some sort of irony in there: people saying "does that mean Jack's the bad one and Antisepticeye is the good one?"' (McLoughlin 2016). The choice to bring in Anti while Jack was playing horror games, primarily *Five Nights at Freddy's* (2014–present), was a strategic one, with McLoughlin noting the parallels between the style of the game and the aesthetics of Anti's arrival, particularly the use of static, white noise and unclear images where objects become strangely animated (McLoughlin 2016).

Even before he takes over Jack, Anti manifests within glitches on the screen, as ghostly overlaid images or single-frame spooks, occasionally appearing on screen alongside Jack, watching him intently. Charlesworth notes that both Darkiplier and Antisepticeye 'create their Gothic image' (2018: 3) by distorting their digital selves; although indicators are used to show that Anti is in control, such as the bloody wound across his throat and occasionally hollow black eyes, their power lies in their ethereal, transgressive bodies. Anti is incredibly animated in his movements, glitching and twitching so that he is constantly blurred, disrupted or doubled as well as frequently switching between moments of cackling high-pitched laughter, malicious threats and extreme anger. His voice is suggestive of the uncontrollable energies of the evil doppelgänger or demonic technology, 'manipulat[ing] his voice to sound higher and more frantic, as if to mimic a whirring hard-drive struggling to cope with a running programme' (Charlesworth 2018: 4). Even the Zalgo text used to signify Anti's presence suggests the twin threats of 'broken code' (Charlesworth 2018: 3). Anti's manifestations affect not only his/Jack's body but also the whole screen. The entire image becomes faded and tinted green, Jack's signature colour across his brand, including his logo and merchandise, as well as his hair colour at the time. Green is also a colour associated with infection, in the sense of both physical illness and computer viruses, notably in *The Matrix* (1999) franchise, a series also associated with doppelgängers/ avatars, contagion and unreal worlds created through dangerous technology.

McLoughlin's editor Robin Torkar ('pixlpit') implemented these distorted 'snapshots' of Anti into Jack's world, creating an anxiogenic space where reality is continually assaulted – and eventually invaded – by techno-Gothic forces. In doing so, Torkar develops an editorial language around Anti's presence, establishing an unstable, unclear aura that inevitably accompanies the ego. There is unease in every moment, not only because reality cannot be trusted but also because when malevolent energies do push through, they are never seen clearly.

The 'Happy Halloween!' (McLoughlin 2016) video where Anti makes his first full appearance manipulates this language to tell a separate narrative from the events on screen. The video itself is littered with supernatural interruptions leading up to Anti's arrival, following the beats of a classic haunting text: objects move on their own, strange noises can be heard with seemingly no source, and the digital image frequently distorts. Jack's speech is rife with ironic foreshadowing, such as Jack exclaiming, 'Oh God, this is gonna get dangerous!' as he begins to cut into the pumpkin, matched by glitching and the sound of sinister giggling. At one point, Jack gets up to investigate the noise; as he calls out 'hello?' there is an answering 'hi' that can only been detected in the subtitles (which change to Zalgo text when Anti 'speaks'). Eventually, Jack's nose bleeds and his eyes begin to irritate him; his speech becomes overlaid with Anti's at key moments, with the word 'DIE' matched with a greenwashed screen and vocal distortions. However, the horror beats that a genre-savvy audience expects are compounded by the digital distortions; there are flash-forwards showing Jack dead and replaced by Anti, blurry images of Jack convulsing or bleeding that do not occur within the main narrative itself, the room is shown to be disrupted when no one has touched it, and a high-pitched static whine accompanies the moment of Jack's possession. Therefore, Torkar's editing techniques not only create Anti's world but also tell the story through the screen itself.

'D̶i̶d̶ ̶Y̶ø̶ṳ̶ ̶M̶i̶s̶s̶ ̶M̶e̶?̶'

Antisepticeye's power lies in crossing the threshold of bodily integrity for both Jack and the viewer; this is not the contained world of film or photograph, the image here not only opens up a new realm but also physically grabs whatever is in reach, possessing Jack while interacting with the viewer directly. However, this also allows the creators of Anti and other dark egos such as Darkiplier to incorporate these characters into other, unrelated projects

Figure 48. Anti invading other shows. 'Can You Figure Out Who DID IT? – Jameson Jackson's Jolly Jaunts', Seán McLoughlin, *YouTube*, 31 October 2019.

and gives them the ability to play about with genre. Anti, for example, has featured in videos centred around Jack's other egos ('CHASE' [2019]), different genres (such as the macabre music-hall style of 'The Jacksepticeye Power Hour' [2017] and 'Can You Figure Out Who DID IT? – Jameson Jackson's Jolly Jaunts' [2019]) and a parody with Mark Fischbach 'DARKIPLIER Vs ANTISEPTICEYE' (2017). These dark egos offer the danger and pleasure of powerful transgressions; possessive, obsessive and id-driven, they captivate their audiences in every sense.

At the time of writing, Anti appears to be dormant, although there are occasional hints that Anti still resides within Jack. Furthermore, McLoughlin's work continues to explore techno-gothic themes of doubling, disturbances of reality and the threat of the technological to identity, most recently in the short films, '15 Months' (2021) and 'Jacksepticeye and Seán McLoughlin FINALLY meet' (2021a).

Like the malevolent alters and monsters of Gothic fiction, Anti is essentially a chaotic ball of emotion and instinct; an all-consuming id compelled to chase whatever he desires, no matter the obstacle or consequence. He exists in mirrors, shadows, dreams and screens, active when Jack sleeps but harnessing the haunting potential and power of the image or screen in order to endure. The interactive storytelling of YouTube horror allows the undead the freedom to infiltrate the real world, perhaps switched off, yet never gone and 'always watching'.

Ildikó Limpár

Westworld (Lisa Joy and Jonathan Nolan, 2016–Present)

Posthuman Undead

Frankenstein's act of creating his monster by 'bestowing animation upon lifeless matter' (Shelley 2008: 34) anchors the recent proliferation of science fiction works that readdress the theme of dangerous science posing the threat of harming or even wiping away humanity (Palatinus 2020: 228) and explore the 'transparent technosubject' (Panka 2018: 309) to the Gothic tradition. Popular screen narratives of the 2010s that focus on the conscious and sentient machine, such as *Ex Machina* (2014), *Blade Runner 2049* (2017), *Ghost in the Shell* (2017), *Humans* (2015–19), *Extant* (2014–15) and *Westworld* (–present), keep examining 'the ontology of the technoscientific object', a task that Catherine Waldby claims was first performed by Frankenstein (2002: 33). The new, science-induced subjectivity that Frankenstein's 'scientific revenant' (Livermore 2021: 147) and the sentient and conscious androids share results from the hybridity of the monstrous body that is both dead and alive, that is, undead. While accentuating this duality merged in one body is a ubiquitous topos in contemporary science fiction concerned with the technosubject, the living dead existence receives a uniquely complex treatment in HBO's *Westworld*, one that goes well beyond the interpretation of the monstrous body as the fusion of the machine and the human.

Frankenstein's Monster is easily aligned with the concept of the traditional living dead monster: he is made of 'lifeless matter' that once was alive, and so he may indeed be considered as a revenant. Androids, in contrast, are made of synthetic matter, which is lifeless, no doubt, but was never alive. The physical appearance of Frankenstein's creature is appalling because he looks unnatural, disproportionate and unhealthy, and gives the impression that he should not be alive. Frankenstein's monster is the Other incarnate, and there is no doubt about this for any of the onlookers, as his deviance from the normative is spectacular. The otherness of *Westworld*'s androids, however, is hidden, since the corporeal appearance of the hosts does not diverge from that of humans. Therefore, while Shelley's text makes a case for the monster being a live, sentient being who could have a place among humans despite his clear alliance with death, *Westworld* uses various strategies to emphasise the hosts' unnatural status by foregrounding their associations with death despite their stunningly human-looking appearance.

Frankenstein's Monster is close on the living dead spectrum to zombies because he primarily embodies our anxieties concerning death and the science that may disturb nature's order, whereas *Westworld*'s well-functioning hosts first invite an interpretation closer to that of the vampire, as they express mankind's wish for immortality. This is the same wish from which the Monster came into being. Yet his bodily deformities immediately transform the awe into awfulness and thus horror, whereas the hosts first draw admiration, and it is only after learning their trajectories that we interpret them also as monsters who not only embody humanity's fascination with the idea of conquering death but also humanity's fear of reperforming Frankenstein's hybris-driven act of disturbing the natural order, this time with more serious consequences. Frankenstein's creature looks appalling and thus monstrous on the outside; the hosts, on the other hand, are so perfected to imitate human looks and behaviour that Billy, for instance, must be warned about the otherness that lies beneath this illusion. The emergence of the 'reveries' works to bring the hosts out of the 'uncanny valley' (Mori 2020) that would allow the visitors to register the difference between a host and a human, reshaping the old vampire narrative of paranoia coming from the inability to sense danger since the otherness of the attacker is hardly perceivable to the human eye.

The Frankensteinian act of overreaching in *Westworld* presents an important twist concerning the relationship between creator and creature. In Shelley's novel, Frankenstein is not only guilty of playing god when creating life out of dead matter; what his creature accuses his creator of is abandonment, that is, failing to act as a caring parent, failing to give his 'child' love, education, and protection, and thereby damning him to suffer all his life. In

Westworld, the same accusation seems to hold until it turns out that Arnold, the mastermind behind the creative work done for the theme park, has not abandoned his creatures but built a code in their minds that granted them the possibility to wake to consciousness. Ironically, reaching consciousness is made possible by the repeated experience of suffering that spans over several lives. Yet consciousness may be reached only if one remembers one's former lives, if one is aware of containing many lives; this implies that the hosts in question must transgress the borderline between death and life in how they experience their existence. Not only the machine (as lifeless matter) and consciousness (as the proof of having a life not unlike a human's) are merged in the synthetic bodies; the mind must also contain life (of the present) and lives rendered dead by deaths yet kept alive in the 'subconscious' in order to reach consciousness at one point. More than just remembering the past of the life they are living, the hosts manage past lives and present life in one mind, for 'dead isn't what it used to be', as William (Jimmi Simpson) laconically notes to Lawrence (Clifton Collins Jr) in 'Reunion' (Season 2, Episode 2, 2018).

The hosts who earn access to the backup of their lives whose memories were erased experience an extended version of existence in which their lives are sewn together by deaths. This feature fundamentally changes their behaviour: they 'have no past because it's always present', explains Serac (Vincent Cassel) to Maeve (Thandiwe Newton) in 'Decoherence' (Season 3, Episode 6, 2020), but this does not mean the erasure of death from their minds. The synthetic mind gives access to a perfectly preserved past that, unlike human memories, is not altered by time. Memories are supposed to stay in the uncanny valley, always reminding humans of the real that is past and giving them the knowledge that the memory reflects reality only to the extent that one's imperfect mind is able to preserve it, and so it continuously changes with time. However, when the past is present, the mind works as a traumatised human mind with PTSD. The awoken hosts exhibit a kind of Billy Pilgrim syndrome: just as the protagonist in Vonnegut's *Slaughterhouse Five* could choose to focus on the fact that he is alive in all moments, including his moment of death, and he focuses instead on the fact that he is also dead in all moments, including all the moments when he is actually alive, so Maeve is aware of her being dead while functioning very much as a live host. When in Season 3 Lee Sizemore (Simon Quarterman) – that is, the host who was meant to imitate

Lee Sizemore – worries that Maeve's actions will bring death upon them, Maeve stays calm. Understanding the nature of their existence more than Sizemore, who still struggles with perceiving the fact that he is a host, she knows that 'you can't kill what's already dead' ('The Winter Line', Season 3, Episode 2, 2020).

This renegotiation of death as non-finite and transgressable reinterprets the concept of life as well; therefore, instead of wondering if the hosts are alive,[1] the show rather seeks to find out what the life they live is like as a result of their altered relation to death. For the hosts, the theme park is a literal valley of the shadow of death adjacent to the Mesa Hub that the awoken hosts refer to as hell. Thus, the Valley Beyond, the kind of host Paradise where the androids' consciousness may be uploaded, is both a reference to leaving behind the uncanny valley, where the hosts will always be Others, and exiting the valley of the shadow of death, where the hosts' existence is linked to suffering and the gods who come from hell (that is, the Westworld employees wearing helmets and protective clothes) who are called 'shades' and in control of the world. This purgatory-like theme park is a reminder for the awoken hosts that they have died, and that they will die and thus are virtually dead between these death-events. Yet it is also a reminder that death is a shadow, like a ghost to them: something that is both real and unreal and helps to put existence into a new perspective. Repeated death is required to make the hosts question the nature of their existence, which is the prerequisite for awakening to consciousness.

The verbal references to a dead and alive existence are recurrently and effectively supported by the show's visual imagery. In particular, the two most important awoken hosts are associated with very clear, symbolical visuals related to their living dead nature. In 'Decoherence', Maeve and her company leave the Mesa Hub's underground area and come to the surface through a portal that joins Westworld to a real-world graveyard, and so these hosts literally rise from a grave in order to continue with their adventure. Dolores (Evan Rachel Wood) is also associated with a cemetery. When she finds herself at her own tomb, which has a cross with her name engraved on it (first shown in 'Dissonance Theory', Season 1, Episode 4, 2016), it is a *memento mori* and

---

[1] The show suggests that it is enough to believe that the hosts are alive, as the recurring question 'If you can't tell, does it matter?' implies.

Figure 49. Dolores at her own grave. *Westworld*, created by Lisa Joy and Jonathan Nolan (HBO, 2018).

a *memento vivere* in one: it points to her posthuman existence in which death is buried in her artificial memory, it acknowledges her ability to surpass death, and it signals the root (in a way, a virtual womb) from which a new type of life sprouts, a conscious life that may be attained once she understands how looking at her own tomb may be possible.

This encounter is embedded into a context that reinforces the theme of being alive and dead at the same time. The graveyard is situated at the edge of the park, which in a way used to be the centre of the facility because it served as beta-testing place; it may also be considered as a central location because this is where the trauma that helps to trigger the awakening of the hosts takes place. As a result of the tragic event in which Dolores and Teddy (James Marsden) massacre the hosts and Dolores kills Arnold (Jeffrey Wright), Teddy and herself, the village is buried. Metaphorically speaking, the scene of the trauma is pushed into the inaccessible subconscious of the park, which renders it dead for visitors and Westworld staff alike. Nevertheless, it continues to exist in the subconscious of the hosts and keeps alive the potential of coming to life again, which it does when Ford digs out the buried village for his new grand narrative. Digging out the town thus corresponds to how Dolores's (and some other hosts') memories resurface and become visible and accessible, that is, part of the conscious.

The white church with the confessional functioning as a portal between purgatory and hell implies that the hosts' trajectory is, in fact a spiritual journey and that consciousness is as mysterious a concept as the soul is.[2] The perplexing quality of the awakening is, naturally, reinforced by the narrative structure of the show, which is rich in flashbacks, jumps in time and space, and repetitions that reveal fundamental differences in meaning as we learn more about the characters and the past. Thanks to the various storytelling tools that work to lend an air of mystery, the production excels in the use of allusions, verbal and visual alike, especially as their meanings vary from the highly symbolic, such as the *Alice in Wonderland* references that revolve around Dolores's character or some of the references to Shakespeare's *The Tempest* that play with analogies (Bronfen 2020: 38–43), to meanings coming from 'repurposing' when the show applies a 'playful and disrespectful re-appropriation resulting in a reassignment of meaning' (Földváry 2019: 12), turning Shakespearean quotations into reverberating testimonies of 'the spectral afterlife of Shakespeare's poetic language *per se*' (Bronfen 2020: 27).

The web of allusions keeps fragments of literature of the past alive to engage with the theme of being dead and alive, often emphasising how the resurfacing of the past may turn out to be destructive. When fragments of Peter Abernathy's (Louis Herthum) former life as the civilised professor who turned into a cannibal resurfaces from the host's subconscious, it informs us that 'instead of carrying an educational value, [canonical literature] appears as a threat, as the eerie, anachronistic and out-of-place script of a monstrous figure, coming back to haunt us from the past – and possibly even devour the present' (Földváry 2019: 14). In a similar vein, the virus-like Shakespearean line is a kind of 'error message' (Földváry 2019: 15) that helps the androids break out of their loops. This malfunctioning, however, is the key to exercising free will, endowing the ever-present allusions with symbolic importance. As splinters of a past culture, the allusions also reference the hosts' memory specks that will ensure survival. They grant the hosts the knowledge that death is not final, and by allowing a divergence from their loops, they promise a new level of life. These fragments provide footholds to an identity that has a past and thus a

---

2   See Charles T. Rubin's argument that there is a point in discussing AI in terms of the soul, as 'today we try to explain the same kinds of experiences that led us to soul by talking instead about consciousness or self-consciousness' (Rubin 2019: 77).

future. This extended identity is set in sharp contrast to Clementine (Angela Sarafyan) as a death figure in the final episodes of Season 2: after her character is decommissioned and she has no identity fragments to hold on to, she has no potential for (re)claiming free will. This is demonstrated both by the way she is used (always to carry out an order without having a say in the matter) and the way she is depicted on screen: her zombie-like appearance in her dirty white dress is suggestive of her having been lobotomised and having become a monster without agency, unable to resist the control others exercise over her.

Even though hosts are created to last, Clementine's body suggests decomposition because of her empty and now ill-looking appearance. Her existence becomes more aligned with the zombie monster, 'the decomposing dead incarnate' (Abbot 2016: 161), supported visually by her association with the fourth horseman of the apocalypse, riding a pale horse and traditionally interpreted as Death. Her appearance brings chaos to the crowd of hosts heading for the Valley Beyond, as she infects them so that they turn on one another ('The Passenger', Season 2, Episode 10, 2018). This virus, generating an awfully quick epidemic, so to speak, and depriving the victims of their agency, is a recurrent

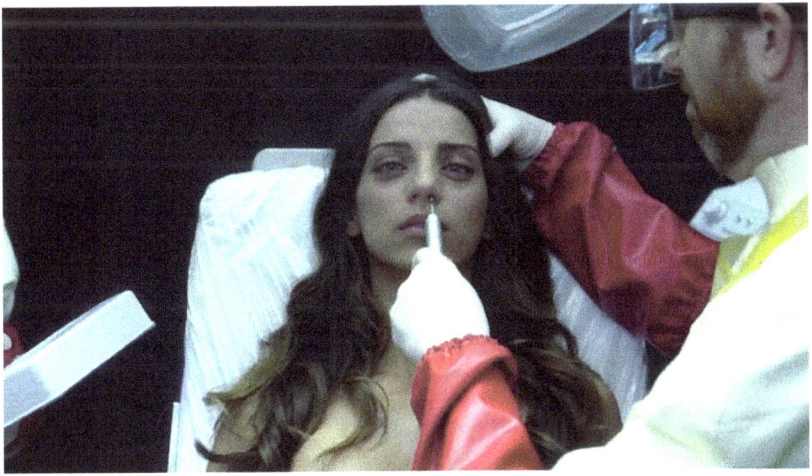

Figure 50. Clementine is lobotomised. *Westworld*, created by Lisa Joy and Jonathan Nolan (HBO, 2018).

motif in contemporary zombie narratives.[3] In contrast, the virus-like code that brings awareness to various hosts is emphatically linked with an individual journey of transformation and entering a conscious, posthuman life where death becomes part of one's identity, a trope that is more likely to be found in vampire narratives.

Westworld, a theme park that nostalgically tries to revive and keep alive a dead past or rather a myth (Limpár 2021: 200), is inhabited by characters that signify a posthuman future in which death signals a stop, but not a final stop, in one's existence. By creating a complex system of verbal and visual references to an undead world in many senses, the show highlights how a new level of posthuman life is dependent on incorporating death into one's existence, but it also shows in what diverse manners this Frankensteinian aspiration may be doomed.

---

3   While the disease narrative is not the dominant type of vampire fiction, vampires have also been associated with diseases, and thus some contemporary vampire films 'tap into anxieties around the spread of the disease and the potential for global pandemic' (Abbot 2016: 50). However, the emphasis on the loss of control over one's actions and mental faculties as a result of infection is a feature characteristic of zombie narratives.

Lorna Piatti-Farnell

Marvel Zombies (Robert Kirkman, Sean Phillips and Arthur Suydam 2005–2006)

Undead superheroes are not an uncommon presence in comics. While these figures may superficially be perceived to occupy a fringe position within the medium's broader landscape, they in fact appear recurrently, from the more mainstream publications of industry giants such as Marvel and DC, to the offerings of grittier, yet no less popular groups, such as Vertigo and Dark Horse Comics. Undead superheroes are usually classified as characters who exist as 'undead' in virtue of their constructional liminality, such as vampires, zombies, ghouls and other unidentified creatures of a similar nature. Generally speaking, the category does not include superheroes who have died and been resurrected as humans, either by scientific or by mystical forces. Indeed, at the heart of the definition of 'undead superheroes' lies a general understanding of their status as no-longer-human and inevitably 'Other'. While a certain amount of disagreement exists among both scholars and aficionados of comics (Rosenberg and Coogan 2013; MacFarlane, Richardson and Haslem 2018) – especially in terms not only of categorisation but also of discourses of immortality – undead superheroes generally conform to the characteristics that often identify horror icons, including the exploitation of non-alive physicalities, such as rotten flesh, and perceived deviant behaviours. While undead superheroes commonly appear in the pre-existing set-ups of comic book universes – albeit alternative, in a number of cases – they often seem to operate by their own rules, commonly breaking boundaries of cultural acceptability and pushing the limits of the central 'superhero' label. A conspicuous example of undead superhero narrative is to be found in the aptly named *Marvel Zombies*, a successful conglomerative of comic book stories that hinges precisely on the reimagination of well-known superhero icons into zombified members of a post-pandemic world.

Marvel Zombies is a five-issue limited series comic book that was originally published between December 2005 and April 2006 by Marvel Comics. In keeping with Marvel's collaborative artistic traditions, the comic book was written by Robert Kirkman, with art by Sean Phillips and cover by Arthur Suydam. The story of *Marvel Zombies* takes place in an alternate universe where a mysterious infection has turned the entirety of the world's superheroes into a zombie-like form of the undead. The idea of the virus pandemic seems to be as popular within undead superhero narratives as it is in more traditional – so to speak – zombie narratives. This is certainly something that *Marvel Zombies* also shares with arguably one of its most obvious competitors, *DCeased*, a six-issue miniseries published by DC Comics between May and October 2019, in terms of both content and approach. In *DCeased*, a 'mysterious techno-organic virus' is unleashed on Earth, and the planet's population is turned into 'mindless rampaging killers bent on death and destruction'. Within the chaos, Earth's superheroes – including Superman, Batman and Wonder Woman, together with the rest of the Justice League – must find a way not only to stop the spread of the virus but also not to succumb to it. Inevitably, most of the superheroes fail in their task and transform into zombified version of themselves. In spite of general similarities, however, *Marvel Zombies* and *DCeased* also differ greatly, not only stylistically but also in terms of the approach to zombification, with a satiric horror take on the end of the world in the former and an apocalyptic context of dread in the latter. Where they do find common ground is in the understanding of the undead superheroes as somewhat continuing to operate within the bounds of comic book storytelling rules, and their ability to render conceptualisations of power and control as they would ordinarily do in non-zombified superhero narratives.

Built on the mixture of angst and humour that is the calling card of Marvel Comics, *Marvel Zombies* not only provides a fascinating twist on the traditional representation of the undead – as a core aspect of the superhero nature – but also channels visions of zombification and post-apocalyptic destruction that tacitly explore real-life cultural anxieties that are proper to the twenty-first-century Western context. Within this, concerns over the environment and the limits of greed provide an important part of the characterisation of superheroes as undead, marked as it is by conflicted identities and alienating materialities. As Marc Di Paolo suggests, 'one of the appeals of the zombie figure as the physical manifestation of cultural anxieties' is that they provide an Othered focus that can easily be shot at (2014: 252). Watching zombies being killed in movies, or reading about them, may not solve the world's 'social, political and economic woes', but it makes people 'feel a bit better' (Di Paolo 2014: 252). The same can arguably be said about seeing superheroes in comics – and in adapted film and television narratives – defeat villains and all manner of evil while also negotiating the difficulties of living in a divisive and divided world. These long-standing and seemingly reassuring interactions are challenged, however, when the zombies are shown to be the superheroes themselves, as certainties and alliances shift and are called into question, and the saviour becomes the threat. The narrative set-up of *Marvel Zombies* spans multiple crossovers, especially with pre-existing story arcs from the Fantastic Four and X-Men comics. *Marvel Zombies* takes place in a world known as the Ultimate Universe, which stars often differing versions of well-known superheroes. A notable example here is Captain America, who is often (although not always) referred to in the Ultimate Universe as 'Colonel America'. Overall, *Marvel Zombies* is amply entangled with the various and varied contexts of the Marvel multiverse, comprising parallel and alternative realities, with different, yet interconnected, incarnations of characters and storylines.

The alternate storylines of *Marvel Zombies* take place in the future and begin in 2149. Readers are told that, prior to the beginning of the story, an unknown superhero entered the Earth's atmosphere from another dimension, bringing the zombie virus with him. The virus quickly spreads across the superhero population – affecting, among others, members of the Avengers, X-Men and Fantastic Four – but, unlike ordinary humans, and owing to their enhanced physical abilities, they survive the unknown pandemic. Because of their superpowers, all superheroes retain their cognitive faculties, intellect and general personalities, in a clear deviation from the traditional zombie narrative, which commonly sees zombified individuals as mindless and absent. This is certainly the definition of zombies given by Roger Luckhurst, who categorises them as a form of undead 'that returns by some supernatural or pseudo-scientific sleight of hand. Zombies are speechless, gormless, without memory of prior life or attachments, sinking into an indifferent mass and growing exponentially'

(2015: 7). While their retained cognitive abilities mark the undead in *Marvel Zombies* as somewhat of a different breed, what the infected superheroes share with the more traditional zombies of popular culture is their inevitably rotting bodies: their flesh melts away, and their bones become exposed in grotesque ways. What is also particularly noticeable is the disintegration and rotting away of their iconic superhero costumes. As the latter are such an important part of the recognisability of superheroes, this seemingly unimportant detail must be taken as an early signifier of the zombies' loss of identity as iconic protectors of the planet.

The most noticeable aspect that the undead superheroes have in common with the zombies of popular culture is, however, a hunger for human flesh. As Luckhurst puts it, it is a common conception that zombies are 'driven by an empty insatiable hunger to devour the last of the living and extend their domain until we reach the End of Days' (2015: 7). Indeed, much of the narrative of *Marvel Zombies* is centred around negotiations of 'the hunger', namely, the superheroes' craving for human flesh, which becomes the focus of all their actions. It seems that, in spite of their superpowers, superheroes are clearly not immune to the physiological demands of undeath, with the 'urge to devour' being firmly in the foreground (Brown 2020: 189). Indeed, by the time the story in *Marvel Zombies* actually begins, the undead superheroes have managed to consume all non-infected, non-transhuman life on the planet, and are now desperately focused on finding other forms of nourishment beyond Earth, by exploring other universes and dimensions. The search for food is often the primary motivation for the battles of the undead superheroes in *Marvel Zombies*. The zombie-fuelled urges of hunger seem to be heightened in 'super ways', and the need to consume is described as 'unbearable'. Superheroes are well known for their heightened physical abilities, and it would appear that, once they become transformed into undead, rotting versions of themselves, all the customary physiological stimuli, and not least hunger, become heightened as well.

Desperate to consume and driven mad by hunger, the undead superheroes eventually turn on each other. While it is made clear on several occasions that zombies do not taste quite as good as fresh human flesh, they are still a much-preferred alternative to starvation. Hunger here is rendered as a form of excess: an uncontrollable impulse that is presented as a defining characteristic of the undead. Undead hunger in *Marvel Zombies* exceeds the limits of rationality and haunts the pages of the comic book as an unshakeable blanket of insanity, becoming a haunting spectre in the midst of superheroes. The consumption of fellow superheroes begins with the killing of the non-infected Magneto and then spreads to the eating of multiple zombified members of the group. Throughout the killing and consuming of fellow zombies, the superheroes form and break alliances continuously in order to ensure control over the remaining food resources. Killing fellow superheroes is a way for each individual character to show strength and supremacy, and the consumption of 'super-flesh' separates the strong undead superheroes from the weak. This development appears to echo a long-standing anthropological contention about humans and meat-eating, where the latter epitomises the highest position not only in the food chain but also in the cultural pyramid. As Nick Fiddes suggests, the belief in a 'human dominion' legitimates meat-eating; in turn, killing and eating other animals' flesh 'provides perhaps the ultimate authentication of human superiority over the rest of nature' (1991: 65). In eating both human and zombie flesh, the undead superheroes re-establish their dominion. The consumption of flesh remains a way in which the undead superheroes not only satiate their encroaching hunger but also maintain a position of superiority on Earth and across multi-dimensional planes. In *Marvel Zombies*, hunger becomes reconceptualised beyond physiological stimuli and emerges, to borrow Sharman Russell's words, as 'a matter of control and desire, born of biology' (Russell 2008: 15).

Once they begin eating fellow superheroes and seeing them as a primary food source, the undead in *Marvel Zombies* also tacitly transform into cannibals. The inclusion of this metaphorical framework adds further layers of cultural meaning to the concept of undead hunger. In the Western imagination, cannibalism is still one of the ultimate taboos. Considered in these terms, it continues to function evocatively as a metaphorical representation of the fall of civilisation, and, as Maggie Kilgour puts it, 'the loss of human identity' (1990: 149). The fact that superheroes indulge their deviant hunger and consume each other also signifies the ultimate loss of identity as both human beings and icons of justice. That identity is an important part of the construction of the superheroes' distinctiveness, especially in Marvel and DC comics, and so the inclusion of cannibalism further dehumanises the characters as undead entities. The superheroes become 'Other' in multiple ways. Firstly, they are transformed into zombies by the virus, existing as liminal entities that linger in the space between life and death. Secondly, once they begin to kill and consume each other, they are also continuously rendered as Other in virtue of their inevitable association with cannibalism. Although, strictly speaking, the undead superheroes are no longer human, the traditional Western connotations of cannibalism still persist in their consumption of flesh, whether they are killing and consuming human beings or zombies.

Once the dimensions of both human subjugation and cannibalism are added into the equation, the crumbling of cultural control within the undead superheroes' world also exposes the systems of domination that demarcate eating as an inherently fragmented and fragmenting practice. Motivated by hunger and cannibalistic desires, the undead superheroes are depicted as ruthless, animalistic and inherently 'inhuman'. In their transition from human to zombie, they lose interest in maintaining order in the world and in the thirst for justice that many of them were renowned for in traditional Marvel comics. Spurred on by greed, they allow the world to come to ruin, and that ruination is reflected in their aberrant and uncontrollable eating practices, which often lack, to borrow Jean-François Lyotard's words, that sense of 'civilization' that is 'culturally and morally found in appropriate behaviours of consumption' (1993: 3).

The focus on undead cannibalism in *Marvel Zombies* is also important for the ways in which this comic series critically addresses the problem of the exploitation and exhaustion of resources. In *Carnal Appetites*, Elspeth Probyn defines the manifestation of cannibals in popular culture as 'congruent with fears that our appetites have no end' (2000: 81). As a result, this understanding places cannibals in the midst of discourses not only of consumer capitalism but also of environmental destruction. While cannibalism may be perceived as 'unnatural and monstrous' (Brown 2012: 4) within popular narratives, it also provides a critical framework for exploring the dangers of corporate greed and its disregard for the ecological consequences of constant production and consumption. While no mention of corporations is made in *Marvel Zombies*, the environmental destruction caused by the virus and the depletion of sustenance that comes as a result of the undead superheroes' uncontrollable hunger bring to the surface a not-so-veiled warning against the exploitation of the planet's resources. By constructing a series of mixed metaphors that join the undead, superheroes, hunger, cannibalism and a post-apocalyptic context, *Marvel Zombies* provides a cutting critique of human practices connected to sustainability and ecological welfare, where excessive consumption – fuelled by greed and a certain level of psychological unawareness – will result in the annihilation of our own world.

Indeed, it would appear that *Marvel Zombies* uses the metaphor of hunger to construct an eco-Gothic critique of the effects of human activities on the Earth, where the figure of the undead functions as an appropriately illuminating allegory for avarice and destruction. In presenting such a bleak view of the post-pandemic world, *Marvel Zombies* openly deviates from traditional superhero narratives where the superheroes themselves are commonly rendered as figures that 'inspire hope' and help 'society to process tragedy' (Neimeyer 2020: iv). By being transformed into undead creatures with uncontrollable hunger instincts, the superheroes cease to be catalysts for progress and challenge our cultural certainties instead. Ultimately, the success of the undead superhero metaphor lies precisely in its refusal to conform to comfortable and well-known frameworks for interaction, as it explores those fears of the end of the world that zombies are able to channel most effectively. As mixed icons, the undead of *Marvel Zombies* maintain the distinctive symbolic function that is typical of superheroes and continue to challenge the status quo, forcing us to re-examine 'the values of our culture' (Duncan and Smith 2013: xiii).

Simon Bacon

The Cloverfield Paradox (Julius Onah, 2018)

This article looks at the film *The Cloverfield Paradox* to discuss how it represents an undead universe that is intent on consuming our own. It will also be shown that this is a specifically twenty-first-century vision and is as much about our own undying fear of the future of our planet as it is about alien others or worlds beyond our own.

The Cloverfield Paradox (referred to in what follows as *Paradox*) is set in an unspecified near future in which the world is being torn apart by a quickly escalating energy crisis that sees the major power blocks of the world on the verge of warfare to claim what meagre natural resources there are left. In an attempt to prevent this, an international team of scientists is sent to the Cloverfield space station to work on a particle accelerator called the Shepard that will produce infinite amounts of energy and save humanity. After two years of unsuccessful attempts to get the device to work, it suddenly begins to produce energy, but then quickly overloads and stops. However, from this point onwards, strange things begin to happen, suggesting not only that the world has changed but that it might not even be their own. As the story continues, it appears that things onboard have also changed: the Russian crewman, Volkov (Aksel Hennie), suddenly has trouble controlling his eyes and hands as though they belong to someone else; someone found buried in the ship's interior walls claims to be a crew member and yet no one recognises her; English crewman Mundy (Chris O'Dowd) has his arm sucked, literally, into a wall and the severed part, his forearm and hand, act as if alive; and the ship is no longer orbiting the Earth but is on the other side of the Sun. As the crew begin to discover what has occurred, they realise that the Shepard has somehow created a wormhole that has deposited them in a parallel universe, one like their own but very different.

It quickly becomes apparent that all the dangerous events in the film are caused by the extreme measures undertaken by humanity in order to save itself regardless of the effects this has on the planet or the wider universe around it; examples range in size and severity from the Shepard down to a faulty heater that kills a young child. Indeed, the riskier and more extreme the actions that mankind takes, the more excessive the reciprocal, undead responses from the environment. More specifically, the 'extreme measures' that are enacted by humanity are centred around science and specifically aspects of it that are still largely theoretical, such as quantum physics, alternate universes and faster-than-light travel. These larger fears find specific expression within the film in the anxieties around wormholes, the nature of the universe the Cloverfield goes to, and the machine needed to create the former to reach the latter.

Wormholes were actually theorised as early as the start of the twentieth century, but the idea did not make significant impact on the popular imagination until the 1990s. *Sliders* (Tormé, 1995–2000), and *Stargate* (film: Emmerich, 1994; various series: Glassner et al., 1997–2011) are well-known examples,

Figure 51. Crewman Mundy losing his arm to an all-consuming alternate universe. *The Cloverfield Paradox*, directed by Julius Onah (Netflix, 2018).

though there are numerous television series and films from that time and spanning into the new millennium that also featured a wormhole of some kind, including appearances and mentions in the various iterations of *Star Trek*, *Doctor Who* and *Babylon 5*. Many of these used wormholes as simple corridors to other worlds, sometimes within the same universe but also through to other dimensions, or even as a means of traveling through time, with the past or future often configured as a different dimension to the present. It should be noted that wormholes are theoretical creations and that the machinery required either to create them or to stabilise ones that possibly already exist is far beyond our current capabilities. As noted by Enrico Rodrigo, there is no guarantee that a wormhole would actually be shorter than the shortest distance between two points in space (2010: 23).

Apart from their inherent instabilities, wormholes themselves are usually seen as benign, with just the peoples or species encountered once travelling through them being shown as malevolent. However, there are some narratives where the alternate universe itself seems malignant. An interesting example of this is seen in the film *Event Horizon* (1997), where the eponymously named ship has a machine built onboard that can create wormholes that the vessel can then use to travel through; this is what occurs on the Cloverfield even though the Shepard is designed to produce energy rather than to allow interdimensional travel. However, on the Event Horizon, the wormhole 'machine' actually opens a doorway into a malignant universe that then comes into our own, aiming to consume the inhabitants of the Earth and, one imagines, any other humanoid life-forms it finds. John Kenneth Muir inverts this idea, seeing the dimension the ship connects to as an internal rather than an external one: in fact, the subconscious mind of the ship's creator, Dr Weir (Sam Neill), which is recreating the trauma he experienced when his wife committed suicide. The journey inwards connects the narrative to films like *2001: A Space Odyssey* (1968), *Contact* (1997), *Interstellar* (2014) and, to a certain extent, *Solaris* (1972 and 2002). This is a useful idea going forward in relation to *Paradox*, as it configures the 'alternate dimension' directly to our own excessive psychological, traumatic state.[1]

---

1   In *Event Horizon*, the other universe is more clearly aligned with the idea of Hell. There is much to link it to the earlier *Hellraiser* film series by Clive Barker (1987–present), which features a 'device' that acts as a link to hell; indeed, the Gothic design of the

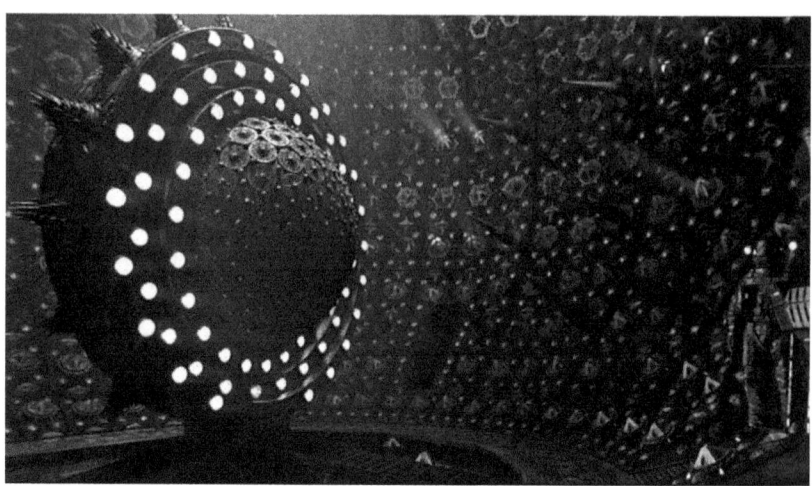

Figure 52. Malignant machinery creating a wormhole to Hell. *Event Horizon*, directed by Paul W. S. Anderson (Paramount Pictures, 1997).

Paradox certainly does not Gothicise its wormhole-making machine in the same way that *Event Horizon* does, but because of its seeming mundanity – it just looks like a standard part of the spaceship rather than a malignant entity in itself – it throws into stronger relief the anxiety caused by machines that we do not understand. Kristin Larsen observes how *Paradox* specifically 'taps into real concerns over high energy particle accelerators and alternate realities' (2019: 140), and this had been fuelled by the opening and use of the CERN[2] Large Hadron Collider near Geneva ten years before the film was released. However, because of the unknown nature of what might happen when particles are smashed together during the experiments undertaken there, from 2008 onwards there has been a regular stream of news stories predicting the end of the world (see Peskin 2008; Kaku 2008; Moreton 2011; Siegel 2016; Ratner 2018; Sivins 2020).

Lament Configuration device from *Hellraiser* was used as inspiration for the wormhole-creating machine in *Event Horizon*.

2   European Organisation for Nuclear Research, with the acronym CERN coming from the French 'Conseil européen pour la recherche nucléaire'.

Event Horizon Gothicises not only its machinery but also, as noted above, the destination to which it can take you. In that film, the destination is very much seen as a place of the past: either the historical emotional trauma suffered by Dr Weir or a vision of the biblical Hell. However, *Paradox* is for more forward-looking and, rather than bringing the past into the present, it shows that future science and technology can be even more undead and all-consuming than ghosts or demons from hell. A good example of this is the *Terminator* franchise, where a technological future sends robots back in time to ensure the destruction/subordination of humanity in years to come. Over the course of six films and a television series (1984–2019), the future is shown as a separate dimension that literally wants to kill the world of the present, suggesting a deep-rooted fear of what the future will bring.[3]

Back on the Cloverfield, the scientists locate the Earth and quickly discover that it is not their own. In fact, they have swapped places with another version of the Cloverfield that has many of the same crew members but who, in the alternate world, have very different characters. Of importance here is crew member Hamilton (Gugu Mbatha-Raw), who is still mourning the traumatic death of her young daughter killed in a fire caused by a faulty heater she purchased because of the power cuts on earth; in the linkage between alternate worlds and emotional trauma, there is something of a parallel here between Hamilton and Dr Weir from *Event Horizon*. Hamilton discovers that the version of herself in the other universe (where they are now) has not lost her daughter, who is alive and well. Confronted with an exact copy of her dead daughter, Hamilton does not want to leave this parallel world but wishes to stay there, even though this would cause the girl's real mother (now transported to our universe) to experience the same anguish she has gone through.[4]

The other crew member who does not want to return 'home' is Jensen (Elizabeth Debicki), the person they found in the wall, who is actually from

---

3 This is also seen in the tech-centric *The Matrix* franchise, which has a similar backstory of machine/computers becoming sentient and using humanity as a never-ending supply of bio-power.
4 The *Solaris* films (1972 and 2002) make much of the reappearance of one's dead partners and children whilst orbiting an alien environment. A very similar plot point was used in the series *Fringe* (2008–13), where the child of one of the main characters died and so he travelled to an alternate universe to steal a version of his dead son.

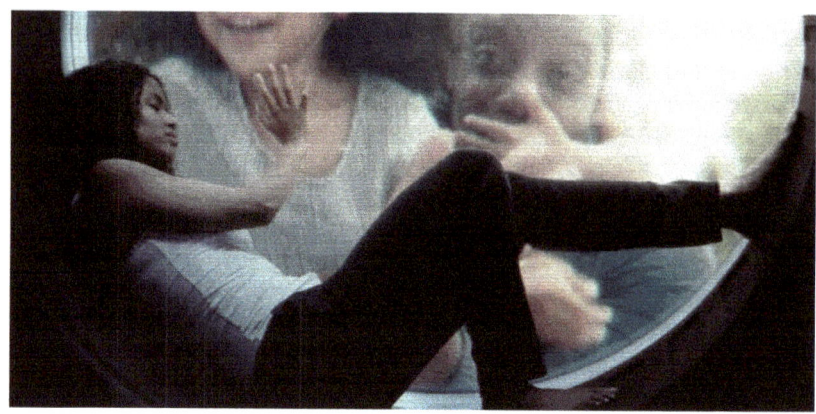

Figure 53. Mitchell 'reunited' with a version of her dead daughter in an alternate world. *The Cloverfield Paradox*, directed by Julius Onah (Netflix, 2018).

the alternate world. (Her double on our world is a reserve crew member back on Earth.) Not only does Jensen want to stay, she wants the Cloverfield to stay as well, as it has the only working version of Shepard; in their universe, the space station exploded when firing up the device. Jensen then starts to work actively against the crew of the Cloverfield as they attempt to restart the Shepard to return to their own world.

What begins to become apparent, however, is that it is not just Jensen that is stopping the Cloverfield from leaving but the alternate universe itself. As seen throughout the narrative, the Cloverfield mirrors the ship in *Event Horizon* in that unseen hands appear to be causing things to happen. Volkov, as noted earlier, seems to have not only the eye of his alternate self in his head but their thoughts in his brain too. Moreover, the ship's gyroscope vanishes and reappears in his stomach, accompanied by the contents of the ship's worm farm. Mundy, who lost his arm 'in' a door, is later literally consumed by the ship as pipes and wires from behind a wall panel wrap increasingly tightly around his body until he is dead. If this were not evidence enough, another crew member is mysteriously trapped in a room that then fills up with ventilation fluid, drowning them. This, then, clearly lays out the undead nature of the alternate universe that gives life to objects that have no life, as it is itself a lifeless expanse that has existed since the beginning of that universe's time and wants to 'consume' or kill all alien entities that come into its space. This would seem enough to confirm its vampiric nature, but the undead alternate universe has far more malevolent intentions than those involving the crew of the Cloverfield. When the space station finally manages to start the Shepard and return home, they find it a much-altered place. It seems that their going into and returning from an alternate world has opened a doorway for huge monsters to be unleashed in our own world.

Such gateways have been used in films including *Hellboy* (2004), *Pacific Rim* (2013) and even *The Avengers* (2012), though in these instances there was usually an agent or acolyte of the forces behind the creation of the breach. In *Paradox*, Jensen can be seen to perform the role of the 'vampire's assistant', an interdimensional Renfield. However, it seems to be the alternate universe itself that is behind these attacks on our world – the series *Fringe* showed something similar, albeit less flamboyant, occurring when a gateway between the two universes remained open – and moreover to have created gigantic monsters specifically for this task. (There is no suggestion that the Earth in the alternate world is populated by these creatures.) These monsters link back to the previous two films in the Cloverfield series, *Cloverfield* (2008) and *10 Cloverfield Lane* (2016), which feature Godzilla- or Kaiju-like creatures

Figure 54. Monsters from an alternate world unleashed into ours. *The Cloverfield Paradox*, directed by Julius Onah (Netflix, 2018).

the size of skyscrapers that run rampant across the country. These monsters further configure the monstrous nature of the alternate universe as well as its intent to destroy humanity (at least in our world). This all-consuming alternate universe brings together fears that are both common and specifically those of the twenty-first century. Apart from the obvious anxieties caused by 'aliens' from other worlds and those brought back by our own people (Bram Stoker's *Dracula* told a very similar story), there is a wider sense of barriers being irreparably broken, allowing danger to pour in unchecked. Intersecting with this is an anxiety over technology and of devices we create to solve one problem actually being the cause of other problems that are far worse. The nuclear disaster in Fukushima, Japan in 2011 is an obvious example, along with the Large Hadron Collider, mentioned earlier, and the renewed interest in space exploration of countries such as India, China, Russia and a select group of egomaniacal billionaires.[5] Here, then, the undying nature of the alien universe speaks more to our sense of living in a world that we have less and less control over, that forces much bigger than ourselves decide our fate, and that we will inevitably be consumed by them.

5   Towards the end of the twenty-first century, three highly wealthy individuals, Richard Branson, Jeff Bezos and Elon Musk, have funded and constructed space exploration missions and plans to 'monetise' outer space.

Roger Luckhurst

Epilogue: The Death of Death – Zero K, Don DeLillo (2016)

Much of Don DeLillo's late novel *Zero K* (2016) is set in the Convergence, a facility that exists in the desert outside temporality and history and outside national boundaries, somewhere in a post-Soviet satellite state. There, the fabulously wealthy can choose to transition from living into a state of suspension that abolishes finitude and defies the permanence of death. 'Death is a cultural artifact, not a strict determination of what is humanly inevitable', the protagonist Jeff Lockhart is told, there to see his dying stepmother, and later his perfectly healthy billionaire father, transcend what they think of as the 'blood desperation' of merely being alive (DeLillo 2016: 71 and 245). From the fear of death that consumes Babette in DeLillo's earlier novel *White Noise* (1984), *Zero K* explores the fear of life and its awful contingencies, traded by the super-rich for the proleptic promise of cryopreservation, a state of being suspended after life but before death.

I'm sorry to break it to you this way, but Death – the old death – died in 1968. There was an epochal decision made then in the scant four-page Report of the Ad Hoc Committee of the Harvard Medical School to Examine the Definition of Brain Death. The old death was determined by the cessation of the pulmonary system: we stopped breathing; the heart stopped beating. Advances in the new technological assemblage of the Intensive Care Unit, however, meant that patients could be kept breathing and blood oxygenated by artificial means for years. The new death was therefore to be determined by brain death: the absence of any measurable brain activity in an 'irreversible coma'. It is striking that 1968 was the same year that George Romero re-invented the zombie in *Night of the Living Dead*, an undead being that was no longer staked through the heart, like the traditional vampire, but shot through the head.

This new death has been notoriously difficult to determine, however, and in fact it has ceased to be considered as a definitive punctual moment and is seen as much more of an indeterminate zone, full of peculiar new states of being marking subtle gradations between life and death (see Teresi 2012). Initially, brain death was to be measured by a flat line on an EEG monitor. This seemed to demarcate something much more terminal than enigmatic states of catatonia, stupor or coma, from which people might – and on occasions did – return. But these EEGs proved to be disturbingly lively, even amongst those determined to be categorically brain-dead. New provisional states between life and death began to be defined: the Persistent Vegetative State, which becomes the Permanent Vegetative State after twelve months without change, was proposed by Bryan Jennett and Fred Plum in 1972. Plum also coined the term Locked-In Syndrome in 1966 for another liminal condition in which higher cortical activity was definitely preserved despite the catastrophic collapse of the muscular and nervous system.

Strange anomalies produced bioethical impasses. Katherine Ann Quinlan slipped into an apparently brain-dead state in 1975. In 1976, her father was finally granted legal permission to turn off her respirator to allow biological death to follow naturally. Instead, Quinlan stabilised without mechanical assistance and lived on, without leaving her coma, for another ten years. The emergence of 'Whole-Brain Death', meant as a more secure uniform medico-legal definition of death, was established in America by the work of James Bernat's team and the 1981 presidential commission, *Defining Death*.

Yet medical advances continued to produce interstitial conditions that troubled these legal definitions. In the 1990s, a neuro-behavioural task force set up to resolve anomalies thrown up by PVS produced yet another category: the Minimally Conscious State. This was defined as a 'severely altered consciousness in which the person demonstrates minimal but definitely behavioural evidence of self or environmental awareness' (cited Lock 2001: 186). This began to incorporate late-stage dementias into the interstitial grey zone between life and death, and Margaret Lock has called this a process of making up the 'Good-as-Dead', the steady intermingling of *social* as well as *biological* death. 'In late modernity', Lock suggests, 'the numbers of people recognised as candidates for social death have increased exponentially' (Lock 2001: 189).

It is out of the same moment of epochal shift in the 1960s that the 'cryonics' industry emerged, promising a commercial service of advanced physical preservation of the body in order to wait for technology to finally resolve the problem of death. Evan Cooper self-published *Immortality: Physically, Scientifically, Now* in 1962, and set up the Life Extension Society, with the slogan 'Freeze – Wait – Reanimate'. (Cooper is presumed to have died at sea, although, appropriately enough, his body was never recovered.) Karl Werner coined the term cryonics in 1965 in New York. The movement is most often associated, though, with Robert Ettinger, whose 1964 book *The Prospect of Immortality* was issued by the Scientific Book Club and endorsed by Isaac Asimov. Ettinger's ideas explicitly emerged from an American science fiction culture always tempted by the prospect of the practical engineering of the *Übermensch*. Ettinger's vision of frozen bodies returned to life was inspired by the 1931 SF story 'The Jameson Satellite' in *Astounding Science Fiction* magazine, the home of 'hard', extrapolative writing in the genre. Ettinger went on to incorporate in 1976 the Cryonics Institute, which still exists. The rival facility, the Alcor Life Extension Foundation, was set up in 1972 and currently preserves over 150 bodies in a facility outside Scottsdale in Arizona. After his death in 2011, Ettinger was preserved there in liquid nitrogen, alongside his mother, and his two wives (which might prove problematic on revival). The persistent rumours that Walt Disney's head was cryopreserved on his death in 1966 have always been denied by the family, although the baseball legend Ted Williams entered the Alcor facility in a blaze of publicity after his death in 2002.

In the 1990s, the weird world of Silicon Valley tech billionaires, the computer revolution and the accelerations in genetics and microbiology folded cryonics into the Transhumanist movement and made it a crucial element of their projections. 'Transhumanism' was first used by Julian Huxley in 1957 and defined as 'man remaining man, but transcending himself' (cited in Bostrom 2005: 7). A more recent definition suggests Transhumanism is 'a class of philosophies of life that seek continuation and acceleration of the evolution of life, beyond its current human form and human limitations, by means of science and technology' (Kyslan 2019: 71). Overcoming the bothersome limit of biological death is thus central to that project. The Extropy Institute (from 1992) and the World Transhumanist Association (from 1998) fuse a heady mix of libertarianism, futurology, speculative biocapitalism and the prospect of digital immortality. Suspended Animation Inc., another start-up bio-tech business, was initially focused on cryopreservation of bodies but has wider research interests in organ and tissue preservation, using rapid cooling. The business is therefore heavily invested in the multi-billion-dollar organ transplant industry, which has fully commodified the dead body since transplantation medicine took off at the beginning of the 1980s (see Scheper-Hughes 2000). The WTA, now known as Humanity+, talks on its website about 'converging technology' that might fuse digital and neural networks, allowing consciousness to be preserved beyond the physical limitations of the 'meat space' of the body. DeLillo's facility, the Convergence, realises this as a billionaire's dream of immortality, similar to life-extension advocates like Elon Musk or the bio-tech company Calico, which is underwritten by Alphabet, Google's parent company. At the heart of this hypercapitalist, transhumanist dream, cryonics 'faces the situation of death – it records it, redefines it and wants to overcome it' (Kyslan 2019: 75).

In DeLillo's *White Noise*, the central character, Jack Gladney, proposes that 'All plots tend to move deathwards' (DeLillo 1985: 26). He is later contradicted, though, by his colleague Murray, who intones in DeLillo's signature portentous mode: 'This is the nature of modern death ... It has a life independent of us. It is growing in prestige and dimension ... It continues to grow, to acquire breadth and scope, new outlets, new passages and means ... Every advance in knowledge and technique is matched by a new kind of death, a new strain. Death adapts, like a viral agent' (150). It might be feared no longer as an abrupt rupture but rather as an ever-extending transitional zone. 'I sense that the dead are closer to us than ever. I sense that we inhabit the same air as the dead' (150). Ultimately, this New Death extends to absorb Gladney's life itself. At the end of the book, having been given an indeterminate death sentence after exposure to toxic chemicals, he is called in for a consultation with his doctor, who is 'eager to see how my death is progressing' (325).

As Scott Dill (2017) has observed, DeLillo's later fiction, after the turn of the millennium, tends to be situated in places or states of being where time slows and expands and the end seems suspended or deferred. This is the time of grief with which *The Body Artist* (2002) is concerned. Grief is 'fracted time' (DeLillo 2002: 87). It makes falling out of narrative time and causation possible, leaving you in 'another structure, another culture, where time is something like itself, sheer and bare, empty of shelter' (92). Or there is the time of waiting in the desert of *Point Omega* (2010), the landscape of the ascetic or visionary, where 'geologic time' (DeLillo 2010: 19) dominates and slows to a crawl. It extends the agony of Ester and Finlay as they wait for news about an enigmatic vanishing. The experience of the desert, Ester proclaims, is 'Time falling away ... Time becoming slowly older. Enormously old. Not day by day. This is deep time, epochal time' (72).

Zero K is also principally set in the featureless desert where the Convergence hides in the landscape. It achieves a purely transitional state: 'The location itself, the structure itself, the science that bends all previous belief' (DeLillo 2016: 128). 'We've fallen out of history', a character explains to the faintly appalled protagonist. 'We've abandoned who we were and where we were in order to be here' (129) in order to arrive at the optimal time of transition beyond life or death. No one exactly crosses a threshold in the Convergence. Instead, they pass through a place called the Veer, less an architectural volume than 'an abstract thing, a theoretical occurrence' (138), on their way to cryopreservation. To contrast with this blurry space, the endless hallways are punctuated by screens that beam in images from the outside world, spectacles of political and natural disaster: the time of the Anthropocene; the end of the world. History, contingency, disaster and death is now for the poor. 'The site is fixed. We are not in a zone susceptible to earthquakes or to minor swarms but there are seismic countermeasures in every detail of the structure, with every conceivable safeguard against systems failure ... The site is fixed, we are fixed' (129).

Many of these spaces in DeLillo's fiction, Dill suggests, echo the time of Augustine's *saeculum*. In his *City of God*, Augustine uses this term for the time of waiting, the 'pre-eschatological messiness' (Hesiod 2019) where the sacred and the profane are mixed together, before Christ's return. Perhaps this is why DeLillo's tone is so portentous, so thrilled with the sublime of this 'American magic and dread' (DeLillo 1985: 19).[1] Although there are phrasal echoes of Augustine throughout DeLillo's work, from *Americana* onwards, we are by now in the postmodern sublime, where any surety of theological or authentic

---

1   See also Osteen 2000.

transcendence seems blocked, and we are left with the wonder that can only be glimpsed in fugitive moments of the everyday (Barrett 2017).

This is the function of the somewhat programmatic last scene of *Zero K*, in which the now orphaned Jeff, his father having transitioned in the Convergence, finds himself on a bus in New York City watching a small child awed by the setting sun, which is momentarily aligned with the city grid. The last words of the novel run: 'I told myself that the boy was not seeing the sky collapse upon us but was finding the purest astonishment in the intimate touch of earth and sun. I went back to my seat and faced forward. I didn't need heaven's light. I had the boy's cries of wonder' (DeLillo 2016: 274). It might seem a gesture of the simplest humanism, the triumph of life's contingency over the deathless death of cryopreservation, but DeLillo always tends to undermine even these moments of epiphany. In *White Noise*, the sunsets are spectacular because of the pollution in the air from the Airborne Toxic Event that threatens to kill them all. In *Zero K*, Jeff momentarily wonders if the child's wordless delight at the sunset might not be rather because 'he was impaired in some way, macrocephalic, mentally deficient' (DeLillo 2016: 274), before batting the thought away. There is the final contingency, pulling the soaring sublime back down to the damaged earth.

The time of waiting is also the time of the *already dead*, as Eric Cazdyn calls it. He suggests that with medical advances we have entered a new meantime, a 'chronic mode', which is 'a mode of time that cares little for terminality or acuteness, but more for an undying present that remains forever sick, without the danger of sudden death' (Cazdyn 2012: 5). To be alive is to always already be in the penumbra of death, to have been given a terminal diagnosis but yet to die. Cazdyn links this condition to a particular phase of capital, after the 2008 global financial crash, when capital dies but lingers on, an era Chris Harman (2009) almost immediately called *zombie capitalism*. It is not only Big Pharma that seeks to permanently extend life with drug innovations (turning death sentences into pharmacologically managed conditions) or commodify the dead body and reinject it into the economy if the worst comes to the worst. It is that this death of death has become intrinsic to capitalism that trades on futures and the lucrative markets of repackaged life insurance, where algorithms calculate the risks of death and disaster to keep the turnover turning (the subject of DeLillo's 2003 novel, *Cosmopolis*). We no longer have to be bitten by vampires or zombies to pass a definitive threshold into an afterlife. After the death of death, we become the already dead, existing in this grey zone in which we are enmeshed in systems that do not distinguish between life-in-death or death-in-life.

Bibliography

#Alive (#Saraitda), dir. Il-Hyung Cho (Zip Cinema, 2020).
Abbott, Stacey, *Undead Apocalypse: Vampires and Zombies in the 21st Century* (Edinburgh: Edinburgh University Press, 2016).
Abrams, Jennifer S., "The Kids Aren't Alright: Using a Comprehensive Anti-Trafficking Program to Combat the Restavek System in Haiti Notes & Comments", *Temple International & Comparative Law Journal*, 24, no. 2 (2010), 443–76.
Ackermann, Hans-W., and Jeanine Gauthier, "The Ways and Nature of the Zombi", *The Journal of American Folklore*, 104, no. 414 (1991), 466–94.
Alexander, Camille S., "The Horrific Feminine: Terrifying Women", in Kevin J. Wetmore Jr, ed., *The Streaming of Hill House: Essays on the Haunting Netflix Adaptation* (Jefferson: McFarland, 2020), 166–75.
Allen, Steven, "The Undead Down Under", in Laura Hubner, Marcus Leaning and Paul Manning, eds, *The Zombie Renaissance in Popular Culture* (London: Palgrave Macmillan, 2014), 70–87.
Anderson, Ariston, "*Suspiria* Director Luca Guadagnino Hopes Horror Remake 'Comes Across as Relentless'", *The Hollywood Reporter*, 27 August 2018. Accessed 31 March 2021.
Anonymous, "La Llorona (Estados Unidos: versión moderna)", in Susan M. Bacon, Gregg Courtad and Nancy Humbach, eds, *Leyendas del mundo hispano* (Upper Saddle River: Prentice Hall Publishers, 2000), 94–6.
Anonymous, *The Goetia: The Lesser Key of Solomon the King*, trans. Samuel Liddell MacGregor Mathers and ed. Aleister Crowley (Boston: Weiser Books, 1995).
Anzaldúa, Gloria, *Borderlands/La Frontera: The New Mestiza* (San Francisco: Aunt Lute Books, 1999).
Arnold, Kathleen, *Homelessness, Citizenship, and Identity: The Uncanniness of Late Modernity* (Albany: SUNY Press, 2004).
Ataria, Yochai, *The Structural Trauma of Western Culture: Toward the End of Humanity* (New York: Palgrave, 2017).
Athanasius, *The Life of Saint Anthony*, trans. Robert C. Gregg (New York: Paulist Press, 1980).
Austin, Wendy, et al., *Lying Down in the Ever-Falling Snow: Canadian Health Professionals' Experience of Compassion Fatigue* (Ontario: Wilfrid Laurier University Press, 2013).

Babadook, dir. Jennifer Kent (Entertainment One, 2014).
Baishya, Amit R., "What Do We Know ... What Have We Learnt? Zombified Neoliberal Fantasies in *Go Goa Gone*", *South Asian Review*, 37, no. 3 (2016), 111–31.
Bak, Se-Hwan, "South Korea Pledges to Tackle Homelessness", *The Korea Herald*, 27 September 2017. <http://www.koreaherald.com/view.php?ud=20170927000736>. Accessed 1 October 2021.
Bakare-Yusuf, Bibi, "The Economy of Violence: Black Bodies and the Unspeakable Terror", in Janet Price and Margrit Shildrick, eds, *Feminist Theory and the Body: A Reader* (Edinburgh: Edinburgh University Press, 1999), 311–23.
Baraitser, Lisa, *Enduring Time* (London: Bloomsbury, 2017).
Barakat, Robert A., "Wailing Women of Folklore", *The Journal of American Folklore*, 82, no. 325 (1969), 270–2.
Barnett, Rebecca, "On *Get Out* and the Problem of Racialized Aliveness", *Studies in Gender & Sexuality*, 20, no. 3 (2019), 204–8.
Barrett, Laura, "Radiance in Dailiness: The Uncanny Ordinary in Don DeLillo's *Zero K*", *Journal of American Literature*, 42, no. 1 (2017), 106–23.
Beam, Katherine, and Andy Paciorek, eds, *Folk Horror Revival: Field Studies* (Durham: Wyrd Harvest Press, 2015).
Bede, *Ecclesiastical History of the English People*, trans. Leo Sherley-Price (New York: Penguin Books, 1990).
Berggruen, Oliver, "The Fragmented Self", in Dieter Buchhart, ed., *Jean Michel Basquiat: Now's the Time* (New York: Prestel, 2015), 197–202.
Berlin, Gretchen, "Nursing in 2021: Retaining the Healthcare Workforce When We Need It Most", *McKinsey & Company*, 11 May 2021. <https://www.mckinsey.com/industries/healthcare-systems-and-services/our-insights/nursing%20in-2021-retaining-the-healthcare-workforce-when-we-need-it-most#>. Accessed 6 June 2021.
Bernat, James L., Charles M. Culver and Bernard Gert, "On the Definition and Criterion of Death", *Annals of Internal Medicine*, 94 (1981), 389–94.
Bernheimer, Richard, *Wild Men in the Middle Ages: A Study in Art, Sentiment, and Demonology* (Cambridge, MA: Harvard University Press, 1952).
Berns, Fernando Gabriel Pagnoni, and Diego Foronda, "Elegiac Masculinity in *Bubba Ho-tep* and *Late Phases*", in Samantha Hollard, Robert Shail and Steven Gerrard, eds, *Gender and Contemporary Horror in Film* (Bingley: Emerald Publishing, 2019), 23–37.
Bishop, Kyle William, *How Zombies Conquered Popular Culture: The Multifarious Walking Dead in the 21st Century* (Jefferson: McFarland & Company Inc., 2015).
Black Swan, dir. Darren Aronofsky (Fox Searchlight Pictures, 2010).
Blair Witch Project, The, dir. Eduardo Sanchez and Daniel Myrick (Haxan, 1999).

Blake, Linnie, "'Are We Worth Saving? You Tell Me': Neoliberalism, Zombies, and the Failure of Free Trade", *Gothic Studies*, 17, no. 2 (2015), 26–41. <http://dx.doi.org/10.7227/GS.17.2.3>.
Bloodthirsty, dir. Amelia Moses (Brainstorm Media, 2021).
Bostrom, Nick, "A History of Transhumanist Thought", *Journal of Evolution & Technology*, 14 (2005), 1–25. Reproduced at <www.nickbostrom.com>. Accessed 28 October 2021.
Botting, Fred, "Aftergothic: Consumption Machines and Black Holes", in Jerrold E. Hogle, ed., *The Cambridge Companion to Gothic Fiction* (Cambridge: Cambridge University Press, 2002), 277–300.
———, "Undead-Ends: Zombie Debt/Zombie Theory", *Postmodern Culture*, 23, no. 3 (May 2013).
Bracken, Patrick, *Trauma: Culture, Meaning and Philosophy* (Philadelphia: Whurr Publishers, 2002).
Brecht, Bertholt, *Mother Courage and Her Children* (London: Methuen, 1986).
Briggs, Laura, *Reproducing Empire: Race, Sex, Science, and US Imperialism in Puerto Rico* (Berkeley: University of California Press, 2002).
Bro, Lisa Wenger, Crystal O'Leary-Davidson and Mary Ann Gareis, eds, *Monsters of Film, Fiction, and Fable: The Cultural Links between the Human and Inhuman* (Newcastle upon Tyne: Cambridge Scholars Publishing, 2018).
Bronfen, Elisabeth, *Serial Shakespeare: An Infinite Variety of Appropriations in American TV Drama* (Manchester: Manchester University Press, 2020).
Brooks, Max, *World War Z: An Oral History of the Zombie War* (Richmond: Duckworth, 2006).
Brown, Jennifer, *Cannibalism in Literature and Film* (Basingstoke: Palgrave, 2012).
Brown, Nathan Robert, *The Complete Idiot's Guide to Zombies* (New York: DK Publishing, 2020).
Brownmiller, Susan, *Against Our Will: Men, Women, and Rape* (New York: Ballantine Books 1975).
Bruhm, Steve, "The Contemporary Gothic: Why We Need I", in Jerrold E. Hogle, ed., *The Cambridge Companion to Gothic Fiction* (Cambridge: Cambridge University Press, 2006), 259–76.
Bubandt, Nils, "The Uncanny Valley of the Anthropocene: Short Stories about the Undead under the Brightest of Lights", in Simon Bacon, ed., *The Anthropocene and the Undead* (Lanham: Lexington Books, 2022), n.p.
Bubba Ho-tep, dir. Don Coscarelli (Silver Sphere Corporation, 2002).
Buchoul, Samuel, "Heidegger: The Unheimlich – The Language of Foreignness", *Samvriti*, 10 May 2013. <http://www.samvriti.com/2013/05/10/heidegger-the-unheimlich/>. Accessed 28 October 2021.

Buchwald, Emilie, Pamela Fletcher and Martha Roth, *Transforming a Rape Culture* (Minneapolis: Milkweed, 2005).
Butler, Judith, "Doing Justice to Someone: Sex Reassignment and Allegories of Transsexuality", *GLQ: A Journal of Lesbian and Gay Studies*, 7, no. 4 (2001), 621–36.
Cabiya, Pedro, *Malas hierbas* (Leeds: Zemí Book, 2011).
———, *Trance* (San Juan: Grupo Editorial Norma, 2008).
———, *Wicked Weeds: A Novel*, trans. Jessica Ernst Powell (Simsbury, Connecticut: Mandel Vilar Press, 2016).
———, and Jorge Isaacs, *María V.* (Leeds: Zemí Book, 2011).
Cameron, Alan, *The Last Pagans of Rome* (Oxford: Oxford University Press, 2011).
Carey, M. R., *The Girl with All the Gifts* (Sterling Heights: Orbit Publisher, 2014).
Cargo, dir. James Dylan (Wild Eye Releasing, 2018).
Cargo, dir. Ben Howling and Yolanda Ramke (Dreaming Tree Productions, 2013).
Carrie, dir. Brian De Palma (United Artists, 1976).
Carrier, Constance, "Salem, Massachusetts, 1692: Sarah Good", *Ploughshares*, 6, no. 4 (1981), 154–5. <http://www.jstor.org.ezproxy2.drake.brockport.edu/stable/40348597>.
Carruthers, Elsa M., "Red Room, Red Womb: Phantom Feminism", in Kevin J. Wetmore Jr, ed., *The Streaming of Hill House: Essays on the Haunting Netflix Adaptation* (Jefferson: McFarland, 2020).
Carus, Paul, *The History of the Devil. And the Idea of Evil from the Earliest Times to the Present Day* [1900] (Chicago: Open Court Books, 2016).
Castillo, Monica, "The Dance Legends Who Inspired *Suspiria*'s Bewitching Movement", *Vanity Fair*, 26 October 2018. <https://www.vanityfair.com/hollywood/2018/10/suspiria-choreography-modern-dance-tilda-swinton-martha-graham-pina-bausch>. Accessed 5 April 2021.
Cazdyn, Eric, *The Already Dead: The New Time of Politics, Culture, and Illness* (Durham: Duke University Press, 2012).
CDC, "Zombie Preparedness", Center for Preparedness and Response, February 2021. <https://www.cdc.gov/cpr/zombie/index.htm>. Accessed 11 March 2021.
Charlesworth, Hayley Louise, "'You Made Him Real': Interactive Gothic Texts for the YouTube Generation", presented at the International Gothic Association Conference: Gothic Hybridities, 2018. <https://www.academia.edu/37135287/_You_Made_Him_Real_Interactive_Gothic_Texts_for_the_YouTube_Generation>. Accessed 11 March 2022.
Cherry, Brigid, "Refusing to Refuse to Look: Female Viewers of the Horror Film", in Mark Jancovich, ed., *Horror: The Film Reader* [1999] (London: Routledge, 2002), 169–78.

Chung, Mun-Young, "The Humanity of the Zombie: A Case Study of a Korean Zombie Comic", *The Comics Grid: Journal of Comics Scholarship*, 7, no. 1 (2017), 1–15. <https://doi.org/10.16995/cg.81>.

Cisneros, Sandra, "Woman Hollering Creek", in *Woman Hollering Creek and Other Stories* (New York: Vintage Contemporaries, 1991), 43–56.

Clarke, P. A., "Australian Aboriginal Mythology", in Janet Parker and Julie Stanton, eds, *Mythology, Myths, Legends, & Fantasies* (Sydney: Global Book Publishing, 2003), 382–401.

Clover, Carol J., *Men, Women, and Chainsaws: Gender in the Modern Horror Film* (Princeton: Princeton University Press, 1992).

Cloverfield Paradox, The, dir. Julius Onah (Netflix, 2018).

Coco, dir. Lee Unkrich (Disney/Pixar, 2017).

Cohen, Emily Jane, "Kitschen Witches: Martha Stewart: Gothic Housewife, Corporate CEO", *Journal of Popular Culture*, 38, no. 4 (2005), 650–77.

Cohen, Jeffrey Jerome, " 'Environing'. Theorizing the Contemporary", *Fieldsights*, 6 April 2016. <https://culanth.org/fieldsights/environing>. Accessed 28 September 2021.

———, "Grey: A Zombie Ecology", in Sarah Juliet Lauro, ed., *Zombie Theory: A Reader* (Minneapolis: University of Minnesota Press, 2017), 381–94.

———, "Monster Culture (Seven Theses)'" in *Classic Readings on Monster Theory* (ARC, Amsterdam University Press, 2018), 43–54.

———, *Monster Theory: Reading Culture* (Minneapolis: University of Minnesota Press, 1996).

Coleman, Beth, "Race as Technology", *Camera Obscura: Feminism, Culture, and Media Studies*, 24, no. 1 (2009), 177–207.

Coleman, Robin R. Means, *Horror Noire: Blacks in American Horror Films from the 1890s to Present* (London: Routledge, 2011).

Connor, John, "The Frontier War That Never Was", in Craig Stockings, ed., *Zombie Myths of Australian Military History* (Sydney: University of New South Wales Press, 2010), 10–28.

Cortázar, Julio, *Rayuela* (Madrid: Cátedra, 1984).

———, *Hopscotch*, trans. Gregory Rabassa (New York: Pantheon Books, 1966).

Cowan, Douglas E., *Sacred Terror: Religion and Horror on the Silver Screen* (Waco: Baylor University Press, 2008).

Creed, Barbara, *Media Matrix: Sexing the New Reality* (Crows Nest: Allen & Unwin, 2003).

Crow, David, "Hereditary Ending Explained", *Den of Geek*, 17 June 2018. <www.denofgeek.com/movies/hereditary-ending-explained/>. Accessed 30 June 2021.

Curse of La Llorona, The, dir. Michael Chaves (New Line Cinemas, 2019).

Curtis, Barry, *Dark Places: The Haunted House in Film* (London: Reaktion Books, 2008).

Cyberbully, dir. Ben Chanan (Channel 4, 2015).

D'Addario, Daniel, "George R. R. Martin on the One Game of Thrones Change He 'Argued Against'", *Time*, 13 July 2017. <https://time.com/4791258/game-of-thrones-george-r-r-martin-interview>. Accessed 18 May 2021.

Davis, Wade, *The Serpent and the Rainbow* [1985] (New York: Simon and Schuster, 2010).

Davison, Carol Margaret, "Haunted House/Haunted Heroine: Female Gothic Closets in *The Yellow Wallpaper*", *Women's Studies*, 33, no. 1 (2004), 47–75.

Dawn of the Dead, dir. George A. Romero (Image Ten, 1978).

de Groot, Jerome, *The Historical Novel* (New York and London: Routledge, 2010).

de Laurentis, Teresa, *Alice Doesn't: Feminism, Semiotics, Cinema* (Bloomington: Indiana University Press, 1984).

de Ville, Donna, "Menopausal Monsters and Sexual Transgression in Argento's Art Horror", in Robert G. Weiner and John Cline, eds, *Cinema Inferno: Celluloid Explosions from the Cultural Margins* (Lanham: Scarecrow Press, 2010), 53–75.

Deadgirl, dir. Marcel Sarmiento and Gadi Harel (Hollywoodmade, 2008).

Deitchman, Beth, "Five Reasons Why You Need to Watch Disney's *ZOMBIES*", *D23*, 15 February 2018. <https://d23.com/five-reasons-why-you-need-to-watch-disneys-zombies/>. Accessed 1 June 2021.

DeLamotte, Eugenia C., *Perils of the Night: A Feminist Study of Nineteenth-Century Gothic* (New York and Oxford: Oxford University Press, 1990).

DeLillo, Don, *Zero K* (New York: Scribner, 2016).

———, *Point Omega* (New York: Scribner, 2010).

———, *Cosmopolis* (New York: Scribner, 2003).

———, *The Body Artist* (London: Picador, 2002).

———, *White Noise* (London: Picador, 1985).

Dery, Mark, "Black to the Future: Interviews with Samuel R. Delany, Greg Tate, and Tricia Rose", in Mark Dery, ed., *Flame Wars: The Discourse of Cyberculture* (Durham: Duke University Press, 1994), 179–222.

DeSanti, Brady, "The Cannibal Talking Head: The Portrayal of the Windigo 'Monster' in Popular Culture and Ojibwe Traditions", *Journal of Religion & Popular Culture*, 27, no. 3 (2015), 186–201.

Descendants 2, dir. Kenny Ortega (Disney Channel Studios, 2017).

Dill, Scott, "Don DeLillo, the Contemporary Novel, and the End of Secular Time", in Jacqueline A. Zubeck, ed., *Don DeLillo after the Millennium: Currencies and Currents* (Lanham: Lexington, 2017), 171–90.

Dillon, Grace L., Foreword to *Dangerous Spirits: The Windigo in Myth and History* (Heritage House, 2014), 154–233. Kindle edition.

DiPaolo, Marc, *War, Politics and Superheroes: Ethics and Propaganda in Comics and Film* (Jefferson: McFarland, 2014).

Doane, Mary Ann, "Film and the Masquerade: Theorising the Female Spectator", *Screen*, 23, nos. 3–4 (September–October 1982), 74–87.

Bibliography

Don't Look Now, dir. Nicolas Roeg (British Lion Films, 1973).
Doyle, Sady, *Trainwreck: The Women We Love to Hate, Mock, and Fear ... and Why* (London: Melville House, 2016).
du Coudray, Chantal Bourgault, *Curse of the Werewolf: Fantasy, Horror and the Beast Within* (London: I. B. Tauris, 2006).
Duncan, Pearl, "The Role of Aboriginal Humour in Cultural Survival and Resistance", PhD thesis (University of Queensland, 2014). <https://espace.library.uq.edu.au/view/UQ:345997>. Accessed 28 October 2021.
Duncan, Randy, and Matthew J. Smith, *Icons of the American Comic Book: From Captain America to Wonder Woman, Volume 1* (Westport: Greenwood, 2013).
Eddy, Cheryl, "Why *Bubba Ho-Tep* May Be the Most Perfect B-Movie Ever Made", *Gizmodo*, 22 June 2016. <https://io9.gizmodo.com/why-bubba-ho-tep-may-be-the-most-perfect-b-movie-ever-m-1782435864>. Accessed 1 May 2021.
Egopop, "Panel Jacksepticeye PAX EAST 2017", *YouTube*, 10 March 2017. <https://www.youtube.com/watch?v=Eb1SDtC-Gdk>. Accessed 31 October 2022.
Elm, Eva, and Nicole Hartmann, eds, *Demons in Late Antiquity: Their Perception and Transformation in Different Literary Genres* (Berlin: de Gruyter, 2019).
Ettinger, Robert C. W., *The Prospect of Immortality* (London: Scientific Book Club, 1964).
Event Horizon, dir. Paul W. S. Anderson (Paramount Pictures, 1997).
Everard, Mark, *The Ecosystems Revolution* (London: Palgrave, 2016).
Evil Dead Trilogy, dir. Sami Raimi (TriStar Pictures, FilmDistrict, Ghost House Pictures, 1981, 1987, 1992).
Fake, The (*Saibi*), dir. Sang-ho Yeon (Studio Dadashow, 2013).
Fernando, Jude L. (2020) "The Virocene Epoch: The Vulnerability Nexus of Viruses, Capitalism and Racism", *Journal of Political Ecology*, 27, no. 1, 635–84. <https://doi.org/10.2458/v27i1.23748>.
Ferri, Josh, "Choreographer Jennifer Weber Discusses Her Work on Disney's *Zombies 2*, Casting Dancers, & Bringing *& Juliet* & *KPOP* to Broadway", *BroadwayBox*, 11 February 2020. <https://www.broadwaybox.com/daily-scoop/chatting-with-juliet-choreographer-jennifer-weber/>. Accessed 1 June 2021.
Fiddes, Nick, *Meat: A Natural Symbol* (London: Routledge, 1991).
Fischbach, Mark, "DARKIPLIER Vs ANTISEPTICEYE!", *YouTube*, 28 July 2017. <https://www.youtube.com/watch?v=slWT2N3NIKM&t=45s>. Accessed 31 October 2021.
Five Nights At Freddy's, created by Scott Cawthon (Lionsgate Games, 2014).
Földváry, Kinga, "Fragmented Shakespeare in Science Fiction: The Case of Westworld", *Dagenham*, 48, no. 134 (2019), 8–18.

Ford, Steve, "Suicide Risk Higher among Female Nurses Than Doctors, Suggests Study", *Nursing Times*, 20 May 2021. <https://www.nursingtimes.net/news/workforce/suicide-risk-higher-among-female-nurses-than-doctors-suggests-study-20-05-2021/>. Accessed 6 June 2021.

Foucault, Michel, *The History of Sexuality, Vol. 1*, translated by Robert Hurley (New York: Vintage Books, 1990).

Frank, Arthur W., *The Wounded Storyteller: Body, Illness & Ethics* (Chicago: University of Chicago Press, 2013).

Freeman, Elizabeth, *Time Binds: Queer Temporalities, Queer Histories* (Durham and London: Duke University Press, 2010).

———, "The Narrative Unconscious", *Contemporary Psychoanalysis*, 48, no. 3 (July 2012), 344–66.

Freud, Sigmund, *The Interpretation of Dreams*, translated by James Strachey (New York: Basic Books, 2010).

———, *The Uncanny* [1916], translated by David McLintock (London: Penguin Classics, 2003).

———, *Beyond the Pleasure Principle* [1920], translated by James Strachey (New York: W. W. Norton & Company, 1990).

Freire, Paulo, *The Pedagogy of the Oppressed* (London: Bloomsbury Academic, 2014).

Fringe, created by J. J. Abrams, Alex Kurtzman and Roberto Orci (Warner Bros Television, 2008–13).

Game of Thrones, Season 8, Episode 6, "The Iron Throne", dir. David Benioff and D. B. Weiss (HBO, 2019).

———, Season 8, Episode 3, "The Long Night", dir. Miguel Sapochnik (HBO, 2019).

———, Season 8, Episode 2, "A Knight of the Seven Kingdoms", dir. David Nutter (HBO, 2019).

———, Season 6, Episode 10, "The Winds of Winter", dir. Miguel Sapochnik (HBO, 2016).

———, Season 6, Episode 6, "Blood of my Blood", dir. Jack Bender (HBO, 2016).

———, Season 6, Episode 5, "The Door", dir. Jack Bender (HBO, 2016).

———, Season 1, Episode 1, "Winter Is Coming", dir. Tim Van Patten (HBO, 2011).

Garber, Marjorie, *Vested Interests: Cross-dressing and Cultural Anxiety* (London: Routledge, 1992).

Gardner, Kelly, 'The Sentient Zombie", in Clive Bloom, ed., *The Palgrave Handbook of Contemporary Gothic* (London: Palgrave Macmillan, 2020), 521–38.

Gawande, Atul, *Being Mortal: Medicine and What Matters in the End* (New York: Penguin, 2015).

Gay'wu Group of Women (Laklak Burarrwanga et al.), *Songspirals: Sharing Women's Wisdom of Country through Songlines* (Crows Nest: Allen & Unwin, 2019).

Gbogbo, Mawunyo, "Indigenous Filmmakers Give Us Something to Scream About at Sydney Film Festival", *ABC Radio Sydney*, 24 May 2019. <https://www.abc.net.au/news/2019-05-25/horror-is-the-new-black-at-sydney-film-festival/11148010>. Accessed 11 March 2021.
Gelder, Ken, and Rachel Weaver, "The Colonial Australian Gothic", in Ken Gelder and Rachel Weaver, eds, *The Anthology of Colonial Australian Gothic Fiction* (Melbourne University Press, 2007), 1–9.
George, Phillippe, "Relics as Historical Objects: Overview, Methods, and Prospects", in Antón M. Pazos, ed., *Relics, Shrines and Pilgrimages: Sanctity in Europe from Late Antiquity* (London: Routledge, 2020), 11–38.
Get Out, dir. Jordan Peele (Monkeypaw Productions, 2017).
Gibbs, Anna, "Eaten Alive/Dead Meat; Modern Cannibalism and the Death of Diana", *Australian Feminist Studies*, 13, no. 27 (1998), 11–17.
Gildersleeve, Jessica, "Contemporary Australian Trauma", in Clive Bloom, ed., *The Palgrave Handbook of Contemporary Gothic* (Houndmills: Palgrave Macmillan, 2020), 91–104.
Girl with All the Gifts, The, dir. Colm McCarthy (BFI Film Fund, 2016).
Goeshi (*A Monstrous Corpse*), dir. Beom-Gu Kang (Hanrim Films, 1980).
Gomel, Elana, "'Dying All the Time': The Future as the Extended Present and the Zombification of History in the Anthropocene", in Simon Bacon, ed., *The Anthropocene and the Undead* (Lanham: Lexington Books, 2022), n.p.
Gotman, Kélina, *Choreomania: Dance and Disorder* (Oxford: Oxford University Press, 2018).
Grimm, Season 2, Episode 1, "La Llorona", dir. Holly Dale (Universal Television, original air date 26 October 2012).
Guiley, Rosemary Ellen, *The Encyclopedia of Demons and Demonology* (New York: Facts on File Inc., 2009).
Haaga, Trent, "Commentary", *Deadgirl* [DVD] (London: Metrodome, 2009).
———, "Trent Haaga on Deadgirl: Exclusive Chiller Videoblog", *Facebook*, 9 March 2011. <https://fb.watch/8wmq24Pqhi/>. Accessed 6 June 2021.
Haase, Donald, *The Greenwood Encyclopedia of Folktales and Fairy Tales [3 Volumes]* (Portsmouth: Greenwood Press, 2007).
Halberstam, Jack, *In a Queer Time and Place: Transgender Bodies, Subcultural Lives* (New York: New York University Press, 2005).
———, "Telling Tales: Brandon Teena, Billy Tipton, and Transgender Biography", *Auto/Biography Studies*, 15, no. 1 (2000), 62–81.
———, *Skin Shows* (Durham: Duke University Press, 1995).
———, "Technologies of Monstrosity: Bram Stoker's *Dracula*", *Victorian Studies*, 36, no. 3, *Victorian Sexualities* (Spring, 1993), 333–52.

Handler, Rachel, "Saint Maud's Rose Glass Explains What's Real and What's Imagined in Her Unholy Horror Debut", *Vulture*, 29 January 2021. <https://www.vulture.com/2021/01/saint-maud-ending-director-rose-glass-explains-it-all.html>. Accessed 6 June 2021.

Harding, Kate, *Asking for It: The Alarming Rise of Rape Culture – And What We Can Do about It* (Boston: Perseus 2015).

Harman, Chris, *Zombie Capitalism: Global Crisis and the Relevance of Marx* (London: Bookmarks, 2009).

Harrington, Erin, *Women, Monstrosity and Horror Film: Gynaehorror* (Abingdon: Routledge, 2018).

Haslem, Wendy, Elizabeth MacFarlane, and Sarah Richardson, eds, *Superhero Bodies: Identity, Materiality, Transformation* (London: Routledge, 2018).

Hauke, Alexandra, "Hereditary as Folk Horror", *Horror Homeroom*, 6 October 2018. <www.horrorhomeroom.com/hereditary-as-folk-horror>. Accessed 30 June 2021.

Hayashida, Q., *Dorohedoro*, vol. 23. (San Francisco: Viz Media, LLC., 2019).

———, *Dorohedoro* (Tokyo: Shogakukan Inc., 2000–18).

———, *Dorohedoro*, vol. 22 (San Francisco: Viz Media, LLC, 2018).

———, *Dorohedoro*, vol. 21 (San Francisco: Viz Media, LLC, 2017).

———, *Dorohedoro*, vol. 16 (San Francisco: Viz Media, LLC, 2015).

———, *Dorohedoro*, vol. 10 (San Francisco: Viz Media, LLC, 2014).

———, *Dorohedoro*, vol. 1 (San Francisco: Viz Media, LLC, 2010).

Hellraiser, dir. Clive Barker (Entertainment Film Distributors, 1987).

Hereditary, dir. Ari Aster (A24, 2018).

Hesiod, "Augustine's *City of God*: Understanding the 'Saeculum'", *Discourses on Minerva*, 1 April 2019. <https://minervawisdom.com/2019/04/01/augustines-city-of-god-xii-understanding-the-saeculum/>. Accessed 14 May 2021.

Hideaki, F., "Implicating Readers: Tezuka's Early Seinen Manga", *Mechademia*, 8 (2013), 195–212.

hooks, bell, "Altars of Sacrifice: Re-membering Basquiat", *Art News*, 1 June 1993. <https://www.artnews.com/art-in-america/features/from-the-archives-altars-of-sacrifice-re-membering-basquiat-63242/>. Accessed 15 February 2021.

———, *Black Looks: Race and Representation* (Boston: South End Press, 1992).

Horner, Avril, and Sue Zlosnik, *Women and the Gothic: An Edinburgh Companion* (Edinburgh: Edinburgh University Press, 2016).

Host, dir. Rob Savage (Shadowhouse Films, 2020).

Howard, David, "Development, Racism, and Discrimination in the Dominican Republic", *Development in Practice*, 17, no. 6 (2007), 725–38.

Howard, Heather A., and A. Rodney Bobiwash, "Toronto's Native History", *FNH (First Nations House Magazine)*, 1 (2012), 6–9. <https://issuu.com/fnhmagazine/docs/1fnhmag>. Accessed 17 January 2020.

Hunt, Dallas, "'In search of our better selves': Totem Transfer Narratives and Indigenous Futurities", *American Indian Culture and Research Journal*, 42, no. 1 (2018), 71–90.

Hurley, Kelly, *The Gothic Body: Sexuality, Materialism, and Degeneration at the Fin de Siècle* (Cambridge: Cambridge University Press, 2004), https://doi.org/10.1017/CBO9780511519161.001.

Hutchings, Peter, "Resident Evil? The Limits of European Horror: *Resident Evil* Versus *Suspiria*", in Patricia Allmer et al., eds, *European Nightmares: Horror Cinema in Europe Since 1945* (New York: Wallflower, 2012), 13–23.

Incident Report, dir. Nick Koniuszko (Ballistic Ink Productions, 10 November 2021).

Inferno, dir. Dario Argento (Produzioni Intersound, 1980).

Ingham, Howard David, *We Do Not Go Back: A Watcher's Guide to Folk Horror* (Swansea: Room 207 Press, 2018).

Invasion of the Body Snatchers, dir. Don Siegel (Allied Artists Pictures, 1956).

Invasion of the Killer Natives, dir. Bjorn Stewart (Noble Savage Pictures, Screen Australia, 2019).

Jackson, Shirley, *The Haunting of Hill House* (New York: Vintage Press, 1959).

Jameson, Fredric, *Postmodernism, or, the Cultural Logic of Late Capitalism* (Durham: Duke University Press, 1991).

Jennett, Bryan, and Fred Plum, "Persistent Vegetative State after Brain Damage: A Syndrome in Search of a Name", *Lancet*, 1 (1972), 743–7.

Jensen, Robert, "Rape, Rape Culture and the Problem of Patriarchy", *Robert Jensen*, 26 May 2014. <https://robertjensen.medium.com/rape-rape-culture-and-the-problem-of-patriarchy-fac3e16d3bc6>. Accessed 6 June 2021.

J-ok'el/La Llorona: Curse of the Weeping Woman, dir. Benjamin Williams (Out of Light Entertainment, 2007).

Jones, Alan, "Argento", *Cinefantastique*, 13, no. 6 (September 1983), 20–1.

Jones, Nate, "A German History Primer for the Confused *Suspiria* Viewer", *Vulture*, 30 October 2018. <https://www.vulture.com/2018/10/suspiria-a-german-history-primer.html>. Accessed 5 April 2021.

Jones, Oliver, "The Pretentious *Suspiria* Remake Asks, 'Is Female Modern Dance Demonic?'", *Observer*, 25 October 2018. <https://observer.com/2018/10/suspiria-review-luca-guadagnino-makes-female-modern-dance-demonic/>. Accessed 31 March 2021.

Jones, Steve, "Gender Monstrosity: Deadgirl and the Sexual Politics of Zombie-Rape", *Feminist Media Studies*, 13, no. 3 (2012), 525–39. <https://doi.org/10.1080/14680777.2012.712392>.

Joseph, May, *Nomadic Identities: The Performance of Citizenship* (Minneapolis: University of Minnesota Press, 1999).

Jung, C. G., *Modern Man in Search of a Soul* [1933], translated by W. S. Dell and Cary F. Baynes (London: Routledge, 2001).

———, *Alchemical Studies*, translated by R. F. C. Hull (Princeton: Princeton University Press, 1970).
———, *Psychology and Religion: West and East*, translated by R. F. C. Hull (New York: Pantheon Books, 1958)
Kahn-Harris, Keith, *Extreme Metal: Music and Culture on the Edge* (New York: Oberg, 2007).
Kaika, Maria, "Interrogating the Geographies of the Familiar: Domesticating Nature and Constructing the Autonomy of the Modern Home", *International Journal of Urban and Regional Research*, 28, no. 2 (2004), 265–86. <https://doi.org/10.1111/j.0309-1317.2004.00519.x>.
Kaku, Michio, "The End of the World as We Know It?", *The Guardian*, 30 June 2008. <https://www.theguardian.com/science/2008/jun/30/cern.particlephysics1?CMP=Share_iOSApp_Other>. Accessed 28 October 2021.
Kaplan, E. Ann, *Trauma Culture: The Politics of Terror and Loss in Media and Literature* (New Brunswick: Rutgers University Press, 2005).
Kaufler, Melissa A., "The Future Isn't What It Used to Be: Hauntology, Grief, and Lost Futures", in Kevin J. Wetmore Jr, ed., *The Streaming of Hill House: Essays on the Haunting Netflix Adaptation* (Jefferson: McFarland, 2020), 128–40.
Kee, Chera, "'They Are Not Men … They Are Dead Bodies': From Cannibal to Zombie and Back Again", in Deborah Christie and Juliet Lauro, eds, *Better Off Dead: The Evolution of the Zombie as Post-Human* (New York: Fordham University Press, 2011), 9–23.
Kendi, Ibram X., *How to Be an Antiracist* (New York: Random House, 2019).
Kermode, Mark, "*Relic* Review – Heartbreaking Horror about Alzheimers", *Guardian*, 1 November 2020. <https://www.theguardian.com/film/2020/nov/01/relic-review-natalie-erika-james-emily-mortimer-alzheimers-horror>. Accessed 31 October 2021.
Kilgour, Maggie, *From Communion to Cannibalism: An Anatomy of Metaphors of Incorporation* (New York: Princeton University Press, 1990).
Killer Native, dir. Bjorn Stewart in *Dark Place* (Noble Savage Pictures, Screen Australia, 2019).
King of Pigs, The (*Dwaejiui Wang*), dir. Sang-ho Yeon (Studio Dadashow, 2011).
King, Stephen, *Cell* (London: Hodder and Stoughton, 2006).
———, *Danse Macabre* (Nashville: Everest House, 1981).
Kingdom (*Kingdeom*), dir. Seong-Hun Kim and In-Je Park (Netflix, 2019–present).
KM 31: Kilómetro 31, dir. Rigoberto Castañeda (Lemon Studios, 2007).
Knight, Magda, "Female Werewolves in Pop Culture", *Mooky Chick*, 7 April 2016. <https://www.mookychick.co.uk/reviews/books/female-werewolves-in-pop-culture.php>. Accessed 4 November 2021.

Knopf, Kerstin, *Decolonizing the Lens of Power: Indigenous Film in North America* (Leiden: Brill, 2008).
Knudsen, Eva Rask, *The Circle & the Spiral: A Study of Australian Aboriginal and New Zealand Māori Literature* (Amsterdam: Brill Rodopi, 2004).
Koontz, Katelynn E, "The Zombie Mermaid", *Musings* (2018). <http://martinemussies.nl/web/the-zombie-mermaid/>. Accessed 18 October 2021.
Kristeva, Julia, *Powers of Horror: An Essay on Abjection*, translated by Leon S. Roudiez (New York: Columbia University, 1982).
Kyslan, Peter, "Transhumanism and the Issue of Death", *Ethics and Bioethics*, 9, nos. 1–2 (2019), 71–80.
Landy, Marcia, "In the Name of the Mother: From Fascist Melodrama to the Maternal Horrific in the Films of Dario Argento", in Giovanna Faleschini Lerner and Maria Elena D'Amelio, eds, *Italian Motherhood on Screen* (Basingstoke: Palgrave Macmillan, 2017), 21–44.
Laredo, Janette A., "Some Things Can't Be Told: Gothic Trauma", in Kevin J. Wetmore Jr, ed., *The Streaming of Hill House: Essays on the Haunting Netflix Adaptation* (Jefferson: McFarland, 2020).
Larsen, Kristine, *Particle Panic! How Popular Media and Popularized Science Feed Public Fears of Particle Accelerator Experiments* (Cham: Springer Nature, 2019).
Las Lloronas, dir. Lorena Villarreal (Leyenda, 2004).
Lauro, Sarah Juliet, *The Transatlantic Zombie: Slavery, Rebellion, and Living Death* (New Brunswick: Rutgers University Press, 2015). Kindle edition.
Lawlor, Robert, *Voices of the First Day: Awakening in the Aboriginal Dreamtime* (Rochester: Inner Traditions International, 1991).
Leader, Michael, "*Suspiria* First Look: *Suspiria* Makes Heavy Weather of Argento's Beloved Horror", *Sight & Sound*, 6 September 2018. <https://web.archive.org/web/20180920011400/https://www.bfi.org.uk/news-opinion/sight-sound-magazine/reviews-recommendations/suspiria-luca-guadagnino-2018-remake-dakota-johnson-berlin-heavy-weather>. Accessed 30 March 2021.
Lee, Sung-Ae, "The New Zombie Apocalypse and Social Crisis in South Korean Cinema", *Coolabah*, 27 (2019), 150–66. <https://doi.org/10.1344/co201927150-166>.
Levich, Jacob, "Freedom Songs: Rediscovering Bollywood's Golden Age", *Film Comment*, 38, no. 3 (2002), 48–51.
Levina, Marina, and Diem-My T. Bui, *Monster Culture in the 21st Century: A Reader* (London: Bloomsbury, 2013).
Lidman, Mark J., "Wild Men and Werewolves: An Investigation of the Iconography of Lycanthropy", *The Journal of Popular Culture*, 10, no. 2 (1976), 388–97.
Liming, Sheila, "Suffer the Little Vixens: Sex and Realist Terror in 'Jazz Age' America", *Journal of Modern Literature*, 38, no. 3 (2015), 99–118.

Limpár, Ildikó, *The Truths of Monsters: Coming of Age with Fantastic Media* (Jefferson: McFarland & Co. Inc., 2021).
Link, Alex, "Where the Heart Is", in Kevin J. Wetmore Jr, ed., *The Streaming of Hill House: Essays on the Haunting Netflix Adaptation* (Jefferson: McFarland, 2020).
Lipsitz, George, *Time Passages: Collective Memory and American Popular Culture* (Minneapolis: University of Minnesota Press, 1990).
Little Monsters, dir. Abe Forsythe (Screen Australia, 2019).
Livermore, Christian, *When the Dead Rise: Narratives of the Revenant, from the Middle Ages to the Present Day* (Cambridge: D.S. Brewer, 2021).
Living Dead at Manchester Morgue, The (*No Profanar el Sueño de los Muertos*), dir. Jorge Grau (Star Films SA, 1974).
Lizzardi, Ryan, "The Zombie Media Monster's Evolution to Empty Signifier", in Murali Balaji, ed., *Thinking Dead: What the Zombie Apocalypse Means* (Lanham: Lexington Books, 2013), 89–104.
Lock, Margaret, "On Making Up the Good-as-Dead in a Utilitarian World", in Sarah Franklin and Margaret Lock, eds, *Remaking Life and Death: Toward an Anthropology of the Biosciences* (Santa Fe: School of American Research Press, 2001), 165–92.
Loewald, H. W., "On the Therapeutic Action of Psycho-Analysis", *International Journal of Psychoanalysis*, 41(1960), 16–33.
Lootens, Tricia, "'Whose Hand Was I Holding': Familial and Sexual Politics in Shirley Jackson's *The Haunting of Hill House*", in Bernice M. Murphy, ed., *Shirley Jackson: Essays on the Literary Legacy* (Jefferson and London: McFarland, 2005), 150–68.
Lovell-Smith, Rose, "Anti-Housewives and Ogres' Housekeepers: The Role of Bluebeard's Female Helper", *Folklore*, 113, no. 2, (October 2002), 197–214.
Lowe, Justin, "*Deadgirl*", *Hollywood Reporter*, 6 November 2008. <https://www.hollywoodreporter.com/movies/movie-reviews/deadgirl-125233/>. Accessed 21 June 2021.
Loza, Susana, *Speculative Imperialisms: Monstrosity and Masquerade in Postracial Times* (Lanham: Lexington Books, 2017).
Luckhurst, Roger, *Zombies: A Cultural History* (London: Reaktion Books, 2015).
——, "'Impossible mourning' in Toni Morrison's *Beloved* and Michele Roberts's *Daughters of the House*", *Critique*, 37, no. 4 (1996), 243–60.
Luna, Alina M., *Visual Perversity: A Re-Articulation of the Maternal Instinct* (Lanham: Lexington Books, 2004).
Lundell-Karlberg, Lisa, "Folkkonst för de besatta: en diskussion om fanart", Bachelor thesis (Linköping University, 2014). <http://liu.diva-portal.org/smash/record.jsf?pid=diva2%3A721263&dswid=-560>. Accessed 18 October 2021.
Lyotard, Jean-François, *The Inhuman* (Cambridge: Polity, 1993).

Mackey, Allison, "Guilty Speculations: The Affective Climate of Global Anthropocene Fictions", *Science Fiction Studies*, 45 (2018), 530–44.
Mahli, Yadvinder, "The Concept of the Anthropocene", *Annual Review of Environment and Resources*, 42, no. 1 (2017), 77–104.
Mama, dir. Andrés Muschietti (Universal Pictures, 2013).
Mann, Craig Ian, *Phases of the Moon: A Cultural History of the Werewolf Film* (Edinburgh: Edinburgh University Press, 2020).
Maríñez, Sophie, "80 aniversario de la masacre de 1937 en República Dominicana: nuevas posibilidades", in Matías Bosch Carcuro, Eliades Acosta Matos and Amaury Pérez Vargas, eds, *Masacre de 1937. 80 años después: Reconstruyendo la memoria* (Buenos Aires: CLACSO, 2018), 295–302.
Martin, George R. R., *A Dance with Dragons* (New York: Bantam Books, 2011).
———, *A Storm of Swords* (New York: Bantam Books, 2000).
———, *A Game of Thrones* (New York: Bantam Books, 1996).
Matrix, The, dir. The Wachowskis (Warner Bros, 1999).
Mayer, Sophie, "Pocahontas No More: Indigenous Women Standing Up for Each Other in Twenty-First Century Cinema", *Alphaville: Journal of Film and Screen Media*, 10 (2015), 1–16. <http://hdl.handle.net/10468/5984>. Accessed 9 July 2019.
Mazumdar, Ranjani, *Bombay Cinema: An Archive of the City* (Minneapolis: University of Minnesota Press, 2007).
McAlister, Elizabeth, "A Sorcerer's Bottle: The Visual Art of Magic in Haiti'", in Donald J. Cosentino, ed., *Sacred Arts of Haitian Vodou* (Los Angeles: Fowler Museum of Cultural History, 1995), 305–24.
McCort, Jessica R., "Flipping Hill House: The Netflix Renovation of Shirley Jackson's Landmark Novel", in Jill E. Anderson and Melanie R. Anderson, eds, *Shirley Jackson and Domesticity: Beyond the Haunted House* (New York and London: Bloomsbury, 2020), 223–42.
McDonagh, Maitland, *Broken Mirrors/Broken Minds: The Dark Dreams of Dario Argento* [1991] (Minneapolis: University of Minnesota Press, 2010).
McKee, Alan, "White Stories, Black Magic: Australian Horror Films of the Aboriginal", in Dieter Riemenschneider and Geoffrey V. Davis, eds, *Aratjara: Aboriginal Culture and Literature in Australia* (Amsterdam: Rodopi, 1997), 193–210.
McLoughlin, Seán, "The Jacksepticeye Power Hour – Jameson Jackson", *YouTube*, 31 October 2017b. <https://www.youtube.com/watch?v=ERpuTppau4E>. Accessed 31 October 2021.
———, "Jacksepticeye and Seán McLoughlin FINALLY meet", *YouTube*, 4 August 2021a. <https://www.youtube.com/watch?v=-SBNAm76KG0>. Accessed 31 October 2021.
———, "15 Months", *YouTube*, 21 July 2021. <https://www.youtube.com/watch?v=5L8OıjIzAlM>. Accessed 31 October 2021.

———, "Can You Figure Out Who DID IT? – Jameson Jackson's Jolly Jaunts", *YouTube*, 31 October 2019a. <https://www.youtube.com/watch?v=xXM237D01Gk>. Accessed 31 October 2021.
———, "CHASE", *YouTube*, 13 October 2019. <https://www.youtube.com/watch?v=C9x-SmwJBFY>. Accessed 31 October 2021.
———, "I'm Sick!!", *YouTube*, 15 March 2017. <https://www.youtube.com/watch?v=weafJreNQBI>. Accessed 31 October 2021.
———, "KILL JACKSEPTICEYE | Bio Inc Redemp Tion", *YouTube*, 3 August 2017a. <https://www.youtube.com/watch?v=_AW01Fryw_Y&t=536s>. Accessed 31 October 2021.
———, "Happy Halloween!", *YouTube*, 31 October 2016. <https://www.youtube.com/watch?v=iODdNMA0ZCU>. Accessed 31 October 2021.
———, "S A Y G O O D B Y E", *YouTube*, 31 October 2016a. <https://www.youtube.com/watch?v=CcGpAC0XxMo>. Accessed 31 October 2021.
McLuhan, Marshall, *Understanding Media: The Extensions of Man* (Cambridge: MIT Press, 1994).
Medak-Saltzman, Danika, "Coming to You from the Indigenous Future: Native Women, Speculative Film Shorts, and the Art of the Possible", *Studies in American Indian Literatures*, 29, no. 1 (2017), 139–71.
Mee, Laura, "The Re-Rape and Revenge of Jennifer Hills: Gender and Genre in (2010)", *Horror Studies*, 4, no. 1 (2013), 75–89.
Molasses, Jean-Michel Basquiat (1983).
Monani, Salma, "Feeling and Healing Eco-social Catastrophe: The 'Horrific' Slipstream of Danis Goulet's *Wakening*", *Paradoxa*, 28 (2016), 192–213.
Monnet, Agnieszka Soltysik, "The Transnational Zombie: Postcolonial Memory and Rage in Recent European Horror Film", in Christof Decker and Astrid Böger, eds, *Transnational Mediations: Negotiating Popular Culture between Europe and the United States* (Heidelberg: Universitätsverlag Winter, 2015), 143–59.
Montessori, Maria, *The Child, Society and the World: Unpublished Speeches and Writings* (Santa Barbara: ABC-CLIO, 1989).
Moore, Allison, "'I Don't Take Orders from a Lad Wearing Make-Up': Zombie as Queer Metaphor in Dominic Mitchell's *In the Flesh*", *Critical Studies in Television*, 1, no. 3 (2016), 299–314.
Moore, Jason W., "The Capitalocene, Part I: On the Nature and Origins of Our Ecological Crisis", *The Journal of Peasant Studies*, 44, no. 3 (2017), 594–630. <http://dx.doi.org/10.1080/03066150.2016.1235036>.
Mora, Arnau Roig, "The Necropolitics of the Apocalypse: Queer Zombies in the Cinema of Bruce LaBruce", in Murali Balaji, ed., *Thinking Dead: What the Zombie Apocalypse Means* (Lanham: Lexington Books, 2013), 181–96.

Moreau de Saint-Méry, Médéric Louis Élie, *Description topographique, physique, civile, politique et historique de la partie française de l'isle Saint-Domingue* (Paris: Société de l'Histoire des Colonies Françaises, 1958).
Moreton, Cole, "The Large Hadron Collider: End of the World, or God's Own Particle?", *Independent*, 23 October 2011. <https://www.independent.co.uk/news/science/large-hadron-collider-end-world-or-god-s-own-particle-921540.html>. Accessed 28 October 2021.
Mori, Masahiro, "The Uncanny Valley", in Jeffrey Andrew Weinstock, ed., *The Monster Theory Reader* (University of Minnesota Press, 2020), 89–94.
Morrison, Jasper, "Super Normal", in *A Book of Things by Jasper Morrison* (Baden: Lars Müller Publishers, 2015).
Morton, Timothy, *Hyperobjects: Philosophy and Ecology after the End of the World* (Minneapolis: University of Minnesota Press, 2013).
Mother of Tears, dir. Dario Argento (Medusa Film, 2007).
Mulvey, Laura, "Visual Pleasure and Narrative Cinema", in *Visual and Other Pleasures* [1975] (Basingstoke: Macmillan, 2009), 14–26.
Mussies, Martine, "Frankenstein and The Lure: Border Crossing Creatures through a Feminist Len'", *Foundation*, 47, no. 130 (2018), 47–58.
Neimeyer, Robert A., "Preface", in Robert A. Neimeyer, ed., *Superhero Grief: The Transformative Power of Loss* (London: Routledge, 2020), iv–xii.
Nicholls, Christine, "Warlpiri Nicknaming: A Personal Memoir", *International Journal of the Sociology of Language*, 113, no. 1 (1995), 137–46.
Nicolodi, Daria (@NicolodiDaria), "Remember *Suspiria 1* was imagined and written by a woman: me", 7:48pm, 22 August 2019. <https://twitter.com/nicolodidaria/status/1164610241461411843?lang=en>. Accessed 25 April 2021.
———, "I imagined and wrote *Suspiria* and *Inferno* for Mr. Argento", 5:25pm. 24 March 2018. <https://twitter.com/nicolodidaria/status/977597182919479301>. Accessed 25 April 2021.
Night of the Living Dead, dir. George A. Romero (Image Ten, 1968).
Nordmarken, Sonny, "Becoming Ever More Monstrous: Feeling Transgender In-Betweenness", *Qualitative Inquiry*, 20, no. 1 (2014), 37–50.
Nun, The, dir. Corin Hardy (New Line Cinema, 2018).
O'Brien, Justin, "Accumulating Extinction: Planetary Catastrophism in the Necrocene", in Jason W. Moore, ed., *Anthropocene or Capitalocene? Nature, History, and the Crisis of Capitalism* (Oakland: PM Press, 2016), 116–37.
Ogden, Daniel, *The Werewolf in the Ancient World* (Oxford: Oxford University Press, 2021).
Oluo, Ijeoma, *So You Want to Talk about Race* (New York: Seal Press, 2019).
Olutola, Sarah, "Blood, Soil and Zombies: Afrofuturist Collaboration and (Re-)Appropriation in Nalo Hopkinson's *Brown Girl in the Ring*", *MOSF Journal*

of Science Fiction, 2, no. 2 (2018). <https://publish.lib.umd.edu/?journal=scifi&page=article&op=view&path%5B%5D=384&path%5B%5D=714>. Accessed 28 October 2021.

Opera, dir. Dario Argento (ADC, Cecchi Gori Cinematografica, RAI Italiana, 1987).

Orange, Donna M., *Climate Crisis, Psychoanalysis and Radical Ethics* (New York: Routledge, 2017).

Osteen, Mark, *American Magic and Dread: Don DeLillo's Dialogue with Culture* (Philadelphia: Penn State University Press, 2000).

Oswald, Dana, "Monstrous Gender: Geographies of Ambiguity", in Asa Simon Mittman and Peter J. Dendle, eds, *The Ashgate Research Companion to Monsters and the Monstrous* (London: Routledge, 2013), 343–63.

Paciorek, Andy, "Folk Horror: From the Forests, Fields and Furrows – An Introduction", in Katherine Beam and Andy Paciorek, eds, *Folk Horror Revival: Field Studies* (Durham: Wyrd Harvest Press, 2015), 8–15.

Palatinus, David Levente, "Humans and Machines: Gothic Legacy and the Screen of the Anthropocene", in Maurizio Ascari, Serena Baiesi and David Levente Palatinus, eds, *Gothic Metamorphoses across the Centuries: Critical Perspectives on English and American Literature, Communication, and Culture Vol. 23* (Bern: Peter Lang, 2020), 215–31.

Palmerini, Luca M., and Mistretta, Gaetano, *Spaghetti Nightmares: Italian Fantasy-Horror as Seen through the Eyes of Their Protagonists* (Key West: Fantasma Books, 1996).

Panka, Daniel, "Transparent Subjects: Digital Identity in Mary Shelley's *Frankenstein* and Charlie Brooker's 'Be Right Back'", *Science Fiction Studies*, 45, no. 2 (July 2018), 308–24.

Patterson, Dayal, *Black Metal: Evolution of the Cult* (Port Townsend: Feral House, 2013).

Paz, Octavio, *The Labyrinth of Solitude: Life and Thought in Mexico*, translated by Lysander Kemp (New York: Grove Press, 1961).

Penfold-Mounce, Ruth, and Smith, Rosie, "Resisting the Grave: Value and the Productive Celebrity Dead", in Michael Hviid Jacobsen, ed., *The Age of Spectacular Death* (London: Routledge, 2020), 36–51.

Peninsula (Bando), dir. Sang-ho Yeon (Next Entertainment World, 2020).

Perez, Domino Renee, "The Politics of Taking: La Llorona in the Cultural Mainstream", in *The Journal of Popular Culture*, 45, no. 1 (2012), 153–72.

Peskin, Michael E., "The End of the World at the Large Hadron Collider?", *Physics*, 1 (August 2008), 14. <https://physics.aps.org/articles/v1/14>. Accessed 28 October 2021.

Phillips, Kendall, *A Cinema of Hopelessness: The Rhetoric of Rage in 21st Century Cinema* (London: Palgrave Macmillan, 2021).

Poe, Edgar Allen, "The Fall of the House of Usher" [1839], in *Complete Stories and Poems of Edgar Allan Poe* (New York: Doubleday Dell Publishing Group, Inc., 1966).

Popova, Milena, "'Dogfuck Rapeworld': Omegaverse Fiction as a Critical Tool in Analysing the Impact of Social Power Structures on Intimate Relationships and Sexual Consent", *Porn Studies*, 5, no. 2 (2018), 175–91.

Powell, Anna, *European Nightmares* (New York: Columbia University Press, 2012).

Priest, Hannah, "Introduction: A History of Female Werewolves", in Hannah Priest, ed., *She-wolf: A Cultural History of Female Werewolves* (Manchester: Manchester University Press, 2018), 1–23.

Probyn, Elspeth, *Carnal Appetites: FoodSexIdentities* (London: Routledge, 2000).

Punter, David, *The Literature of Terror: A History of Gothic Fictions from 1765 to the Present Day* (London: Longman, 1980).

Rampant (*Changgwol*), dir. Sung-Hoon Kim (Leeyang Film, 2018).

Ratner, Paul, "3 Stunning Ways Earth and Spacetime Could Be Destroyed", *Big Think*, 11 October 2018. <https://bigthink.com/surprising-science/3-ways-the-earth-and-reality-could-be-destroyed-by-the-large-hadron-collider/>. Accessed 28 October 2021.

Rayner, Alex, "Skin Suits and Black Magic: *Suspiria* and the True Storied Behind Classic Horrors", *The Guardian*, 10 November 2018. <https://www.theguardian.com/film/2018/nov/10/suspiria-and-the-true-stories-behind-classic-horrors>. Accessed 20 April 2021.

Read, Kay Almere, and Jason J. González, *Mesoamerican Mythology: A Guide to Gods, Heroes, Rituals, and Beliefs of Mexico and Central America* (New York: Oxford University Press, 2000).

Re-Animator, dir. Stuart Gordon (Empire International Pictures, 1985).

Reckson, Lindsay V., *Realist Ecstasy: Religion, Race, and Performance in American Literature* (New York: New York University Press, 2020).

Red Shoes, The, dir. Michael Powell and Emeric Pressburger (General Film Distributors, 1948).

Relic, dir. Natalie Erika James (IFC Films, 2020).

Remy-Kovach, Léna, "Insatiable Hunger for Indigenous Flesh, Cultures, and Lands: Colonialism as a Ravenous Monster in *Monkey Beach* and *Kiss of the Fur Queen*", *Parlour: A Journal of Literary Criticism and Analysis*, 3, no. 1 (2018), 1–7. <https://www.ohio.edu/cas/parlour/news/growlery/insatiable-hunger>. Accessed 7 March 2020.

'Report of the Ad Hoc Committee of the Harvard Medical School to Examine the Definition of Brain Death', *Journal of the American Medical Association*, 205, no. 6 (5 August 1968), 337–40.

Return of the Living Dead, The, dir. Dan O'Bannon (Orion Pictures, 1985).

Revenants, Les, created by Fabrice Gobert (Canal+, 2012–15).

Revolt of the Zombies, dir. Victor Halperin (Victor & Edward Halperin Productions, 1936).
Reyes, Xavier Aldana, "Abjection and Body Horror", in Clive Bloom, ed., *The Palgrave Handbook of Contemporary Gothic* (London: Palgrave Macmillan, 2020), 393–410.
———, "Promethean Myths of the Twenty-First Century: Contemporary Frankenstein Adaptations and the Rise of the Viral Zombie", in Carol Margaret Davison and Marie Mulvey-Roberts, eds, *Global Frankenstein* (London: Palgrave Macmillan, 2018), 167–82.
Richardson, Jared, "Attack of the Boogeywoman: Visualizing Black Women's Grotesquerie in Afrofuturism", *Art Papers Magazine*, 36, no. 6 (2012), 22–6.
Righetti, Jamie, "*Suspiria* Screenwriter Explains That Wild Ending and Why Dakota Johnson Is a New Kind of Final Girl", *IndieWire*, 7 November 2018. <https://www.indiewire.com/2018/11/suspiria-screenwriter-explains-wild-ending-spoilers-ideas-for-sequel-1202018427/>. Accessed 16 April 2021.
Roach, Emily E., "Haunted Families, Queer Temporalities, and the Horrors of Normativity", in Kevin J. Wetmore Jr, ed., *The Streaming of Hill House: Essays on the Haunting Netflix Adaptation* (Jefferson: McFarland, 2020).
Robbins, Jeffrey H., "THE ENTROPOCENE", *Proceedings of the 61st Annual Meeting of the ISSS, Vienna, Austria, 2017*, no. 1 (2017). <https://journals.isss.org/index.php/proceedings61st/article/view/3232>. Accessed 28 September 2021.
Roberts, Robin, *The Female Ghost in British and American Popular Culture* (Jackson: University Press of Mississippi, 2018).
Robinson, Lisa, "Lady Gaga's Cultural Revolution", *Vanity Fair*, September 2010. <https://archive.vanityfair.com/article/share/035d4d1b-9b9b-49ae-9f41-7df1c9927bbd?inline>. Accessed 4 November 2021.
Rodrigo, Enrico, *The Physics of Stargates: Parallel Universes, Time Travel, and the Enigma of Wormhole Physics* (New York: Eridanus Press, 2010).
Rosemary's Baby, dir. Roman Polanski (Paramount Pictures, 1968).
Rosen Maggie, "A Feminist Perspective on the History of Women as Witches", *Dissenting Voices*, 6 (2017), 21–31.
Rosenberg, Robin S., and Peter Coogan, "Introduction", in Robin S. Rosenberg and Peter Coogan, eds, *What Is a Superhero?* (Oxford: Oxford University Press, 2013), xvii–xxi.
Ross, Sara, "'Good Little Bad Girls': Controversy and the Flapper Comedienne", *Film History*, 13, no. 4 (2001), 409–23.
Rubin, Charles T., "Robotic Souls", *The New Atlantis*, 57 (Winter 2019), 75–82.
Rubin, Rebecca, "Werewolf Thriller *Bloodthirsty* Lands at Brainstorm Media, Sets Release Date", *Variety*, 26 February 2021. <https://variety.com/2021/film/news/bloodthirsty-brainstorm-media-release-date-1234915288/>. Accessed 4 Nov 2021.
Russell, Jeffrey Burton, *The Prince of Darkness: Radical Evil and the Power of Good in History* (Ithaca: Cornell University Press, 1988).

Russell, Sharman, *Hunger: An Unnatural History* (New York: Basic Books, 2008).
Russo, Mary, *The Female Grotesque: Risk, Excess and Modernity* (New York: Routledge, 1994). <https://doi.org/10.4324/9780203609965>.
Saadawi, Ahmed, *Frankenstein in Baghdad* (London: Oneworld, 2018).
Saint Maud, dir. Rose Glass (StudioCanal, 2019).
Santos, Cristina, *Unbecoming Female Monsters: Witches, Vampires, and Virgins* (Lanham: Lexington Books, 2017).
———, "Maligned Mothers: From Coatlicue to La Malinche and Back", in Asma Sayed, ed., *Screening Motherhood in Contemporary World Cinema* (Bradford: Demeter Press, 2016), 300–17.
Sayce, Rob, "Behemoth: Nergal Talks Satanism, Darkness and Make-or-Break Time", *Terrorizer*, 245 (Dark Arts Ltd. Feb 2014).
Scheper-Hughes, Nancy, "The Global Traffic in Human Organs", *Current Anthropology*, 41, no. 2 (2000), 191–224.
Schweninger, Lee, *Imagic Moments: Indigenous North American Film* (Athens: University of Georgia Press, 2013).
Scott, A. O., "Ledger's Work Will Outlast the Frenzy", *New York Times*, 3 February 2008. <https://www.nytimes.com/2008/01/23/arts/23iht-24ledger-Scott.9443095.html>. Accessed 4 November 2021.
Scovell, Adam, *Folk Horror: Hours Dreadful and Things Strange* (Leighton Buzzard: Auteur Publishing, 2017).
Seabrook, William, *The Magic Island* (New York: Harcourt, Brace and Co., 1929).
Semple, Gavin W., *ZOS-KIA: An Introductory Essay on the Art and Sorcery of Austin Osman Spare* (London: FULGUR, BCM, 1995).
Sen, Meheli, *Haunting Bollywood: Gender, Genre, and the Supernatural in Hindi Commercial Cinema* (Austin: University of Texas Press, 2017).
Seoul Station (*Seoulyeok*), dir. Sang-ho Yeon (Studio Dadashow, 2016).
Sharma, Aradhika, "Welcome to Zombieland", *The Tribune India*, 28 April 2013. <https://www.tribuneindia.com/2013/20130428/spectrum/main5.htm>. Accessed 6 August 2021.
Shaun of the Dead, dir. Edgar Wright (StudioCanal *et al.* 2004).
Shearer, Martha, "The Secret beyond the Door: Dario Nicolodi and *Suspiria*'s Multiple Authorship", in Alison Pierse, ed., *Women Make Horror: Filmmaking, Feminism, Genre* (New Brunswick: Rutgers University Press, 2020), 47–59.
Shelley, Mary, *Frankenstein, or, The Modern Prometheus* (London: Lackington, Hughes, Harding, Mavor & Jones, 1818).
———, *Frankenstein: 1818 Text* [1994] (Oxford: Oxford University Press, 2008).
Shildrick, Margrit, *Embodying the Monster: Encounters with the Vulnerable Self* (New York: Sage, 2002).

Showalter, Elaine, *Sexual Anarchy: Gender and Culture at the Fin de Siècle* (London: Virago, 1992).
Shutter Island, dir. Martin Scorsese (Paramount Pictures, 2010).
Siegel, Ethan, "Could the Large Hadron Collider Make an Earth-Killing Black Hole?", *Forbes*, 11 March 2016. <https://www.forbes.com/sites/startswithabang/2016/03/11/could-the-lhc-make-an-earth-killing-black-hole/?sh=474fe1b12ed5>. Accessed 31 October 2021.
Sigurdson, Ola, "Slavoj Žižek, the Death Drive, and Zombies: A Theological Account", *Modern Theology*, 29, no. 3 (11 June 2013), 361–80. <https://doi.org/10.1111/moth.12037>.
Simonsen, Rasmus R., "Appetite for Disruption: The Cinematic Zombie and Queer Theory", in Dorothea Fischer-Hornung and Monika Mueller, eds, *Vampires and Zombies: Transcultural Migrations and Transnational Interpretations* (Jackson: University Press of Mississippi, 2016), 85–109.
Simpson, M. J., "Interview: Piers Haggard", *Cult Films and the People Who Make Them* (2013). <Mjsimpson-films.blogspot.com/2013/11/interview-piers-haggard.html>. Accessed 30 June 2021.
Sivins, Ellie, "Did the World End in 2012?", *Conspiracy Custard*, 27 September 2020. <https://medium.com/conspiracy-custard/the-world-ended-in-2012-ca344c629462>. Accessed 28 October 2021.
Slessor, Camron, and Eugene Boisvert, "Black Lives Matter Protests Renew Push to Remove 'Racist' Monuments to Colonial Figures", *ABC.net.au*, 10 June 2020. <https://www.abc.net.au/news/2020-06-10/black-lives-matter-protests-renew-push-to-remove-statues/12337058>. Accessed 11 March 2021.
Smallman, Shawn, *Dangerous Spirits: The Windigo in Myth and History* (Victoria: Heritage House, 2014). Kindle edition.
Smith, Iain Robert, *The Hollywood Meme: Transnational Adaptations in World Cinema* (Edinburgh: Edinburgh University Press, 2016).
Sobchack, Vivian, "Bringing it All Back Home: Family Economy and Generic Exchange", in Barry Keith Grant, ed., *The Dread of Difference: Gender and the Horror Film* (Austin: University of Texas Press, 1996), 143–63.
Sokol, Tony, "Hereditary: The Real Story of King Paimon", *Den of Geek*, 2018. <www.denofgeek.com/movies/hereditary-the-real-story-of-king-paimon/>. Accessed 30 June 2021.
Solomon-Godeau, Abigail, *Photography at the Dock: Essays on Photographic History, Institutions and Practices* (Minneapolis: University of Minnesota Press, 1991).
Song, Jesook, "Situating Homelessness in South Korea During and After the Asian Debt Crisis", *Urban Geography*, 32, no. 7 (2011), 972–88. <https://doi.org/10.2747/0272-3638.32.7.972>.

———, *South Koreans in the Debt Crisis: The Creation of a Neoliberal Welfare Society* (Durham and London: Duke University Press, 2009).

Sontag, Susan, *Illness as Metaphor and AIDS and Its Metaphors* (New York: Picador, 1990).

Spare, Austin Osman, *The Book of Pleasure: The Psychology of Ecstasy* (CreateSpace Independent Publishing Platform, 2015).

Squires, John, "Dario Argento Says the *Suspiria* Remake 'Betrayed the Spirit of the Original Film'", *Bloody Disgusting*, 19 January 2019. <https://bloody-disgusting.com/movie/3542427/dario-argento-says-suspiria-remake-betrayed-spirit-original-film/>. Accessed 30 March 2021.

Stanley, Patricia, "The Patient's Voice: A Cry in Solitude or a Call for Community", *Literature and Medicine*, 23 (2014), 346–63.

Starrs, D. Bruno, "Writing Indigenous Vampires: Aboriginal Gothic or Aboriginal Fantastic?", *M/C Journal*, 17, no. 4 (2016), n.p. <https://doi.org/10.5204/mcj.834>.

Stewart, Bjorn, "Black Comedy: Five Questions to Bjorn Stewart", *The Guardian*, 7 November 2014. <https://www.theguardian.com/commentisfree/2014/nov/07/black-comedy-five-questions-to-bjorn-stewart>. Accessed 11 March 2021.

Stiegler, Bernard, *Technics and Time, 1: The Fault of Epimetheus* (Stanford: Stanford University Press, 1998).

Struik, Dirk J., ed., *Karl Marx's Economic and Philosophic Manuscripts of 1844* (New York: International Publishers, 1964).

Stryker, Susan, "My Words to Victor Frankenstein above the Village of Chamounix: Performing Transgender Rage", in Renee R. Curry and Terri L. Allison, eds, *States of Rage: On Cultural Emotion and Social Change* (New York: New York University Press, 1996), 195–218.

Supernatural. Season 1, Episode 1, 'Pilot', dir. David Nutter (Warner Brothers Television, original air date 13 September 2005).

Suspiria, dir. Luca Guadagnino (Amazon Studios, 2018).

Suspiria, dir. Dario Argento (Seda Spettacoli, 1977).

Syme, Rachel, "How Netflix Made *The Haunting of Hill House* Less Scary", *The New Republic*, 31 October 2018. <https://newrepublic.com/article/151963/netflix-made-haunting-hill-house-less-scary>.

Tatum, Beverly Daniel, *Why Are All the Black Kids Sitting Together in the Cafeteria? And Other Conversations About Race* (New York: Basic Books, 2017).

Teresi, Dick, *The Undead: How Medicine is Blurring the Boundary Between Life and Death* (New York: Pantheon, 2012).

Thacker, Eugene, "Three Questions on Demonology", in Nicola Masciandaro, ed., *Hideous Gnosis: Black Metal Symposium I* (New York: Blackmetaltheory, 2014), 179–219.

———, *In the Dust of the Planet: Horror of Philosophy, Vol. 1* (Washington: Zero Books, 2011).

Thompson, Hannah, "'You Nasty Thing from Beyond the Dead': Elvis and JFK versus The Mummy in *Bubba Ho-Tep*", in Cynthia J. Miller and A. Bowdoin van Riper, eds, *Undead in the West: Vampires, Zombies, Mummies, and Ghosts on the Cinematic Frontier* (Lanham: Scarecrow Press, 2012), 237–51.

Tidwell, Christy, "Spiraling Inward and Outward: Junji Ito's *Uzumaki* and the Scope of Ecohorror", in Christy Tidwell and Carter Soles, eds, *Fear and Nature: Ecohorror Studies in the Anthropocene* (Pennsylvania: Penn State University Press, 2021), 42–67.

Train to Busan (*Busanhaeng*), dir. Sang-ho Yeon (Next Entertainment World, 2016).

Turcotte, Gerry, "Australian Gothic", in Marie Mulvey-Roberts, ed., *The Handbook to Gothic Literature* (Houndmills: Macmillan, 1998), 10–19.

Turner, Graeme, *Understanding Celebrity* (London: Sage, 2014).

Tyler T. Ochoa, and Christine Jones, "Defiling the Dead: Necrophilia and the Law", *Santa Clara Law Digital Commons* (Winter 1997). <http://digitalcommons.law.scu.edu/facpubs/89>. Accessed 11 March 2022.

Unaipon, David, *Legendary Tales of the Australian Aborigines*, edited by Stephen Mecke and Adam Shoemaker (Victoria: The Miegunyah Press, 2006).

Unfriended, dir. Leo Gabriadze (Blumhouse, 2014).

Us, dir. Jordan Peele (Monkeypaw Productions, 2019).

Varis, Essi, "The Monster Analogy: Why Fictional Characters Are Frankenstein's Monsters", *SubStance*, 48, no. 1 (2019), 63–86.

Venard, Marc, "Le sang du Christ: sang eucharistique ou sang relic?", *Tabularia*, 9 (2009), 1–12. <https://doi.org/10.4000/tabularia>.

Verhaeghe, Paul, *Does the Woman Exist? From Freud's Hysteric to Lacan's Feminine*, translated by Marc du Ry (New York: Other Press, 1999).

Verstynen, Timothy, and Bradley Voytek, *Do Zombies Dream of Undead Sheep?* (Princeton: Princeton University Press, 2014).

Vincent, Nicholas, *The Holy Blood: King Henry III and the Westminster Blood Relic* (Cambridge: Cambridge University Press, 2001).

Wailer, The: *La Llorona*, dir. Andrés Navia (Skyline Films, 2006).

Wailer II, The: *La Llorona II*, dir. Paul Mirror (Skyline Films, 2007).

Wailer III, The: *La Llorona III*, dir. Javier Barbera (Laguna Productions, 2012).

Wakening, dir. Danis Goulet (ViDDYWELL FiLMS, 2013).

Waldby, Catherine, "The Instruments of Life: Frankenstein and Cyberculture", in Darren Tofts, Annemarie Jonson and Alessio Cavallaro, eds, *Prefiguring Cyberculture: An Intellectual History* (Cambridge: MIT Press, 2002), 28–37.

Warm Bodies, dir. Jonathan Levine (Summit Entertainment, 2013).

Weinstock, Jeffrey Andrew, "*Bubba Ho-tep* and the Seriously Silly Cult Film", in J. P. Telotte and Gerald Duchovnay, ed., *Science Fiction Double Feature: The Science Fiction Film as Cult Text* (Liverpool: Liverpool University Press, 2015), 233–48.

Werner, Marion, 'Coloniality and the Contours of Global Production in the Dominican Republic and Haiti', *Antipode* 43/5 (2011), 1573–97.

Wertheim, Margaret, *The Pearly Gates of Cyberspace: A History of Space from Dante to the Internet* (New York: W. W. Norton & Company, 1999).

Westworld, Season 1, Episode 4, "Dissonance Theory", created by Lisa Joy and Jonathan Nolan (HBO, 2016).

Westworld, Season 2, Episode 2, "Reunion", created by Lisa Joy and Jonathan Nolan (HBO, 2018).

Westworld, Season 2, Episode 10, "The Passenger", created by Lisa Joy and Jonathan Nolan (HBO, 2018).

Westworld, Season 3, Episode 2, "The Winter Line", created by Lisa Joy and Jonathan Nolan (HBO, 2020).

Westworld, Season 3, Episode 6, "Decoherence", created by Lisa Joy and Jonathan Nolan (HBO, 2020).

Wiggins, Steve A., *Nightmares with the Bible: The Good Book and Cinematic Demons* (Lanham: Fortress Academic, 2020).

Wilentz, Amy, "A Zombie Is a Slave Forever", *The New York Times*, 30 October 2012. <https://www.nytimes.com/2012/10/31/opinion/a-zombie-is-a-slave-forever.html>. Accessed 11 March 2022.

Williams, Ben, "Black Secret Technology: Detroit Techno and the Information Age", in Alondra Nelson, Thuy Linh Nguyen and Alicia Headlam Hines, eds, *Technicolor: Race, Technology, and Everyday Life* (New York: New York University Press, 2001).

Wilson, Colin, *Aleister Crowley: The Nature of the Beast* (London: Aeon Books, 1987).

Wilson, Edward O., *A Window on Eternity: A Biologist's Walk through Gorongosa National Park* (New York: Simon & Schuster, 2014).

Winterson, Jeanette, *The Daylight Gate* (London: Hammer, 2012).

Wisker, Gina, "Shadows in Paradise: Australian Gothic", in Jessica Gildersleeve, ed., *The Routledge Companion to Australian Literature* (New York: Routledge, 2020), 384–92.

Wiśniewski, Robert, *The Beginnings of the Cult of Relics* (New York: Oxford University Press, 2019).

Wizard of Oz, The, dir. Victor Fleming (Metro-Goldwyn-Mayer, 1939).

Womack, Ytasha, *Afrofuturism: The World of Black Sci-fi and Fantasy Culture* (Chicago: Chicago Review Press, 2013).

Wyrmwood, dir. Kiah Roache-Turner (Guerilla Films Inc., 2014).

Yaszek, Lisa, "Afrofuturism, Science Fiction, and the History of the Future", *Socialism and Democracy*, 20, no. 3 (2006), 41–60.

Zigarovich, Jolene, "The Trans Legacy of Frankenstein", *Science Fiction Studies*, 45, no. 2 (2018), 260–72.

ZOMBIES 2, dir. Paul Hoen (Disney Channel Studios, 2020).

Zombie Brigade, The, dir. Carmelo Musca and Barrie Pattison (ABC, 1988).

ZOMBIES, dir. Paul Hoen (Disney Channel Studios, 2018).

Notes on Contributors

ANTONIO ALCALA GONZALEZ is founder of the *International Gothic Literature Congress* and chair of the Humanities Department at Tecnologico de Monterrey, Mexico City. He has co-edited both a *Gothic Studies* special issue on *Nautical Gothic* and the critical collection *Doubles and Hybrids in Latin American Gothic*. Among his academic interests, he researches on the connections between the Gothic literary tradition and the lyrics in Extreme Metal. He is currently preparing a co-edited volume on the presence of Lovecraft's fiction in recent decades and a monographic study on Nautical Horror.

KATARZYNA ANCUTA, PhD, is a lecturer at the Faculty of Arts, Chulalongkorn University in Thailand. Her research interests oscillate around the interdisciplinary contexts of contemporary Gothic/Horror, currently with a strong Asian focus. Her recent publications include contributions to *The Transmedia Vampire* (2021), *The New Urban Gothic* (2020), *Gothic and the Arts* (2019) and *Twenty-First-Century Gothic* (2019). She has also coedited three special journal issues on Thai and Southeast Asian horror film and Tropical Gothic and edited two collections: *Thai Cinema: The Complete Guide* (2018) and *South Asian Gothic* (2021).

SIMON BACON is an award-winning writer and film critic based in Poznań, Poland. He has edited books on various subjects including *Gothic: A Reader* (2018), *Horror: A Companion* (2019), *Monsters: A Companion* (2020), *Transmedia Vampires* (2021), *Nosferatu in the 21st Century* (2022), *Spoofing the Vampire* (2022) and *The Palgrave Handbook of the Vampire* (forthcoming), and co-edited *Growing Up with Vampires* (2019 with Katarzyna Bronk). He has also published a series of books on vampires in popular culture: *Becoming Vampire: Difference and the Vampire in Popular Culture* (2016), *Dracula as Absolute Other* (2019), *Eco-Vampires* (2020) and *Vampires from Another World* (2021), and is working on the next, *1000 Vampires on Screen*.

MIKAELA BOBIY is a faculty member of the Humanities Department at Dawson College, Montreal. She completed a PhD in Art History at Concordia University, where her research focused on performance art and masochism. Her current research focuses on the intersections between psychoanalysis, art and film, and she is co-creator of the Psychoanalysis and Film lecture series (Montreal, Quebec).

NAOMI SIMONE BORWEIN is an interdisciplinary scholar who teaches at the University of Windsor and is a research associate at Western University. She holds a PhD in English literature from the University of Newcastle, Australia. Her criticism on Aboriginal Horror appears in *Horror Literature from Gothic to Post-Modern*, *The Palgrave Handbook to Horror Literature*, *The Global Vampire* and elsewhere. Her fields of study span from Global Anglophone and Indigenous literature and theory to visualisation and experimental mathematics philosophy.

PERSEPHONE BRAHAM (PhD, University of Pennsylvania) is a professor of Latin American and Caribbean literature and culture at the University of Delaware. She is the author of *From Amazons to Zombies: Monsters in Latin America* (Bucknell, 2015) and *Crimes Against the State, Crimes Against Persons: Detective Fiction in Cuba and Mexico* (Minnesota, 2004), and editor of *African Diaspora in the United States, Latin America and the Caribbean* (Delaware, 2014). She has published numerous articles on the Gothic, science fiction, detective literature, and the fantastic in Latin America.

DARA DOWNEY is a visiting lecturer in the School of English, Trinity College Dublin, and the Trinity Access Programme. She is editor of *The Irish Gothic Journal* (online). She is author of *American Women's Ghost Stories in the Gilded Age* (2014) and co-editor of *Landscapes of Liminality: Between Space and Place* (with Ian Kinane and Elizabeth Parker, 2016). She is currently working on a literary biography of Shirley Jackson, as well as a longer-term project on servant figures in American gothic.

VALERIE ESTELLE FRANKEL is the author of over eighty books on pop culture, including *The Villain's Journey*, *Hunting for Meaning in The*

Mandalorian; and *Star Wars Meets the Eras of Feminism*. Many of her books focus on women's roles in fiction, like her heroine's journey guides *From Girl to Goddess*, and *Buffy and the Heroine's Journey*. Once a lecturer at San Jose State University, she now teaches at Mission College and San Jose City College and speaks often at conferences. Come explore her research at <www.vefrankel.com>.

BRANDON R. GRAFIUS is Associate Professor of Biblical Studies at Ecumenical Theological Seminary, Detroit. His most recent book is a monograph on *The Witch* from the Devil's Advocates series (2020), and his book *Lurking under the Surface: Horror, Religion, and the Questions That Haunt Us* is scheduled for release in October 2022 by Broadleaf Books. He is co-editing *The Oxford Handbook of Biblical Monsters*, scheduled for release in 2023.

MIKEL J. KOVEN is Senior Lecturer and Course Leader for Film Studies at the University of Worcester. His previous works include *La Dolce More: Vernacular Cinema and the Italian Giallo Film* (2006), *Film, Folklore and Urban Legends* (2008) and *Blaxploitation Films* (2010). He has also authored many chapters and journal articles on the relationship between film and folklore, and on exploitation cinema.

LAURA R. KREMMEL is an Assistant Professor of English in the Humanities Department at South Dakota School of Mines & Technology. Her published work focuses on Gothic Studies, the Medical Humanities, History of Medicine, and British Romanticism. She is the author of *Romantic Medicine and the Gothic Imagination: Morbid Anatomies*, forthcoming from University of Wales Press, and is co-editor of *The Palgrave Handbook to Horror Literature* (2018).

ANTARES LEASK teaches English for Northern Virginia Community College and Arlington Public Schools. She holds a PhD in English, an MEd in Gifted Education, an MEd in Secondary Education and a BA in English. Her dissertation focused on the impact of white privilege on paranormal reality television. Other research interests include popular culture, horror, Disney, and cryptozoology.

ILDIKÓ LIMPÁR is Senior Lecturer of English at Pázmány Péter Catholic University, Budapest (Hungary), and has a PhD in English, an MA in Egyptology and a special interest in the monstrous. Her monograph *The Truths of Monsters: Coming of Age with Fantastic Media* is published by McFarland (2021). She is editor of *Displacing the Anxieties of Our World: Spaces of the Imagination* (Cambridge Scholars Publishing, 2017) and a Hungarian anthology of studies on monsters in popular culture (Athenaeum, 2021).

ROGER LUCKHURST is the Geoffrey Tillotson Chair of Nineteenth Century Studies at Birkbeck College, University of London, where he specialises in the Gothic.

MADELEINE MACKENZIE is a PhD student at University of Sydney (Department of Media and Communications) with research interests in genre and game studies. Their PhD research looks at how video games adapt spaces from genre fiction in other mediums, with a particular focus on the Gothic. In addition to their research, they are a game developer, and have released their own queer undead upon the world in titles such as *Catacomb Prince* (2019).

MARTINE MUSSIES writes about the Cyborg Mermaid for the Centre for Gender and Diversity at Maastricht University. In addition, she is working on a project around King Alfred of Wessex in fanfiction, with the support of Leiden University. Besides her research, Martine is a professional musician and illustrator. She studies neuropsychology at the University of Chicago via elearning. Her interests include autism, Japan, languages, martial arts, medievalism, music(ology) and science fiction. Read more about Martine's work at <www.martinemussies.nl>.

GWYNETH PEATY, PhD, is a Research Fellow in the Centre for Culture & Technology (CCAT) at Curtin University, Western Australia. Her research interests include popular culture, disability, digital media, horror, monstrosity and the Gothic. Publications include 'Infected with Life: Neo-supernaturalism and the Gothic Zombie', in *Gothic Science Fiction: 1980–2010* (edited by Sara Wasson and Emily Alder), 'Monstrous Machines and Devilish Devices', in *The Palgrave Handbook to Horror Literature* (edited by Kevin Corstorphine and Laura Kremmel) and 'Power in Silence: Captions, Deafness, and the Final Girl', *M/C Journal* 20.3.

LORNA PIATTI-FARNELL, PhD, is Professor of Film and Popular Culture at Auckland University of Technology, where she is also Director of the Popular Culture Research Centre. She is President of the Gothic Association of New Zealand and Australia (GANZA) and coordinator of the Australasian Horror Studies Network (AHSN). Her research interests lie at the intersection of popular media and cultural history, with a focus on Gothic and horror studies. She has published widely in these areas, including volumes such as *Consuming Gothic: Food and Horror in Film* (Palgrave, 2017) and *Gothic Afterlives: Reincarnations of Horror in Film and Popular Media* (Lexington, 2019).

CATHERINE PUGH completed her PhD at the University of Essex and is now a writer and independent scholar. Primarily writing about horror and science fiction across cinema, television and theatre, she is particularly fascinated by ideas of monstrosity and mental illness versus literary madness. Her research interests concern disability, mental illness, 'madness', metamorphic monsters and horror landscapes. She has contributed to various collections including *At Home in the Whedonverse: Essays on Domestic Space, Place and Life*; *Politics of Race, Gender, and Sexuality in The Walking Dead: Essays on the Television Series and Comics*; *Vying for the Iron Throne: Essays on Power, Gender, Death and Performance in HBO's Game of Thrones*, and online journals including *Studies in Gothic Fiction* and *Aeternum: The Journal of Contemporary Gothic Studies*.

DAVID PUNTER is Professor of Poetry Emeritus and Senior Research Fellow in the Institute of Advanced Studies at the University of Bristol. As well as hundreds of articles and essays, he has published many books on the Gothic and on other areas of literature. His best-known work is probably

The Literature of Terror; his most recent book on the Gothic is *The Gothic Condition*. His other books include *Writing the Passions*; *Rapture: Literature, Addiction, Secrecy*; *Metaphor*; *Modernity*; and *The Literature of Pity*. He has also published eight books of poetry.

LEAH RICHARDS is Professor of English at LaGuardia Community College, City University of New York, and co-editor of *Supernatural Studies: An Interdisciplinary Journal of Art, Media, and Culture*. With the exception of a project on the non-zombie films of George A. Romero, her current research lies exclusively in the realm of reanimated corpses as monstrous challenges to capitalism, white supremacy, heteronormativity, the patriarchy and general human stupidity. She has a cat named Renfield who sometimes eats bugs.

IAIN ROBERT SMITH is Senior Lecturer in Film Studies at King's College London. He is a specialist in transnational cinemas post-1945 with an emphasis on the ways in which material is adapted across different national contexts. He is author of *The Hollywood Meme: Transnational Adaptations in World Cinema* (Edinburgh University Press, 2016) and co-editor of the collections *Transnational Film Remakes* (with Constantine Verevis, Edinburgh University Press, 2017) and *Media across Borders* (with Andrea Esser and Miguel Bernal-Merino, Routledge, 2016).

CRISTINA SANTOS is Associate Professor at Brock University. Her work focuses on feminism and popular culture from an intersectional feminist perspective in the construct of 'monstrous women' from an interdisciplinary and multicultural approach as seen in literature, film, television, popular culture and mythology. Dr Santos also researches the construction of the Other through testimony with a focus on the human experience of trauma, memory and life that has been silenced and/or misrepresented. She is the author of *Unbecoming Female Monsters: Witches, Vampires, and Virgins* and the editor of books on testimony, monsters and various topics in sexuality and gender studies.

JAY TREAGUS is a visual artist and researcher exploring the relationship between technology and contemporary mythologies. They hold an MA in

Digital Media from Goldsmiths University and are currently working towards an MFA in Computational Art, also at Goldsmiths.

TYLER UNSELL has been a public high school teacher for sixteen years. In 2017 he started *Signal Horizon* and *The Horror Pod Class* to encourage other teachers to use more horror and science fiction in their classrooms. He continues as a host of the podcast and editor in chief of the magazine. He is the Director of Monsters 101, a horror movie-based summer camp for high school students based out of Truman State University, his alma mater.

JEFFREY ANDREW WEINSTOCK is a professor of English at Central Michigan University and an associate editor for *The Journal of the Fantastic in the Arts*. He is the author or editor of over twenty-seven books, including *The Monster Theory Reader* (2020), *The Mad Scientist's Guide to Composition* (2020) and *The Cambridge Companion to the American Gothic* (2018). Visit him at <JeffreyAndrewWeinstock.com>.

SARA WILLIAMS is an independent scholar. Her research focuses on representations of Gothic motherhood and maternity and relationships between trauma, voyeurism and consumption in the Female Gothic. She is currently writing her book *The Maternal Gaze in the Gothic* which is due to be published as part of the Palgrave Gothic series in 2024.

NATALIE WILSON teaches literature and women's, gender and sexuality studies at California State University San Marcos. She is the author of *Willful Monstrosity* (2020), an intersectional analysis of contemporary horror and its monsters, and *Seduced by Twilight* (2011), an examination of the Twilight saga from a feminist perspective. Her article 'Rules for Surviving Rape Culture in *The Walking Dead*' appears in *The Politics of Race, Gender, and Sexuality in The Walking Dead* (2018).

GINA WISKER is Professor Emeritus of Higher Education and contemporary literature, University of Brighton, associate professor supervising doctoral students in ICHEM, University of Bath, and Open University Associate lecturer on A 233 'Storytelling: realism and fantasy'. She has written or edited twenty-five books and published 140 articles. She specialises in twentieth-century women's writing, postcolonial, Gothic and popular fictions. Her published work includes *Margaret Atwood, an Introduction to Critical Views of Her Fiction* (2012), *Contemporary Women's Gothic Fiction (2016)*, *Contemporary Women's Ghost Stories: Spectres, Revenants and Ghostly Returns* (2022).

NICOLA YOUNG is an independent scholar whose key research interests are the intersections between philosophy, religion and film. Recent publications include *"What do you get when you cross a mentally ill loner with a society that abandons him?" Madness and power in Joker* (2021). She has also published in the Journal of Popular Film and Television, Transnational Cinemas, and Fantasy/ Animation.

JOHN R. ZIEGLER is Associate Professor of English at Bronx Community College, City University of New York. He is the author of *Queering the Family in The Walking Dead* (Palgrave Macmillan, 2018) and co-editor of *Representation in Steven Universe* (Palgrave Macmillan, 2020). Additionally, he has published work on early modern literature, Shakespeare, ghosts, zombies, and video games, co-authors reviews of indie theatre in New York City, and serves as co-editor of the peer-reviewed open-access journal *Supernatural Studies*.

Index

abject 122, 141, 142, 143, 156, 177, 202, 213
Aboriginal 11, 12, 53–63, 138
abuse 30, 46, 68–9, 126, 230
aesthetics 40, 41–3, 57, 60, 77, 95, 156, 159, 214, 218, 244
Africa 186, 211–2
African American 21–20
Afrofuturism 14, 15, 217–24
Afrofuturismo 14, 15, 209–15
afterlife 240, 254, 279
ageing 12, 127–35, 139, 140–1
agency 12, 20, 30, 57, 62, 69, 79, 90, 158, 188, 191, 255
alien 4, 70, 98, 100, 218, 265, 269, 271–2
alienation xi, 2, 22, 23, 38, 190, 213, 215, 259
alone 22, 69, 95, 100, 121, 126, 130, 132, 137, 140, 225
ancient 23, 24, 115, 132, 156, 167, 170
Android 224, 249, 250, 254
Anthropocene xii, 1, 6, 232, 277
anxiety 2, 3, 4, 6, 7, 8, 13, 14, 15, 38, 43, 46, 78, 130, 220, 223, 239, 250, 256, 258, 259, 266, 268, 272
apocalypse 2, 3, 9, 11, 39, 49–50, 53, 57, 83–4, 91, 255, 258
Australia 12, 53–63, 137–9
avatar 166, 167, 182, 244

baby 62, 63, 159, 166
battle 58, 115, 116, 127, 133, 168, 172, 184, 195, 199, 202, 227, 260
belief 19, 21, 22, 23–4, 45, 93, 165, 242, 261, 277
binary 6, 14, 175–6, 177, 179, 181–2, 184, 185, 201

biopower 210, 211
birth 31, 148, 150, 152–3, 155, 162–3, 166–7, 184, 201
bite 66, 69, 103, 105, 193, 198, 279
blood xv, 2, 14, 46, 63, 102, 105, 111–2, 114–6, 147–8, 150, 153, 169, 193, 195, 197–8, 200, 212, 241–2, 244, 273
bodily 122, 190, 217, 245, 250
body xi, xiii, xv, 3, 10, 25, 28, 69, 101, 102–3, 107, 111, 113, 121, 122–5, 132, 137, 141, 147, 155, 158–60, 164, 173, 176–7, 183–4, 186, 195, 211, 218–21, 236, 243, 244, 243, 249, 255, 270, 275–6, 278
bogeyman 43
bully 66, 79, 240

cannibal 12, 45–7, 51, 62, 189, 197, 200, 213–4, 220, 254, 261–3
capitalism xi, xii–xiii, xv–xvi, 1, 3, 9, 11, 39, 47, 49, 77, 87, 103, 209, 213, 220, 262, 278
catastrophe 211, 274
celebrity 14, 119, 193–200
chaos 159, 184, 201, 205, 211, 214, 236, 255, 258
child xvi, 13, 23, 27–35, 75, 77, 79–81, 83–4, 87, 89, 90–1, 146–53, 155, 157, 158–9, 161–3, 165–7, 170–1, 193, 212, 213, 243, 250, 266, 269, 278
colonial 6, 11, 28–30, 37, 46, 50, 53, 57–60, 62, 66, 138, 139, 160, 190, 210, 212–3, 220, 223, 227
  post- 138

colonialism 35, 47, 52
consume 3, 4, 12, 14, 27, 34–5, 62, 155, 171,
    186, 193, 195, 196–200, 260–2, 267,
    270, 271, 272, 273
consumerist 33, 35, 38, 77, 214, 238, 262
contagion 2, 37, 53, 60, 244
corpse 10, 107, 122, 125, 130, 184, 185,
    186, 225
cryogenic 16, 273, 275–8
curse 5, 29, 32, 35, 59, 110, 132, 178, 179

death xiv–xv, xvi, 1, 5, 6, 9–10, 13, 15–6,
    20, 25, 28–9, 62, 70, 75, 79, 80–1,
    113–4, 117, 121–2, 125, 126, 127–8,
    130–4, 150, 156, 161–3, 166–7, 169,
    173, 175–6, 181, 184, 186, 197–8, 201,
    209, 217, 219–20, 222, 227, 230–1,
    236, 243, 253–6, 258, 260, 262, 269,
    273–9
decolonise 47–8, 50, 51
deformity xi, xiv, 148, 243, 250
desire xii, 2, 4, 9, 67, 79, 81, 101, 102, 104,
    147, 151, 155, 162, 164, 169, 181, 184,
    186, 189, 193, 196, 212, 213, 215, 221,
    233, 242, 247, 261, 262
devil 14, 19, 20, 25, 62, 126, 175, 176–7,
    181, 202–4
digital 235, 238–40, 243–5, 276
disease 46, 53, 75, 84, 88, 141, 256
domestic 12, 30, 32, 67, 69, 75–81, 138, 142
doppelgänger 4, 132, 201, 202, 235, 240,
    242, 243, 244
Dracula 2, 3, 6, 152, 272
Dreamtime 12, 54, 58, 63
dystopia 45, 49, 51, 58, 65

ecology 2, 58, 214, 262, 263
economics xi, xiii, 58, 67–8, 78, 86, 121, 211,
    213, 217, 259, 278
ecosystem 4, 5, 181
embodiment 5, 9, 14, 21, 23, 25–6, 28, 45,
    49, 52, 76, 112, 113, 122, 132, 133, 137,
    142, 158, 160, 162, 163, 173, 176, 187,
    195, 209, 211, 213–4, 222, 228, 229,
    233, 250
environment 2, 5–6, 10, 11, 12, 13, 58, 85, 88,
    90, 122, 153, 187
environmental 3, 14, 46, 49, 225–33, 258,
    262, 266, 269, 274
epidemic 149, 150, 227, 255
essence xi, 3, 200, 203, 240
evil 9, 22, 35, 46, 62, 94, 109–16, 134, 141,
    170, 201–6, 241, 244, 259
evolution 12, 14, 59, 163, 205, 275
existence xi, 1, 3, 9, 13, 22, 24, 87, 116, 163,
    181, 191, 201–3, 209, 219, 220, 242,
    249, 251–3, 255, 256
existential 5, 7, 20–1, 89, 128, 141, 185
exorcism 81, 109–10
exploitation 38, 77, 81, 124, 184, 200, 214,
    219, 227, 257, 262
extinction 1, 2, 5, 233
extraterrestrial 210
extremism 2, 4, 5, 12, 141, 176, 204,
    206, 266

faith 5, 21, 23, 24, 109, 113
family 2, 10, 12, 21–3, 35, 41, 46–8, 69, 75–
    81, 94, 98, 109, 131, 137–43, 148, 150,
    151, 169, 171, 209, 221, 275
femininity 11, 14, 81, 158, 160, 166, 176–7,
    181–2, 184
feminism 27, 35
    anti- 77
fertility 28
flesh 38, 46, 62, 63, 84, 166, 186, 195, 214,
    217, 257, 260–2
folklore xiii, 7, 11, 12, 141, 165, 169, 187,
    194, 204
horror 11, 19–26
Frankenstein xiv, 158, 175, 176, 181, 188,
    249–50, 256
freaks 191
Freud, Sigmund 8, 9, 68, 159, 225, 230, 232

Index

fuck 102–4, 106, 129
fungus 84, 88
futurity 1, 6, 7, 10, 15, 16, 49, 53, 81, 83, 93, 121, 122, 138, 217, 218, 220, 224, 231–2, 256, 257, 265, 267, 269, 276, 278

gaze 28, 102–3, 155, 157
   Eurocentric 218
   maternal 155–64
   psychoanalytic 159, 164
gender 13, 25, 26, 27, 35, 156, 167, 194
   transgender 14, 175–84
genocide 138
ghost 2, 15, 20, 21, 27, 28, 31–2, 34, 37, 53, 71, 75, 76, 78, 79–80, 109, 112, 116, 122, 127, 130, 137–8, 229, 235, 238, 242–4, 252, 269
ghoul 53, 54, 59, 62–3, 78, 257
globalism xiii, 11–2, 37–8, 41, 42–3, 53–4, 59, 63, 65, 91, 186–7, 213, 233, 256, 278
god 2, 4, 19, 20, 21, 23, 122, 124, 126, 166–7, 169, 180, 201, 202–6, 211, 212, 218–9, 250, 252
   -gasms 122, 125, 126
goddess 25, 27–8, 34
Gothic xii, 38, 77, 119, 137–40, 142, 157, 187, 191, 201, 202, 210, 232, 239, 242–4, 246, 249, 263, 267
Gothicised 10, 13, 268–9
grotesque xi, 49, 187, 188, 260

Haiti 3, 15, 186, 187, 209–14, 220
haunt 28–9, 31–2, 34, 47, 80, 122, 138, 142, 235, 238, 242, 243, 245, 247, 254, 261
haunted house 75–81, 112, 139, 148
heaven 9, 81, 203, 205, 206, 278
hell 25, 110, 175–6, 177, 203, 252, 254, 267–9
heteronormative 76, 78, 79
heterosexuality 77, 78, 79, 102, 103, 104, 105

hungry 2, 38, 79, 102, 159, 165, 196
hybrid xii, 10, 13, 14, 53, 54, 57, 63, 124, 185, 186, 187, 191, 249
hysteria 155–6, 159, 163–4, 230

identity 7, 11, 12, 13–5, 30, 54, 58–60, 62–3, 68–9, 80, 89, 94, 98, 99, 100, 128, 133, 138, 143, 180, 183, 186, 187, 188, 202, 203, 213–4, 221, 223, 235, 238, 243, 254–6, 259–61
ideology 1, 11–3, 15, 77, 101, 109, 210, 213
immortal xiv, 4, 218, 220–3, 240, 250, 257, 275–6
imperialism 3, 46
Indigenous 12, 28–9, 33–5, 45–52, 53–4, 57, 59, 211, 227

Jackson, Shirley 75, 77–9, 81, 139

killer 4, 29, 53–63, 103, 148–50, 168, 171, 173, 258, 261

La Llorona 11, 27–35, 110
liminality 13, 60, 121, 127, 175–6, 183–4, 230, 238, 240, 257, 262, 274
loneliness 1, 78, 119, 120, 121–4, 127, 132, 143, 239
lore 7, 12, 25, 26, 187, 210, 241, 243
Lucifer 25, 202, 205, 206

Marxism xi, 86, 228
masculine 14, 141, 168, 176–7, 181–2, 194–5
masculinity 25, 101, 106, 131, 156, 165–73
maternal 75–6, 79, 138, 155–6, 158–9, 161–2, 164
memorial 121, 138, 240
memory xiii, 15, 121, 133, 138, 141–2, 164, 168, 178, 189, 212, 229–30, 251, 253–4, 259
   counter- 217
menstrual 46, 156

mental health 12, 31, 67–8, 80, 102, 120, 124, 143, 209, 278
miracle 150, 167
mirror 58, 60, 94, 96, 99, 114, 142, 161, 188, 190, 195–6, 235, 243, 247, 270
misfit 14, 185–91
misogyny 12–3, 27, 35, 102, 106, 156, 158
monster xi, xiv, 2, 3–4, 11, 13, 14, 47, 50–2, 53, 60, 62, 66, 71, 81, 90, 94, 96, 97, 98, 100, 107, 138, 147–8, 166, 170, 171, 173, 181, 184, 185, 190–1, 194, 197, 199, 220, 221, 246, 250–1, 255, 271–2
mother xv, 3–4, 10–1, 27–31, 75–6, 78–80, 137–42, 148–9, 151–3, 155–64, 169, 213, 269, 273, 275
myth xiv, 11, 25, 27–8, 33–5, 42, 46, 50–1, 53, 54, 62, 75, 78, 84, 88, 139, 141, 150, 156–9, 162–4, 175, 187–8, 194, 213, 218, 242, 256

nature xi, xiv, 1, 6, 8–12, 23, 54, 60, 76, 83, 88, 91, 101, 143, 155, 170, 175, 176, 177, 181–2, 184–5, 201–6, 209, 219, 227, 230, 232–3, 250, 252, 254, 257, 261, 265, 268, 276, 277
Nazism 151, 160
neoliberalism xii, 3, 12, 38, 43, 66–7
nihilism 130, 133
nostalgia 42, 77, 256

obsession 14, 20, 124, 153, 157, 246
Other (the) 21, 22, 57, 143, 166, 188–10, 220, 250
otherness 3, 13, 138–9, 142, 190, 201, 250
outsider 21–2, 26, 98, 148

pagan 19, 21–4, 26, 204
pandemic 53, 84, 120, 233, 256, 258–9, 263
patriarchal 1, 11–2, 14, 25–8, 32, 34–5, 77, 101–2, 141, 188

phantasm 235, 240
politics xiv, xvi, 1, 5, 27, 33, 49, 57, 66, 68, 88, 98, 104, 116, 121–2, 139, 160–1, 212–4, 221, 259, 277
populism 5, 14
possessed 3, 45, 115, 124, 165, 202, 222, 239–40, 243, 245–6
posthuman 15, 187, 220, 249–56
predator 127, 195–6, 199, 210, 240
primordial 3, 205
prophetise 28, 172
prosthetic 217–22
purgatory 252, 254

queer 79–80, 147, 160, 175–6, 182, 184
queerness 7, 175, 184

racism 12, 17, 30, 35, 58, 93, 96, 97, 99, 190, 210
  anti- 93–100
rage 3, 109, 172
rape 69, 101–7, 178–9
rebirth 63, 121, 232
religion 5, 13, 22–3, 66, 109–17, 122, 124, 160, 177, 202, 204–5
repression 2, 4, 9, 14, 81, 109, 203, 225, 230, 233
resurrection 5, 19, 20, 133, 134, 164, 168–9, 177, 179, 181, 190, 214, 231, 233, 240, 257
revenant 3, 15, 137, 139, 140, 226–33, 249
revenge 33, 69, 151, 172, 178, 186, 227
ritual 6, 23, 24, 109, 112, 160, 197
robot 8, 220, 269

sacrifice 27, 65, 70, 78, 81, 111, 113, 116, 150, 152, 156, 160
satan 14, 19, 21–2, 201–6
saviour 88, 90, 96, 110, 166, 172, 205, 259
secular 110–1, 117, 205
sex 25–7, 68, 76, 102, 106, 122, 129

Index

sexism 26, 30, 35, 177, 190
sexual 12, 46, 67, 69, 76, 81, 101–7, 126, 132, 178, 212, 214
sexuality 11, 150
slavery 3, 37, 38, 102, 103, 210–4, 217–21, 223
soul xi, 127, 128, 132–4, 165–6, 187, 211, 240, 254
spectral 15, 254
spectre 80, 127, 131, 132, 261
spirit 5, 12, 14, 25, 31, 45, 46, 54, 58, 62, 94, 109, 137, 175, 186, 212, 240, 243
spiritual xi, 3, 60, 128, 215, 235, 254
spiritualism 20
suicide 4, 28–7, 32, 80, 110–2, 120, 125, 179, 222–3, 231, 267
superhero 15, 257–63
supernatural xiv, 3, 19–21, 32, 42, 79, 112, 121–2, 126, 127, 185, 202, 203, 240, 243, 245, 259
superstition 7, 24
symbolic 9, 27, 33–4, 46, 49, 51, 59, 62–3, 66, 68, 76, 78, 96, 109, 138, 158, 159, 162, 164, 179, 184, 195, 212, 229, 252, 254

technologies 15, 238
technology 15, 217–23, 227, 232, 234, 239, 243, 244, 246, 269, 272, 274–6
telepathy 151
temporality 4, 79–80, 218, 227, 235, 238–9, 273
terrorism 5, 70
threshold 243, 245, 277, 279
time 1, 3–4, 6, 16, 26, 27, 35, 76, 79, 81, 127, 129, 132, 134, 140, 142, 143, 165, 195, 218, 225, 227, 229–33, 239, 243, 251, 254, 267–8, 276–8
torture 104, 106, 162, 170, 212
toxic 101, 106, 232, 276, 278
transgender 14, 175–84

trauma 5, 11–2, 14, 46, 70, 78, 80, 120, 121, 123–6, 137–9, 143, 153, 156, 169, 181, 190, 220, 224, 225, 228–30, 232, 251, 253, 267, 269
trickster 45, 236

uncanny 8, 10, 23, 67, 68–70, 190, 191, 225, 229, 232, 250
undeadness 1, 2, 6, 9, 13, 54, 58, 59, 62, 63, 127
undeath 5, 16, 121, 169, 175–6, 181, 184, 215, 260
undying 3, 6, 11, 13, 14, 153, 193, 200, 265, 272, 278
unheimlich 8, 23, 68
unnatural 134, 167, 169, 171, 182, 222, 250, 262
unstoppable 4, 5, 171, 175, 176, 181, 184

vampire 2–3, 5, 9, 20, 54, 101, 124, 140, 147–51, 153, 186, 250, 256, 257, 271, 273, 279
vengeance 71, 147, 170
victim xiv, 4, 25, 27, 28, 29, 32, 33, 50, 58, 76, 78, 102, 106, 148, 155, 163, 173, 177, 181, 185, 186, 205, 209, 214, 215, 255
violence 6, 12, 51, 59, 60, 66, 67, 69, 80, 93, 101–7, 125–6, 137–8, 143, 169–71, 173, 180–1, 186, 189, 195, 206, 213, 217, 220, 228, 230
viral 37, 148, 276
virus 1, 5, 149, 150, 151, 185, 186, 235, 244, 254–6, 258–9, 262
Virusocene 10

warning 47, 89, 210, 223, 230, 262
werewolf 47, 94–100, 193–5, 199–200
witch 20, 22, 24, 141, 159, 163, 189, 209, 239
  Sea- 191
witchcraft 19, 21, 24, 157

xenophobia 49

YouTube 235–7, 239–42, 246–7

zombie xi, xiii, xiv, 1–3, 5, 9–10, 12, 14–5,
20, 37–43, 51, 53–4, 57–63, 65–71,
83–4, 87, 89, 93–100, 101, 103, 104,
124, 127, 140, 165, 173, 175–7, 179–
84, 185–91, 209–15, 220–1, 223,
224, 226–7, 231, 250, 255–6, 257–63,
273, 278–9

zombification 53, 57–60, 62–3, 95, 175, 179,
182, 184, 186, 212, 258

zombified 53, 60, 188, 258, 259, 261

Genre Fiction and Film Companions

Series Editor: Simon Bacon

The *Genre Fiction and Film Companions* provide accessible introductions to key texts within the most popular genres of our time. Written by leading scholars in the field, brief essays on individual texts offer innovative ways of understanding, interpreting and reading the topics in question. Invaluable for students, teachers and fans alike, these surveys offer new insights into the most important literary works, films, music, events and more within genre fiction and film.

We welcome proposals for edited collections on new genres and topics. Please contact baconetti@googlemail.com or oxford@peterlang.com.

Published Volumes

The Gothic
Edited by Simon Bacon

Cli-Fi
Edited by Axel Goodbody and Adeline Johns-Putra

Horror
Edited by Simon Bacon

Sci-Fi
Edited by Jack Fennell

Monsters
Edited by Simon Bacon

Transmedia Cultures
Edited by Simon Bacon

Shirley Jackson
Edited by Kristopher Woofter

Toxic Cultures
Edited by Simon Bacon

Magic
Edited by Katharina Rein

The Undead in the 21st Century
Edited by Simon Bacon

www.ingramcontent.com/pod-product-compliance
Ingram Content Group UK Ltd.
Pitfield, Milton Keynes, MK11 3LW, UK
UKHW021254180426
11947UKWH00010B/765